THE CHESAPEAKE WATERSHED

Sally,

Thanks so much
for your interest in my
books — here is another one
you might like —

Ned Tillman

The
Chesapeake
Watershed

A Sense of Place and
A Call to Action

NED TILLMAN

BALTIMORE
THE CHESAPEAKE BOOK COMPANY

Library of Congress Cataloging-in-Publication Data

Tillman, Ned.
 The Chesapeake Watershed : a sense of place and a call to action /
Ned Tillman.
     p. cm.
 Includes bibliographical references and index.
 ISBN-13: 978-0-9823049-0-7 (alk. paper)
 ISBN-10: 0-9823049-0-0 (alk. paper)
 1. Human ecology—Chesapeake Bay Watershed. 2. Nature—Effect of
human beings on—Chesapeake Bay Watershed. 3. Coastal ecology—
Chesapeake Bay Watershed. 4. Water—Pollution—Chesapeake Bay
Watershed. 5. Chesapeake Bay Watershed—Environmental conditions.
6. Chesapeake Bay (Md. and Va.)—Environmental conditions. I. Title.

 GF504.C54T55 2009
 508.75--dc22

                                        2009008266

Manufactured in the United States of America on paper containing
30 percent post-consumer waste. The paper used in this publication
meets the minimum requirements of the American National Standard
for Information Sciences Permanence of Paper for Printed Library
Materials ANSI Z39.48-1984.

Available wherever fine books are sold. Distributed by Alan C. Hood &
Co., Inc., P.O. Box 775, Chambersburg, PA 17201. (Phone: 717-267-
0867; Toll-free Fax for orders, 888-844-9433; www.hoodbooks.com.)

COVER IMAGES: TOP LEFT: Severn River Crabbers, courtesy, Chris Edwards
CENTER: Gunpowder Falls & Great Egret | iStockphoto.com
LOWER LEFT & SPINE: Blue Crab courtesy Southeastern Regional
Taxonomic Center/South Carolina Department of Natural Resources

To the planet's caretakers of the past,

the present, and most importantly,

the future

Table of Contents

Appendices

List of Illustrations

Acknowledgments

I would like to thank my extended family and friends who have always shown me new ways to take care of our planet. I also would like to thank the following people for reading and commenting on various parts of the manuscript at different stages of its development or for answering question as they arose: Carolyn Mateer, Jo and Bob Solem, Meg Meyers, Tom Fulda, Sara Taber, Dave and Elaine Pardoe, Kathy Tillman, Leigh Tillman, and Anna Tillman. I would like to acknowledge all those involved with the Commission and the Board of Environmental Sustainability of Howard County, Maryland, and specifically County Executive Ken Ulman and Josh Feldmark for their leadership on sustainability issues. The following technical experts helped me to better understand the complexities of the watershed: Trish Steinhilber of the University of Maryland, Bill Richkus and Mark Southerland of Versar, Julian Levy of Exponent, Jim Reger of the Maryland Geological Survey, Harley Speir and Larry Hindman from the Maryland Department of Natural Resources, and Carlton Haywood from the Potomac River Commission. I would also like to thank all the friends, scientists and authors who over the years have contributed to my deeper appreciation of the watershed. The art included in this book was created by Alice Webb, one of the best-known artists in the region. She has a real gift for capturing the soul of the watershed (http://www.alicewebb.com). Other images are courtesy of Jim Gerhardt and Timothy Auer of the USGS (U.S. Geological Survey Open-File Report 2008-1259).

Prologue

While talking with a friend one day, I found myself describing my family's technique for catching crabs back in the 1950s. How my Dad and I would wade barefoot through the thick aquatic grasses in the shallow, clear waters of the Chesapeake Bay. How we wedged bushel baskets into inner tubes and towed them behind us by tying them with a string to our bathing suits. Holding wire-mesh crab nets with long wooden poles, we would forage in water three feet deep, literally scooping up king-sized, hard-shell blue crabs and an occasional soft-shell crab.

My friend was intrigued with these exploits and how easy I said it was to fill bushel baskets with the Chesapeake's "beautiful swimmers." Then it dawned on me that he and many other people in this area have never gone crabbing. Many have never opened oysters, filled ice chests full of bluefish, or explored the watershed's gorges, mountains, and tributaries. Evidently my life on and near the bay has been nothing like that of many of the fifteen million people living in this vast and beautiful realm. It was an epiphany. Why would my neighbors care about the estuary or even want to go outdoors and explore all it has to offer if the bay isn't in their blood? Though the idea of "Saving the Bay" is set before us more and more often, it may in fact be too abstract for people who have not grown up immersed in the natural wonders of the watershed. Intellectually we may all understand why it is a good idea to save the bay, but on an emotional level how many of us really feel a kinship with it, or an innate responsibility to become better stewards of one of the greatest natural resources on the planet?

In contrast to these friends, my childhood of picking crabs, canoeing wetland swamps, and watching skies darken with enormous flights of migrating ducks and geese is such an important part of my history that I've developed a strong sense of place, a sense of responsibility, and an intimate rapport with all aspects of the bay. I have come to realize that any damage to the bay damages each of us who live here. It also casts a shadow on the future. I have been led to wonder what the impact might be if I could share this deeper, emotional attachment to the bay with newcomers. Could sharing my experiences help readers gain a greater sense of place? Might my stories inspire others to go outside and explore? Would more people learn not just to enjoy the outdoors, but actually benefit from being out in nature? Might these stories result in creating a more committed sense of public stewardship for sustaining and restoring our natural environment.

Extensive and fragile, the Chesapeake Bay watershed is one of the fastest growing regions in the country and is therefore in great peril, but in many ways the stories in this book apply to many places. This watershed is but a microcosm of the planet. The land, the waters, and the mountains described here can be found across America and on other continents. No matter where we live, the challenge is always the same; how do we live in balance with a dynamic earth?

I hope this book will inspire you to go outside and experience the wonders of the region, to walk its rivers, sail or fish in the bay, and get in touch with its natural beauty. Perhaps if more of us take the time to enjoy the outdoors, each of us will become healthier, more creative, and more engaged. Most importantly we will take the individual and collective steps we must take if we are to save the bay (or other places you value) and live more in balance with our planet.

Ned Tillman, 2009

Part I

The Land

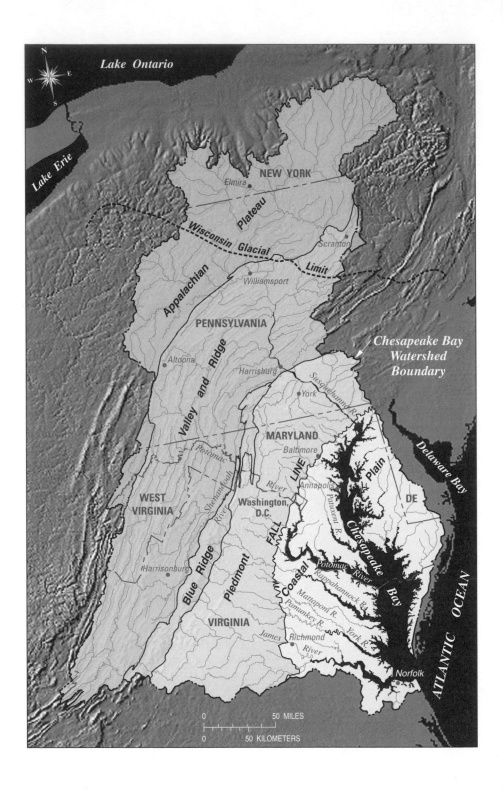

O ur story begins with the land, the earth's surface and the architecture upon which we learn to live our lives. This thin skin of our planet is alive with all the things we need to survive. If we learn to read the land well, it will tell us where to settle and what resources to use to build our dreams. Conversely, if we are not sensitive to how we treat the land, we will face increasingly difficult challenges in the future. Most past civilizations blossomed as people learned to work closely with their environment. These same societies failed once they became overpopulated and destroyed the land that had given them sustenance (Diamond, 2005, Montgomery, 2007). So now, more than ever before on this increasingly crowded planet, it's important that each of us re-establish the necessary balance—this most basic relationship—our covenant with the land.

To understand why the Chesapeake Bay and its watershed, once rich in resources and a hospitable place for the birth and growth of a nation, is now in peril, one has but to explore the timeless geologic and climatic forces that created the bay. They are still at work, and we must learn about them and understand how our ancestors' activities interrupted their natural courses. We must learn to see our history in the geologic record, for only then can we hope to understand the present and gain insights into the future. We can best begin by examining how things were before our ancestors arrived in the Chesapeake, before man began to disrupt the balance of the ecosystem in which we live.

The Chesapeake Watershed. Courtesy U.S. Geological Survey.

Reading the Land

It's a warm summer's day as I walk along the rusted railroad tracks on the banks of the mighty Susquehanna River just north of the sleepy little town of Port Deposit. The river is a mile wide here just before it empties into the Chesapeake Bay. The sun bakes the blackened rocks along the ancient cliff walls. Fragrant honeysuckle and long, leafy grape vines cover most of the steep slopes. I pull the vines back to get a closer look at the cliff walls, for my job as a geologist is to explore the rocks and landforms along the river's edge, to unravel the complex history of this area, to gain a better perspective on how the earth behaves.

To expose the stories sealed in the rocks, I pull a battered geology hammer from my belt and break off a small piece of the cliff wall. The pick strikes a quartz vein and elicits a ping as a chip breaks loose and falls to the ground. Picking it up, I turn it over and over in my hands examining both the fresh and weathered surfaces. One side is lustrous and white, the other black, a piece of crystalline quartz coated with soot from years of coal- and diesel-fired engines rumbling by this spot as they pulled mountaintops of coal from the Appalachians down to the sea. Myriad interwoven tributaries and train tracks connect mountains and coast, providing avenues by which the watershed's mineral and timber resources were shipped downstream for eventual consumption in coastal cities and foreign ports. All that remains along the banks of this river from four centuries of commerce is this blackened residue covering the land.

The pick strikes again. This time, black slate ricochets off the wall and onto the tracks. The rock releases a strong odor of sulfur, an element bound up in the rock when it was deposited in an ancient sea millions of years ago. The rock, an especially hard slate, was once used for roofing tiles on many of the old houses and barns throughout this region. After carefully examining the specimens I reach back and pull a dog-eared notebook from my back pocket to record what I have found: *black, pyrite rich, Peach Bottom Slate with quartz vein, striking North-40East, dipping 75 degrees to the Southeast.*

Feeling hungry, I cross the tracks and sit down on a large slab of black slate under the filtered light of a sumac tree to read over my notes from the morning. My weathered jeans are covered with *hitchhikers*—seeds wanting to travel and be dispersed far from their mother plants. My rough leather boots are covered with the sooty dust of the railroad embankment. Gingerly pulling a flattened, peanut butter and jelly sandwich out of my daypack for a bite of lunch, I look out over the rapidly flowing waters of the river and daydream for a moment about those distant mountains and ports. The rest feels good, but I have to make sense of the data that I've been collecting, it has to all fit together somehow.

The ancient geology around Port Deposit, here at the northern tip of the bay, is fascinating, for I am trying to decipher the history of plate tectonics in this area, speculating on what happened here when Africa collided into North America. Of course that was a long, long time ago, back several hundred million years, during the Paleozoic Era. I am uncovering evidence of a long history of volcanic eruptions, earthquakes, and the creation of mountains, all recorded here in these rocks by the river. Every little piece of information aids in the interpretation of the details of that continental collision. What happened in the depths of the earth long ago is now exposed at the surface for anyone to see, thanks to millions of years of uplift and erosion. Deciphering these rocks helps us better understand what is happening deep in the earth's crust today in modern day collision zones beneath the Andes, the Aleutians, and the Himalayan mountains.

But the ancient geology is not the only thing that captures my interest walking along the tracks this morning. The gigantic size of this river valley itself is puzzling. Below my perch, high up on the bank, the water carries tree branches, leaves, and silt downstream. A lot of water is passing by, for the Susquehanna is one of the largest rivers on the east coast of North America, second only to the St. Lawrence Seaway in Canada. Yet it does not seem big enough to have cut this huge gorge where I am sitting. The walls of the gorge are hundreds of feet high and set back, as if the river has shrunk over the years. In some places, the cliff walls are terraced like giant steps leading away from the water's edge, creating a gorge far wider and deeper than the river requires today. Sitting here on the quiet banks I have a feeling that at one time years ago much more water rampaged down this river. How else could you explain the creation of such an impressive gorge?

I remember arriving at this same conclusion several times before while walking along the Susquehanna in Maryland, Pennsylvania, and in central New York. This river, or some much greater, mythical predecessor, carved out spectacular gorges all along its length. None of the other tributaries to the Chesapeake reveals such a fascinating history. This river could not have done all of this carving and excavation with the volume of water it carries now. The carving of the land had to have been done at the end of a glacial age, when massive amounts of melt water rushed down its veins.

Geologists have been studying the Susquehanna for more than 150 years, mapping the steep walls and accumulating evidence of a much larger river all the way from New York to Maryland. I have climbed inside giant potholes the size of tree trunks along the now dry parts of the ancient riverbed. These could only have been formed by torrential whirlpools carving out the stone over many years, relics of a series of ice ages that wreaked havoc on the planet. Collectively, the evidence indicates that the last of the great ice ages peaked 18,000 years ago, when Earth's climate began to warm. The slow but steady advance of the huge, continent-wide, Laurentian Ice Sheet that had bulldozed its way across Canada and New York State stopped its relentless march to the south. The ice began to melt; the level of the sea rose. The whole complexion of what was to become the Chesapeake watershed began to change.

The scars left from the advance of this massive sheet of ice are spread across New York, Ontario, and Quebec. Most of the topsoil was stripped away. Debris plucked from rock formations many miles to the north sculpted the land beneath the massive, mile-thick ice sheets and then was abandoned as the ice retreated. Advancing ice left deep valleys, kettle ponds, and striations in bedrock surfaces all across the northern states and provinces. Today moraines and hummocky glacial deposits of sands, clays, and endless mounds of boulders dot the countryside throughout the headwaters of the watershed. The Ice Age created these dramatic landforms of the north.

Fortunately, this thick mountain of ice that ruthlessly scoured all soil and life from the land in the north never reached what is now the Chesapeake Bay. The ice sheet reached only into northern Pennsylvania. But the vast floodwaters that issued from the melting of this tremendous volume of ice had nowhere else to go. To the north was the ice mass, thousands of feet thick. So the melt waters flowed southward, flooding and carving the ancestral Susquehanna River gorge. These waters shaped the topography, the history, and eventually the culture of the Chesapeake Bay.

Try to imagine a blanket of ice 3,000 to 8,000 feet thick stretching across the northern tier of the United States from the Atlantic to the Pacific and *at least* six times the height of the dramatic five-hundred-foot walls of the Susquehanna River Valley that dwarf the steeples of Port Deposit. The ice sheet, more than three times the height of the Empire State Building, also covered the northern reaches of Europe and Asia. So much of the earth's water was locked up in the massive polar ice sheets during that last advance of the Wisconsin Ice Age that sea levels worldwide were lowered by about three hundred feet. Try to fathom what that must have looked like. The lower sea level would have exposed vast areas of our continental shelves. Our current coastlines and coastal communities would have been left high and dry, some two hundred miles inland from that Late Pleistocene Ocean.

Now close your eyes and try to conjure up pictures of what it must have been like as the ice melted. Imagine all the glacial melt waters rushing down rivers like the Susquehanna, the Columbia, and the Mississippi on their way to refill the depleted oceans, releasing vast amounts of fresh water captured as snow and held frozen in the ice for thousands of years. The waters from the ice sheet covering New York State would have flushed down the headwaters of the Susquehanna River, flowing into the northern tributaries such as those which now lie near the towns of Cooperstown, Oneonta, Binghamton, and Elmira, New York, and then funneling into the main stem and weaving their way through

Pennsylvania. All that water would have come roaring right down past places now known as Towanda, Wilkes-Barre, Danville, and Harrisburg and then through this gorge where I'm sitting. The water level would have been well over my head where I'm having lunch today on the lowest floodplain. Looking downriver to where the river opens into the bay, I realize that, since the sea level was so much lower, the Chesapeake did not even exist at that time. To get to the Atlantic Ocean, the flood waters traveled through a narrow and much longer river valley that extended for hundreds of miles beneath what is now the deeper part of the bay, all the way to Norfolk, Virginia. From there the river would have continued many more miles to the east, crossing the then-exposed continental shelf. I picture myself and friends kayaking such a river back in the Pleistocene. It would have been one heck of a ride down a raging and swollen river and would have taken weeks to reach the sea.

Today the gorge abruptly disappears near Havre de Grace, Maryland, just south of Port Deposit. The salty waters of the ocean have encroached onto the continent all the way up to that point, leaving the four-hundred-mile-long river valley to the southeast submerged and forgotten, hidden by the waters of the Atlantic and the Chesapeake. The best view of the dramatic topographic change and submersion of this gorge can be seen from the Tydings Memorial Bridge that carries Interstate 95 across the Susquehanna. When you look to the northwest side of this bridge, you can see cliff walls five hundred feet high separating the rolling upland plateaus and sleepy farmlands from the flowing waters in the deeply incised river valley. Looking to the southeast you will see the cliffs falling away and disappearing beneath the Chesapeake. The river opens up here at its mouth, and fresh water pours into the wider and saltier expanse of the bay.

As sea level rose, the ocean began to creep inland, slowly flooding the old river valley and its tributaries. These fluvial tentacles reached their way hundreds of miles back into the countryside and provided wonderful shipping access to many corners of the Maryland and Virginia tidewater. Where the rising water overflowed the banks of the ancient rivers, the bay tends to be very shallow—forty percent of it is less than six feet deep. However, farther from shore and hidden beneath the calm waters of the bay is the deeper trough of the ancestral Susquehanna River gorge that reaches depths of 174 feet. The rising tide brought brackish water and marine life all the way up to Havre de Grace, nearly bisecting what is now Maryland into two regions, known as the Eastern Shore and the Western Shore. The flooding of the Susquehanna River gorge created one of the largest and most productive estuaries on earth.

The quaint little town of Havre de Grace lies at the northern tip of the bay just downriver and on the opposite bank from where I sit. Havre de Grace was built on the fall line, that partly imaginary, partly geologic, and partly topographic line that separates the navigable, tidal waters of the Coastal Plain to the southeast from the water "falls" of the Piedmont to the northwest. Since the fall line marks the northern and western limits of the bay, it was significant historically. Most of the major ports built over the last four centuries in the Mid-Atlantic grew up straddling this line. Philadelphia, Trenton, Wilmington, Baltimore, Washington, and Richmond were all built at the ends of navigable waterways as far inland as possible to serve the greatest number of farms and plantations. These towns flourished, allowing goods and resources of the Piedmont and tidewater to be shipped cheaply by sea up and down the coast, to Europe, the West Indies, and beyond. With the arrival of Europeans in the Chesapeake, the bay became first and foremost an avenue for communication and transportation.

But that is all *recent* history. At this point in our story we want to know what this area looked like 18,000 years ago, when this gorge was churning with melt waters and there was no bay. The area now known as Maryland might have looked a lot more like Pennsylvania with a mighty river running through it. No bay, no crabs, no oysters. The entire region, including the vast, then-exposed parts of the continental shelf, was home to colder weather flora and fauna. Conifers blanketed the landscape. Based on the fossil record, we know that many of the large Ice Age mammals—mammoths, mastodons, saber-toothed tigers, giant sloth, giant bears, and giant beavers, as well as horses and camels—roamed across the savannahs and woodlands in North America during this Late Pleistocene Age before man showed up. Geologically speaking, it really wasn't so long ago.

Then man arrived. One of the more interesting archeological spots on the Eastern Shore of Maryland is Paw Paw Cove on Tilghman Island. Professor Brian Lowery of Washington College and his students have found Clovis-like arrowheads buried in 13,000-year-old soil horizons on this site. This is 2,000 years older than sites in the western U.S. where Clovis arrowheads were initially discovered. Furthermore, Dennis Stanford of the Smithsonian Institute claims that the Paw Paw Cove relics resemble arrowhead styles common to archeological sites in Spain. These two lines of evidence draw into question the common theory that early man migrated from the northwest along a land and ice bridge connection between Alaska and Asia. Although that theory may be true for humans who settled the western U.S., the older sites near the Chesapeake support the idea that humans may have migrated here during an earlier period from a different direction. They might have come from the northeast, along a land and ice bridge between Europe and America. The lower sea levels and the massive continental ice sheet of the Ice Age provided opportunities for either or both of these migrations. We are still struggling with this piece of the puzzle. That's what is so fascinating about research and science—putting all the pieces together. All we have to do is gather enough information.

In addition to raising questions about where early Americans came from, the arrowheads also raise questions about man's impact on the native species, for that is when our tug-of-war with nature here in North America began. Some archeologists link the lethal Clovis arrowheads to the demise of the large Ice Age mammals. All of the thirty-five large Pleistocene mammal species present when man arrived in North America were extinct by the end of the Pleistocene, some 10,000 years ago. They passed from the earth just as early man was spreading across the continent. Others argue that global warming and even an atmospheric meteorite explosion caused their extinction. Those events may have had an effect, but the coincident timing of man's arrival and the end of the large Ice Age mammals is quite compelling. Archeologists and geologists continue to search for the clues that will tell a more complete story of this period. They will keep digging in the rubble of the few dozen remaining archeological sites scattered around the bay, searching until they find answers to these questions.

I've often wondered why more evidence of the people and animals of post-glacial time hasn't been unearthed. Why don't we stumble onto Native American artifacts when exploring river valleys and turning over rocks looking for geologic clues? If man was widespread enough to hunt and kill off all the large mammals, why don't we have more evidence of his villages and burial grounds? An understanding of the last Ice Age and subsequent global warming provides at least some answers.

Early man most likely camped and built villages along the banks of the ancestral Susquehanna River in what is now Maryland and on the continental shelf to the east, to harvest the bounty of the river and the expanding bay. As the waters slowly rose, the inhabitants would have picked up their belongings and moved inland. The game would have moved as well. As the water rose, all of these ancient villages as well as the piles of discarded oyster shells, mastodon bones, and other debris would have been washed away or covered. Just picture all the relics from thousands of years of habitation buried beneath the bay and our coastal waters, buried because of global warming and sea level rise following the last Ice Age.

Sitting here on a very hot day on the banks of the Susquehanna, it's hard to picture the Ice Age, but it does give me a deeper appreciation of how nature works. We should all ponder how this post–Ice Age history can enhance our understanding of the possible outcomes of our current, man-made episode of global warming. Even though the cause may be different, the results will certainly be the same. It is clear that if the current warming trend continues, more ice will melt and sea levels will rise. Based on all the evidence from the past, if we allow this warming trend to continue, sea levels are projected to rise globally at least several feet during this century and maybe more. This may not be significant in the history of the earth, but it will certainly be significant to humans. We have finely tuned our lives to current environmental conditions, and even small changes like this will affect us greatly. Our food, our water supplies, and our cities are all in jeopardy. The Chesapeake, with its 8,000 miles of coastline, is considered one of the areas most at risk to sea level rise in this country. The area around Norfolk at the mouth of the bay is the second most vulnerable city in the country after New Orleans.

Unless we act to slow global warming, the bay will continue to expand, flooding thousands of acres of marshes and currently dry land. As in the past, islands will disappear. Twelve of the thirty-five islands that existed in the bay during the colonial period have already been lost. The best-known islands soon to be lost will be Smith and Tangier, both of which barely stay dry during high tides today. Wetlands will be inundated. Blackwater Refuge and much of the southern part of the Eastern Shore are at risk. Towns, cities, and villages built close to the bay will also be flooded. Since colonial times, more than a hundred historic settlements, forts, and plantations have been lost to rising water and coastal erosion. The effect on Baltimore, Fells Point, and Annapolis was evident when a storm surge flooded parts of them during Hurricane Isabel, which was only a Level II hurricane. Because of a combination of factors it was the costliest and deadliest storm in the 2003 Atlantic hurricane season. The threat is real.

Returning to my perch on the banks of the Susquehanna, I realize that lunchtime is over. I get up, dust off my pants, put my notebook away in my backpack, and continue walking along the cliffs in search of the next outcrop. I have a job to do. But as I walk, I begin to realize that there is other important work that needs doing as well. Yes, we must understand the past, but we must also learn from it if we are to better understand the future. It's time to reflect upon what we've learned, to recognize the impact we have on this landscape and change the way we are contributing to global warming and causing other damage to the environment. While walking along the bank above the river, I decide to do something about my own small impact on the bay and, on a larger scale, on global warming. I decide to identify the other ways my manner of living has affected the environment and to share the information

Tangier Island, one of the disappearing islands of the Chesapeake. (Courtesy of Alice Webb, the artist.)

with others. We must all comprehend the fine balance our society has to maintain with the bay, so we can more clearly see the consequences of our actions. It will take all of us, acting together, to make a difference. We have to move beyond years of apathy and cynicism and into a time of responsibility and caring for our environment. It's the only one we have. Our home is changing, and not for the better. We must do something about it.

What can be done about sea level rise? Following the Ice Age, man had no choice in the matter, he had to adapt to sea level rise. He had no ability to stop the warming trend and had plenty of time and space to adapt. Adapting today would be much more difficult. No longer are there just farms and homes close to sea level but large cities, and there is no more free land to accommodate us if large parts of our society are displaced by rising sea levels. Fortunately, we do have a choice, since much of any rise in sea level will be the direct result of greenhouse gases we are discharging into the atmosphere. We can act now to slow these emissions and slow global warming. It would be foolhardy to ignore the trend, to just wait and try to adapt to the changes, because they will be significant, and destructive.

Individuals can help immediately by changing our wasteful energy practices. We currently waste thirty percent of the energy we use in our homes and offices. We can also support the development of less polluting energy sources by signing up for wind- and solar-generated energy and thereby encourage utilities to move away from fossil fuels. We can stop buying things we don't need, because it takes energy to create, distribute, maintain, and dispose of things. Each of us can also help create and articulate a vision of a healthier earth to our friends, families, and representatives. If people will lead, politicians will follow.

Corporations can help by reducing emissions from power plants, factories, trucks, and automobiles. Cleaner technologies exist; people are ready to support better alternatives. Corporations who harness this trend will do well as they create jobs and help to rebuild our economy. Their marketing power can show the way to a more secure future.

Governments can lead by shifting tax incentives, subsidies, and delivery infrastructure away from fossil fuels to renewable sources of energy. Political leaders can use the bully pulpit to challenge us all to work together toward the goals of clean energy, climate stabilization, and global security.

From the Mountains to the Sea

A watershed is all the land that drains into a particular river or body of water. The Chesapeake Bay watershed is fascinating because it straddles the entire eastern edge of the North American continent. One can explore it by taking a journey all the way from the mountains to the sea, from the Appalachians to the Atlantic. It's a trip that crosses at least three major geologically diverse terrains and one that reveals this area's dynamic history of both continental collisions and continental conquest. If you look closely as we travel, you will see the roots of the ancestral Appalachian Mountains as well as evidence of the breakup of the Pangea Supercontinent. You will also see the barriers to westward migration and the resources that made it possible. It's an amazing example of what can be learned by studying the rocks and landforms in one's own back yard. So come along with me on this trek. You just might enjoy it.

We'll start in the mountainous area geologists refer to as the Valley and Ridge Province in western Maryland, our little section of the Appalachian Mountain chain which runs from Georgia to Maine. One of the best rock exposures, or *outcrops*, in this entire range lies just east of Cumberland. To shorten the trip west, engineers building Interstate 68 literally blasted through the top third of Sideling Hill, a significant hurdle to east-west travel. I stop here regularly, partly for the view and in part to look at such a large exposure of the earth's crust; it's a rare treat here in the East. Perhaps you, too, will find it comforting to see what underlies the land we live upon.

This dramatic, near-vertical road cut exposes a breath-taking expanse of folded Paleozoic strata. It looks like half of a colorful layer cake that sank in the middle. A palette of red, yellow, white, gray, and even black sedimentary rock layers form a broad syncline, a U-shaped fold that seems counter-intuitive to its presence at the pinnacle of this 2,300-foot ridge. The layers of rocks swoop upward at each end of the rock outcrop just as the slopes of the ridge descend into the valleys on each side. You have to see it to believe it. Stop and take a look the next time you drive by.

To understand what is happening, geologically speaking, visit the Exhibit Center on the east side of the ridge. Stroll around looking at the easily understood pictures of *plate tectonics*, 600 million years of geological turmoil that created the bedrock beneath your feet. The best time to stop and visit is when Wally DeWitt is presiding over the exhibit. Wally is retired from the U.S. Geological Survey and lives near Washington, D.C. He has spent his entire career investigating the rocks of the Valley and Ridge Province. Many of the interpretations of the geologic past shown in the displays are ideas he came up with and published over the years. Whenever Wally gets the chance, he volunteers at this roadside exhibit. The Center is a great tribute to a man who has devoted his life to discovering earth's mysteries.

Wally is a stout man with a buzz cut and high forehead. At first he appears a little gruff, but you quickly learn that he is warm and friendly and loves to explain the history of the area. Geologists as a rule would rather be hiking the mountains than talking to people, but at this point in his career, Wally has come in from the woods and seems to really enjoy sharing his deep understanding of the earth. He uses the pictures and the models to explain how the mountains came to be.

Whenever I stop by for a visit, I engage Wally with some challenging questions; that's what geologists do. We are great believers in multiple working hypotheses, the more the better. Sure, the facts are very important, but the fun is coming up with theories on how all the geological observations fit together. The theories that geologists create are subject to debate. When interpreting a complex set of data, nothing is cast in stone, so to speak. There is always room for another interpretation.

As usual, Wally has heard many of these arguments before. He acknowledges mine with a kindly nod and then explains why he rejects it. He has an encyclopedic memory, it appears, remembering every outcrop he has mapped and how each rock fits into his world view. Still, I leave the debate quite pleased. The exchange has prompted deeper thought, and a greater appreciation of the geology and the man.

Then it's outside for a walk where you can get a real feeling for the magnitude of the forces that must have been required to fold these massive layers of rock. Just looking at the curved outcrop is exhilarating. Nothing less than the collision of continents could have produced a fold of this magnitude. You can get a stiff neck looking up at the rocks. A total of 840 feet of strata are exposed at the site, reflecting millions of years of sediment accumulation. The rock layers are made up of conglomerate, siltstone, sandstone, shale, and coal, all of which were deposited in some ancient landscape after eroding from the tops of mountains and traveling long distances down streams and rivers. Plant and animal (brachiopod and bivalve) fossils in some of the rock layers help to establish an age for this part of our geologic past as the early Mississippian Period. That means that these plants and animals lived about 340 million years ago, when these strata were being deposited on an alluvial plain down close to sea level, not up here at 2,300 feet above sea level on top of a mountain. The thin coal deposits exposed in this road cut were once swamps on ancient flood plains, and the sandstone rocks an old river channel.

The rocks we see today once were the sands and organic humus of that ancient plain. They were then buried by thousands of feet of younger sediments on the edge of the continent. This deep burial process compacted and cemented this ancient detritus into the rocks exposed here today. These rocks were subsequently folded and uplifted during the collision of Africa with North America over 200 million years ago, a continental collision that built this area up into a very tall mountain range, possibly the size of the Himalayas. During the millions of years since, erosion has removed thousands of feet of overlying sediments to expose these once deeply buried rocks for our viewing pleasure (Tillman, 1983). It's a site worth visiting and a good place for the start of our journey. Things just get more complex as one moves east across the watershed.

After saying farewell to Wally we drive east, up and down mountains, through the valleys and across the ridges. The ridge top views are spectacular and in places one can almost feel like being in flight high above the wooded stream valleys. After passing Hancock, Williamsport, South Mountain, and High Knob we'll drop down out of the mountains near Frederick and enter into the rolling hills, suburbs, and farmlands of the Piedmont. The rocks of the Piedmont, which extend all the way from Frederick to Baltimore, differ from the broadly folded sedimentary rocks to the west. The Piedmont rocks represent the actual core of the collision zone where the continents came together long ago. In contrast to the sedimentary rocks of the Valley and Ridge, these were buried to greater depths. In fact, they were metamorphosed into more crystalline rocks by the greater heat and pressure found deep within the earth's crust. Under those conditions, sandstone became quartzite, limestone re-crystallized into marble, and shale became schist. At depths of several miles beneath the earth's surface, the metamorphic rocks were also intruded by molten magmas. The magmas later cooled into igneous rocks like the granites now found in the Piedmont near the towns of Woodstock, Granite, Ellicott City, and Guilford. On the far eastern edge of the Piedmont, near Elkridge, large slabs of dark, oceanic crust and ancient volcanic islands were thrust up onto the mélange of continental rocks along the eastern edge of the ancestral North American continent.

So the Piedmont, which underlies parts of Maryland, Pennsylvania, and Virginia, is quite a hodge-podge of different types of rocks. When you look at them closely or examine a map of their distribution patterns, you will see that they have been tightly folded and squeezed as if they were mud, not rock. This is what happens at great depths in the core of a collision zone. The rocks were heated to temperatures where they became ductile and flowed like toothpaste.

Whereas Wally Dewitt was at home in the Valley and Ridge, the Piedmont is my geologic home. I am, in geological terms, a *hard rocker*, one trained to study *hard* metamorphic and igneous rocks in contrast to *soft* sedimentary rocks. I've mapped granites and gabbros, gneisses and schists, and the more contorted the rocks, the more I like them. There are more clues to our past, more geologic history hidden in deformed rocks, more to unravel.

Unlike Sideling Hill, few large rock exposures are visible along the interstate highways within the Piedmont, but bedrock can be seen in the beds of rivers as they descend eastward to the fall line. You just have to get off the highways and walk on the trails to discover the rocks of the Piedmont. The best rock exposures are along the Susquehanna and Potomac rivers where deep gorges reveal many outcrops of Piedmont rocks. The easiest way to get to one of the most dramatic rock exposures is along the Billy Goat Trail on the Potomac River. You can get to the trail from the C&O Canal on the Maryland side of the river. Take a friend and your lunch, and go explore Bear Island, one of the more spectacular views in the entire Mid-Atlantic region.

Let's leave the metamorphic and igneous rocks of the Piedmont and move eastward to explore the relatively young sediments of the Atlantic Coastal Plain that border and underlie the bay. You can see these sediments on a drive across the Severn River Bridge east from Annapolis because they show up on the edges of many bay tributaries as tall yellow, orange, tan, and white cliffs that are easily eroded by wind, rain, and wave action. The sediments appear today just as they were deposited, in horizontal layers of sand and clay, looking like a flat (unfolded) layer cake. They have not yet been buried to depths great enough to deform them into folds or even to turn them into more resistant rocks. In fact, in areas such as Calvert Cliffs in southern Maryland, it is easy to dig through the cliffs with a trowel or shovel and discover fossilized shark teeth and whale vertebrae.

Where did these sediments come from and how do they relate to the Piedmont? After the continental collision that formed the ancestral Appalachian Mountains, Africa was connected to North America. This supercontinent was called Pangea, and it lasted for 165 million years. When what is now Africa eventually separated from the North American continent about 65 million years ago, a new ocean, the Atlantic, opened up along the old suture zone. Erosion of the very high ancestral Appalachian Mountains deposited sand, silt, and clay onto the edge of this new ocean. These loose, unconsolidated sediments now form the Atlantic Coastal Plain, which is an eastward thickening wedge of sediments that lies east of the fall line. This wedge of sediments is only a

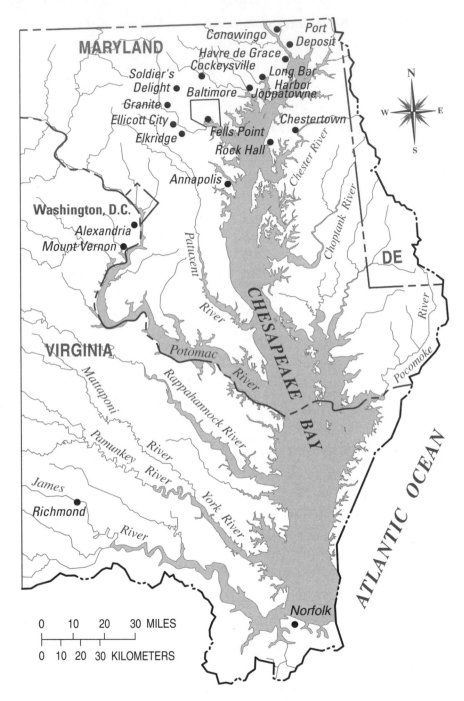

Chesapeake Bay towns. (Courtesy of the U.S. Geological Survey.)

few feet thick along the fall line but becomes more than 7,000 feet thick beneath Ocean City and steadily increases in thickness as the wedge of sediment extends eastward beneath the continental shelf. Geologists have explored this offshore regime in great detail by drilling wells and running seismic surveys along the coastline and far offshore in search of oil and gas deposits.

Our geological field trip across the bay's watershed from the mountains to the sea ends as we leave the watershed to take a stroll along the shores of the Atlantic. Pick up a handful of sand, let the grains flow through your fingers, and try to imagine the various trips that each of these quartz grains has made to arrive here on this sandy stretch of beach. Some may have come from the Atlantic Coastal Plain sediments, some from the granites and quartz veins in the Piedmont, and still others from sandstones way up on Sideling Hill. They were all flushed down tributaries and eventually worked their way out into the ocean to be redirected by the tides and the waves along the Atlantic Coast. Now they rest on the windswept sand dunes of this barrier island. The surf breaks down the sand grains and shells to smaller and smaller fragments and redistributes them in various patterns along the beach. Some day they too will be buried under the sea by thousands of feet of future sediments. They will eventually become caught up in another collision zone and end up as part of a future mountain range accreted onto the eastern edge of the North American continent. That will come to pass at some point because the geological cycle is a continuous, some say relentless, process of erosion, burial, and mountain-building—a process of shifting and transforming matter, and we are just observers, a few carbon molecules playing on this vast continental stage.

Whenever I stand on the shores of the Atlantic thinking about the timelessness of geologic processes, I wonder about the impact man has had on these natural cycles. Has it been significant? We are so small relative to the size of the earth. Yet erosion, which at first appears to be innocuous, is the dominant process occurring in the watershed today. It is the natural process of rock breaking down and the sediment transported by water to lower and lower elevations, all the way from the mountains to the sea. We have greatly altered this process. In many places we have accelerated it by loosening the soil during construction and farming. Our disruptive activities have increased rates of erosion from fifty to four hundred times the natural rates. How many of us understand that we are bankrupting our farms, throwing away our topsoil, wasting an invaluable resource? I don't think we realize this sediment is washing into our streams at an anomalously rapid rate, in many cases faster than it can be removed by natural flushing. In addition to jeopardizing our ability to feed ourselves in the future, these sediments carry toxins, increase turbidity, reduce sunlight, clog waterways, and as a result can dramatically change habitats and threaten the existence of many species.

Several of the watershed's early settlements failed as the result of ruined soils and the silting of their natural harbors. Joppa Town and Elkridge, for example, once thriving ports that served ocean-going vessels, died when their harbors filled with sediment flushed down the Gunpowder and Patapsco Rivers by colonial farming practices. Even today, major dredging operations are required each year to keep our harbors open for shipping. Farming and construction still produce much sedimentation, and significant efforts have been focused on reducing the amount of runoff into our streams. More must be done, lest we end up like Mesopotamia, Egypt, Athens, Rome, and MesoAmerica, where erosion from poor farming habits caused the fall of earlier empires (Montgomery, 2007). We are poised to repeat history if we are not smart enough to learn from it.

In addition to current human activities that accelerate erosion and fill our waterways with silt, a latent source of colonial sediments that could cloud the waters of the bay in the future has recently been documented. I was invited by Dorothy Merritts and Bob Walter to take a look at sediment deposits along several stream valleys within the watershed. Both are professors of geology at Franklin and Marshall College in Lancaster, Pennsylvania. They are a husband and wife team that had never worked together on a project before, but the more they discussed sediment deposits along the Little Conestoga Creek in Lancaster County, the more interested they both became in working together on this project.

Dorothy is a petite, freckled, redhead with a long braid flowing out behind her floppy tan hat and down her back. Her enthusiasm is infectious as we walk along the stream bank. We are all decked out in rubberized waders, carrying trowels, topographic maps, and airborne images of the stream valley and surrounding area. Bob is up ahead, already wading across the stream. He slices into the bank on the far shore with a shovel to expose a fresh cross-section of the sedimentary horizons of what at first appears to be a natural stream bank deposit.

Dorothy is a tectonic geomorphologist who studies landforms and changes to the base levels of streams. She explains that natural and man-made changes to the environment can be documented by studying their effect on stream sediments. She now points out the laminated clays, silts, and sands overlying an organic layer and a basal gravel unit sitting on the limestone bedrock Bob has exposed. We wade across to get a better look at the twenty-foot-high bank of sediments. Historically these occurrences were interpreted as natural floodplain deposits, but this thick section did not look like a natural floodplain deposit to Dorothy and Bob, so they decided to investigate.

The sediments turn out to be what is left of the slack water millpond sediments trapped behind a man-made dam that dates from the colonial period. Dorothy and Bob traced the sediments upstream, and where the sediments petered out they found the remains of another dam. This raised their curiosity about how many dams there might have been in Pennsylvania. With help from their students, they discovered that more than 10,000 dams had been built in the seventeenth, eighteenth, and nineteenth centuries. Literally everywhere a dam could have been built, someone built one. More than 65,000 dams were constructed in the eastern United States during those three centuries. Within the Piedmont, streams were literally choked with dams, which served as the settlers' main source of power. Most are gone now, but the enormous amounts of sediment that collected behind them are still present along many streams throughout the watershed.

Bob is a geochronologist, an age-dater. He utilizes a range of isotopic analyses to determine the age of sediments, rocks, and geologic processes. He used radiocarbon, cesium, and lead age-dating methods to test Dorothy's field observations and wound up confirming the pre- and post-settlement histories of the sediments they found along the rivers in southern Lancaster County.

The sediments commonly contain high concentrations of the residue of man's activities, ranging from nutrients like phosphorus and nitrogen to heavy metals and other toxins in some cases. Merritts and Walter refer to these soils as *legacy sediments* and estimate that they occur along thousands of miles of stream banks throughout the watershed. During construction activity or major storms, sediments and the residues they contain are washed down into the bay. This previously undocumented source of nutrient-laden sediments continues to contribute to the problems of the bay, as widespread construction releases them into the water throughout the watershed.

A few intact dams still lie along the Susquehanna River. Dams at Holtwood, Safe Harbor, York Haven, and the hundred-foot-high Conowingo Dam near the mouth of the Susquehanna, are almost filled with legacy sediments that stretch upriver for many miles. Currently this series of dams captures two-thirds of the three million tons of sediment the river carries each year. What will happen when these reservoirs fill to the brink? That time is only a few years off—we had better start planning for it.

From a single day in the woods, one can come to realize how important it is that basic scientific work continues. Whether it is Wally's work in the Valley and Ridge or Dorothy and Bob's work in the Piedmont, there is still lots to learn and understand from the land. Much of the public works planning and the multi-billion dollar stream restoration efforts undertaken in this country have not taken into account the potential impact of legacy sediments on the bay. With the publication of their work, we should be able to do better in the future. A wealth of knowledge is still waiting to be unearthed, and I hope more young people will take up the challenge and help unlock the natural mysteries so essential to our lives.

I left full of questions after spending the day with Dorothy and Bob.

What should we do about legacy sediments? If we dredge them out of the rivers so they don't wash into the bay, where should we take them? If we don't dredge them out, what happens when the next big storm arrives? Hurricanes Agnes and Isabel taught us what big storms can do—both released large amounts of legacy sediments and nutrients into the bay. The current warming trend will probably produce more big storms in the future. To fix the problem will be expensive. Restoration and regeneration of our resources are invariably more complicated than prevention. It is always far better not to damage the resources in the first place. Everything comes down to understanding how nature operates and how our actions affect our environment. We must find better solutions to uncontrolled storm water runoff, the erosion of our soils, and the flushing of silt, nutrients, and chemicals into our waterways.

What can be done about erosion, siltation, and legacy sediments? We have to take responsibility for the erosion of current and past sediments and the chemical residues they contain. This is a widespread problem that affects our lives, our health, and our environment as well as the non-human species in our interdependent web of life. Our goal must be to slow down the mass movement of the land into the sea, to save our topsoil, and to save our bay. There are several things we can do to help.

Individuals can start learning more about natural processes and how our everyday activities affect the waterways and the bay. Right in our back yards we can begin shifting focus from encouraging water to run off our land and instead encourage it to filter into the soil (see appendices for specific suggestions). That will reduce runoff of water, silt, nutrients, and toxic residue from our homes, yards, and driveways and keep it from damaging our waterways and the bay.

Governments can begin reducing the amount of legacy sediments washing into the bay by requiring their removal from streams during sewer, road, and bridge construction projects and planting better buffers along streams. They can also do a better job of enforcing runoff regulations, encouraging no-till farming, and updating development manuals to require low-impact storm water designs in future development. Most jurisdictions will have to bite the bullet and create a storm water utility to retrofit existing storm water management systems.

Corporations can lead the way in providing many of the solutions to these problems. They can develop expertise in Low Impact Development, in retrofitting the current storm water infrastructure, and in finding economical solutions to the legacy sediment problem. They can enhance their community, while lowering their costs, by demonstrating best sustainability practices in their buildings and on their grounds.

Building Blocks of the Bay

Whenever I'm out leading field trips, participants of all ages ask about the rocks we encounter. There is just something magical about finding a colorful rock or a plant fossil. We seem to tap into some primeval sense of discovery when we pick up a dark gray rock with a bright white calcite vein zigzagging through it. On these field trips, I always stop and do my best to identify even the most nondescript rocks people pick up. If we have time I will discuss how the rock fits into the theory of plate tectonics and the history of the area.

"What's this?" Some kid is tugging on my shirt.

"I'm not sure. Let's see if we can identify it. Can you describe it?"

"It's gray and has a jagged, white line cutting through it. Is it a fossil?"

"No, but that's a good description. Let's see how hard it is. Try to scratch it with this nail. Scratch the white line as well."

"It scratches. Is that good?"

"Well it tells us it's soft like a sedimentary rock. Igneous rocks are usually quite hard, and it's hard to scratch them. It's probably limestone or shale. Let me drop some vinegar on it." We both watch intently as the scratch fizzes and the white line fizzes too.

"What's happening?"

"It's releasing carbon dioxide. That tells me it's limestone. And that's a white calcite vein cutting across it."

The little boy goes away satisfied, thinking he has a pretty neat rock that fizzes. But in addition to the science, the rock, the soils underfoot, and the landforms all around us, are all pieces of the fascinating story of how the region's geology shaped human settlement in the watershed. This story begins when the first colonists settled in the tidewater. The tidal tributaries of the bay offered easy access and transportation. Planters along the bay's tributaries could travel by water along thousands of miles of coastline because of the flat nature of the Atlantic Coastal Plain. The whole tidewater region consists of easily eroded sediments

27

dissected by navigable waters, making the Chesapeake especially attractive for settlement at a time when no roads existed. Furthermore, where the sediments were exposed along cliffs and streams, the settlers could locate and easily quarry unconsolidated sand, silt, and clay for roadbed materials, mortar, and making bricks.

When Captain John Smith sailed up the bay and into the Patapsco River in 1608, he noted the widespread red clay along the banks. What is now Baltimore's Inner Harbor was dominated by Federal Hill, and this massive clay hill became the site of several early brickyards. With time, Baltimore became a city of brick and evolved into a center of brick-making and export, to places like Boston, New York, Philadelphia, and other large ports in the colonies. Bricks were also sent to England as ballast in ships. In addition, Federal Hill was mined for fine white sand, used by a nearby silica glassworks. It was also a source of low-grade iron ore, which was extracted through a labyrinth of tunnels that are said to still exist beneath the hill. German brewers reportedly later used these cool tunnels to store wooden kegs of beer, and Union troops garrisoned on the hill during the Civil War stored ammunition there. The tunnels are also said to have been a secret stop along the Underground Railroad. As they did at Federal Hill, settlers quarried ironstone from sedimentary deposits throughout the Coastal Plain and turned it into iron ore. By the time of the Revolutionary War, the colonies had become the third largest producer of raw iron in the world, and the natural geological resources had made Maryland and Virginia the largest producers in the colonies. Iron was second only to tobacco in revenue for these states. Iron furnaces of the 1700s in Baltimore, Cecil, and Anne Arundel counties (Maryland) produced the best pig and bar iron in the colonies.

Water power was required in order to make the iron, which drove the settlers west into the Piedmont. Forges were built along and just west of the fall line where there was adequate elevation drop for water to run a waterwheel. Water-driven bellows kept the furnaces hot enough to produce pig iron. A forge was then used to refine iron pigs into bar iron by repeated cycles of heating and pounding with a water-driven hammer. This process strengthened the iron and made it easier to work into a finished product. Water-powered iron slitting operations cut the iron into nails. Water-powered and wood-heated rolling mills turned the iron into sheet metal of various thicknesses.

As settlement moved west of the fall line and onto the Piedmont, the settlers found rolling topography and harder metamorphic and igneous rock exposed along stream valleys. Marble, quartzite, serpentine, gneiss, granite, and gabbro were the resources mined and used by settlers during the eighteenth and nineteenth centuries. They built numerous road and railroad bridges and buildings out of these more resistant building materials. Many remain standing. Some of the quarries are also still in use.

White and gray-banded Cockeysville marble is found in the Piedmont and used extensively for building stones, rip rap to armor shorelines and riverbanks, and road material. It is mined from large quarries like those at Cockeysville and Marriottsville, Maryland. Thousands of slabs of this strikingly white marble are now the famous white steps and window sills that adorn Baltimore's well-known red brick rowhouses. The marble was also used to build the 108 columns in the wings of the U.S. Capitol, and Baltimore's City Hall. Cockeysville marble was used for all but four courses of the 555-foot-tall Washington Monument in the District of Columbia.

The large quarry on the south side of the Susquehanna River, which can be seen from the Interstate 95 Bridge, is also an active operation that continues to mine Port Deposit gneiss for shipping to points around the bay. Port Deposit gneiss is a granitic gneiss with large crystals of quartz and feldspar, and a distinctive black mica striped pattern. It was used in the construction of Fort McHenry, Goucher and Haverford Colleges, and the U.S. Naval Academy. Oceanic crust, known locally as Baltimore gabbro, continues to be mined and used for building stone and road materials throughout the region.

During the colonial period, Setters quartzite was used for building homes and is used widely today as flagstone in patios and fireplaces. Most people just walk on the stones without ever noticing their striking, white mica crystals and the one- to four-inch striated black tourma-

Old Ellicott City homes and courthouse built with Ellicott City granite. (Courtesy of Alice Webb, the artist.)

line crystals that decorate the surface. The entire Bon Secours Spiritual Center in Marriottsville, Maryland, was built upon a Setters quartzite ridge and is constructed with these very attractive local flagstones.

Granite from a number of small quarries operated in the early nineteenth century was cut into blocks and used to build houses, commercial buildings, and the old court house in Ellicott City. The granite was also shipped off to build the Baltimore Basilica, parts of the U.S. Capitol, and the Library of Congress. Large blocks of granite were initially hauled from Ellicott City in huge wagons drawn by nine yoke of oxen. Later they were shipped by rail. Abandoned quarries can still be seen along the sides of Old Frederick Road just east of Old Ellicott City. Other outcrops can be seen along Main Street and along the abandoned trolley tracks leading out of town from the Trolley Stop Restaurant.

Hidden within the Piedmont is a narrow, northeast trending, serpentine belt containing chrome ore deposits which became the most significant chromium mining district in the country. Chromite, used in manufacturing chemicals, paints, and dyes, was first discovered in this country in the serpentine area of Bare Hills in Baltimore County in 1810. A Baltimore Quaker, chemist, geologist, abolitionist, and businessman, named Isaac Tyson Jr. developed the mines and by 1825 extended his mining activities to Soldiers Delight. Tyson had the "superior acumen" to recognize "that the chromite always occurs in the serpentine and was able to follow this rock by the barren areas to which it gives rise" (Maryland Geological Survey, 285). He established the Baltimore Chrome Works and had a virtual monopoly on the world chrome market until significant deposits were discovered in Asia Minor (Maryland Geological Survey I, 1897). It is possible to visit and see the old chrome mines at the Natural Environmental Area in Soldiers Delight, Maryland.

There are two legacies to these serpentine deposits. Waste materials from the chromium refining operations have contaminated a large amount of land, some of which juts right out into Baltimore's Inner Harbor. The contamination on this site has been contained at great expense and is not believed to pose any further threat but will require ongoing monitoring. It is currently being developed. In Montgomery County, Maryland, the serpentine was quarried, crushed, and used for paving roads. This proved to be a bad idea, because serpentine contains natural asbestos. As the roads wear, chrysotile fibers are found in the air near the roads at concentrations ten times greater than typically found in air. These are good examples of how, if they are not handled appropriately, our natural resources can become liabilities in the future. Today's mining industry is more knowledgeable, professional, and regulated, and therefore the likelihood of these sorts of problems is far less than in the past.

As the settlers moved west into the Valley and Ridge Province and beyond, they found sedimentary rocks that were used for the construction of roads and buildings, silica sand for glass, and limestone for cement. Unique to this part of the watershed, these rocks also contained coal seams and years later were discovered to contain oil and gas reservoirs. Coal, gas, and oil helped to power the nineteenth, twentieth, and twenty-first centuries, replacing wood as the primary fuel for the nation's growth during the Age of Industry and beyond. Each geologic province offered the settlers a different suite of natural resources. The settlers figured out how to use these resources to build a nation.

Today, some of these quarries and mines are still operating. Visiting them offers a great look into our past and into our planet. Going underground in an active mine offers the ultimate way to see what the earth is made of, especially in this heavily vegetated part of the world. Have you ever gone down into a cave or a mine, beneath all the vegetation and the surficial soils? Down to where there is nothing but rock? A few years ago I was lucky enough to have the opportunity. A marble quarry that you can see from Interstate 83 in Cockeysville lies just north of the Maryland State Fairgrounds. It's a large operation, basically a 550-foot-deep, 100-acre, open pit into the bowels of the earth and a busy site to visit with lots of blasting and mining going on during the week. A group of local geologists was invited in on a weekend when there was less blasting for a look at the mining operation. Page Herbert, a consultant for many of the mining companies in the area, was our guide.

On a beautiful, warm, sunny day, eight of us gathered in the white dust at the entrance to the quarry. The sun reflecting from millions of crushed calcite crystals beneath our feet produced a desert-like glare that made us reach for our sunglasses. After a few minutes, a van pulled up and Page jumped out and warmly welcomed us. He was tall and trim with graying hair and beard and was dressed just like the rest of us with weathered, leather boots and faded blue jeans. While we stood around in a circle, Page led us through a tailgate safety meeting. He alerted us to the hazards of the mine, told us to wear our hard hats at all times, and warned us to stay out of the way of the hundred-ton, fully loaded dump trucks rumbling up and down the dusty roads.

We climbed into the company van feeling like we were back in grad school. Our first stop was at the top of a ridge overlooking the open pit portion of the quarry. A huge gaping hole lay before us. Standing as close as we dared to the edge, we looked down. We could see that the pit had been excavated to a series of terraces, stair steps on the sides of a giant, but empty, hot tub. The large tub, filled with water only at its lowest level, had pumps running around the clock to keep the operations dry. The groundwater table had been breached within the first fifty feet of the surface and a constant battle went on to keep the water from filling up the tub. It was clear that a lot of rock had already been shipped out of this pit. Page assured us that there was a lot more to blast if it became cost-effective to go vertically down to even greater depths.

We left the glare and the warming day and rode in the van down into the mine, following tight curves along the sides of the open pit toward a dark hole in a corner of the quarry. The dark spot grew larger as we approached, and when it finally swallowed us we felt dwarfed by the maw of this tunnel, which was all of thirty feet high. Day became night. Each of us quickly removed our sunglasses and peered out the windows into the dark. The van's headlights cut the only swath as we turned in tight circles and descended to greater and greater depths. Glistening calcite walls lit up as we passed, each crystal face winking at us as they momentarily reflected the lights from the van.

Page brought our van to a stop beside a pile of crystalline rubble and several idle, sleeping trucks with tires eight feet high. Even empty, these gigantic trucks weighed thirty tons each. As we disembarked, the sweat carried down from the warm midday sun quickly cooled in the constant fifty-five degree depths of the mine. Page switched off the headlights and total darkness surrounded us. The van, the walls, and the gigantic trucks and loaders all disappeared. No sight, no sound, except for dripping water. Then one by one we reached up and clicked on the head lamp on the front of our hard hats. Slowly our little cones of light found one another and the walls of the cavern. We spread out like mice scurrying to explore the large calcite crystals in the walls and the tightly folded layers of marble.

Page explained that the calcite in this part of the mine was pure enough to be sold as calcium carbonate for making antacid tablets. Evidently, the calcium carbonate rock, when ground to a fine powder, can be ingested and relieves heartburn by neutralizing stomach acids. It is also used as a whitener for paper products, which would otherwise be brown. Less pure marble from other parts of the mine is still used as dimension stone, road material, and rip rap for holding back the ever eroding sandy shores of the bay. Historically most of the marble mines in the Piedmont had roasting ovens to calcinize the rock into cement and plaster, both much in demand as our cities grew. Marble from the Piedmont was widely used in many of the nineteenth-century buildings in Baltimore and Washington, because by then railroads had been built allowing the mines to ship their products to markets.

We moved on to other locations and finally climbed back up to sunlight. On the way out I was thinking how a mine is where our knowledge of technology and of the earth come together. It's an intersection of disciplines, science, engineering, and commerce used to meet the needs of society with the resources of the planet.

The natural resources of the watershed have been significant to our history and will always be important. Some of the old quarries were abandoned, their resources played out. Others are still actively mined. Some of the abandoned quarries have become swimming holes, lakes, and parks. A great example of what can be done with these old sites can be seen at the 471-acre Fairland Regional Park in Prince George's County, Maryland. As an integral part of the redevelopment of this former sand and gravel pit, good storm water management practices were followed. The design captures the rain that falls onto the buildings, parking lots, and sports fields, and allows this water to filter back into the ground. It's a demonstration of what can be done to better manage storm water runoff. The site was restored in the mid-1990s. Unfortunately, most developments since then have not paid attention and have less protective storm water systems.

It's a rare walk in the woods when I don't see some landform or feature that makes me stop and wonder what caused it. Invariably these landforms show up as unnatural swales or excavations into steep slopes, cuts along banks of rivers, or depressions in the forest floors. I constantly notice features that could not have been formed by natural erosion. A more careful look reveals that sand, gravel, or building stones have been quarried, or an old road or foundation has been abandoned. Leaves and trees have reclaimed the land, trying to cover and heal the scars we have left.

Since our history is so deeply tied to the character of the land, the next time you are out and about, take a good hard look at the landforms, the rock outcrops, the building stones, and the names of towns like Granite and Chrome. You'll gain a deeper appreciation for how geology has affected the settlement of this region and how it contributes to the shape of the land and even the flora and fauna that inhabit different areas of the watershed. You will also begin to see how our re-engineering of the earth's surface is changing the health of our ecosystem. Sometimes we do things well and sometimes we do not. It is so easy to upset the balance if one does not realize the effects of one's actions.

What can be done about abandoned mines and quarries? Many old mines and quarries have been reclaimed as forests, meadows, lakes, and ponds, and others as building sites for offices or cities. Since the natural soils have been removed and mining residues can be hazardous, it is important to reclaim the surface so that any remaining contaminants do not migrate directly into either the surface water or ground water.

The extensive coal mines in the Appalachian Mountains have caused significant degradation to mountain habitats and to streams. Some strip mines and debris piles have been contoured and seeded with grasses.

It is better to re-establish the soil and flora to their natural state. When done poorly, mining and remediation can be an expensive and toxic legacy that we leave to our children.

Governments, in most cases, have laws on the books that require full reclamation of mines. Enforcement and monitoring are required to see that these mined areas do not damage our local habitat and the bay.

Corporations exist that specialize in restoration. Experts with good track records should be brought in to work with mine owners to ensure adequate reclamation is done.

Individuals may have to ensure that regulations are enforced and that full restoration is done. Since reclamation and long-term monitoring will take many years, a local non-profit group may have to be established to monitor the impacts over time.

Part II

The Bay

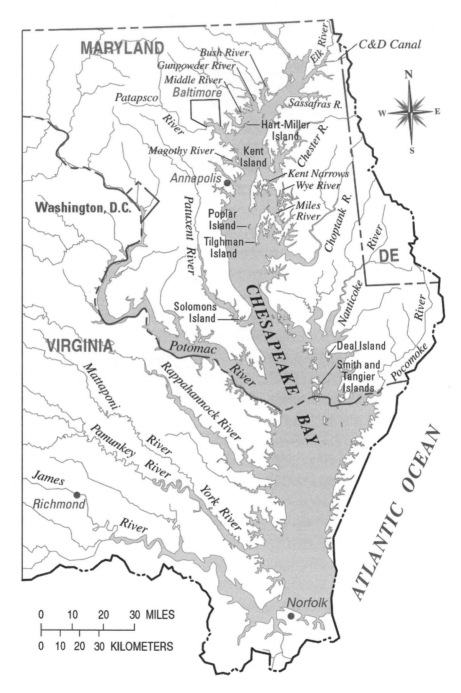

Major Chesapeake Bay Tributaries (Courtesy of the U.S. Geological Survey.)

As a young boy I knew the bay was big. It took forever to motor across it in our five-horsepower fishing boat. But I had no idea that the bay was the largest estuary in the country, with hundreds of tributaries reaching back into the woods and mountains, collecting waters from parts of six states. It is a giant mixing bowl of nutrient-rich freshwater from the tributaries mixing with saltwater from the Atlantic Ocean. With so many habitats it is one of the greatest marine nurseries in the country. H. L. Mencken, the "sage of Baltimore" during the early twentieth century, referred to it as "the great protein factory."

I also saw large numbers of geese and ducks coming here in the winter but did not fully appreciate how unique that was. The bay lies at the narrow funnel end of the Atlantic Flyway and is a major wintering spot for many species of birds. Its location, size, and diverse habitats have created a natural paradise unequalled in the country. It's not just a local resource, it's a national treasure.

The Great Chesapeake Bay Fishery

I raise the Teflon, ultra-light spinning rod to make yet another cast. Salty water from the line sprinkles my face, cooling it for just a moment. The red and white "Daredevil" artificial lure sails out toward a dark green clump of floating grass off the bow. I hold my breath, hoping a large, hungry bass is lurking under the grasses looking for lunch. Then again it could be any number of types of fish and I would be happy. I'm just waiting for some action here on a late spring morning that's turning out to be a beautiful but uneventful day on the bay.

I'm sitting in the bow of our tiny, aluminum boat. Dad is aft, down by the outboard motor. I say "down" because his weight combined with that of the motor, gasoline tanks, assorted tackle boxes, and the stern of the boat lifts the narrow bow with me in it. I can see right over his head, all the way to the Eastern Shore. We've occupied these same positions in this same boat for over forty years. He is the consummate fisherman, I am the son. He picks the spots to fish. I just try to keep the knots out of my line.

Dad sits there, intent on what he is doing. He casts in every direction he can without snagging me. Normally a quiet and industrious man, Dad loves fishing and will drop whatever he's doing for a chance to go out on a river or the bay. Once on the water he's all about the art of fishing. I've always wondered what goes on in his head when he's deciding which lure to use, where to cast, how quickly to retrieve the line, and when to move on. He never taught me anything about fishing, but I learned a lot by watching.

When I was nine, I remember tagging along to buy our rooftop launch, the one we're sitting in four decades later. We went up the street to where old man Kimmel had a hand-lettered, "BOAT 4 SALE" sign posted in his front yard. They had upgraded to a thirteen-foot Boston Whaler and were selling their old, twelve-foot aluminum boat with motor, seat cushions, anchor, and oars, all for $125. That was a hefty sum in 1959, but it proved to be a good investment in more ways than one.

Most importantly, it was a two-man boat. It took two of us to get it up on the roof of the various cars it outlived. It also took two of us to carry it down to the river, two of us to bail it in heavy rains, and two of us to get its flooded outboard motor started after many tugs on the cord.

I learned many things in that boat, not the least being that my father cursed a flooded engine with carefully chosen words like "sugar" and "durn." Most importantly, I learned patience. One has to learn patience when fishing. But this morning we have had no problem with boat or motor. It's the fish we curse. Things are slow here on the bay. Gazing out to the horizon I see a thin, endless row of green trees, loblollies I'd bet, on the very flat, almost monotonous Eastern Shore. In stark contrast, looking to the west there are yellow sand and clay cliffs, maybe fifty to a hundred feet high, capped with majestic white oaks. Both sides of the bay have a mix of modest and fancy houses with wooden steps down to wooden piers. White sails appear in all directions. There is just enough breeze to bring out boats of all sizes and shapes. Scanning the horizon, I try to find some of the old classics that still ply the water, ships like bugeyes, pungies, sloops, bay schooners, skipjacks, and log canoes. A rust-colored cargo ship, ten stories high, is coming up from Norfolk, riding low on its way to deliver goods to East Coast households. Gulls fly overhead and fish swim below, at least that's the theory. We haven't had a bite all morning so we're starting to wonder what happened to them all. I can't complain, I've landed my share of fish over the years. There just seem to be fewer fish every time I go out and far fewer than when I was a boy.

Growing up in the Fifties with a bamboo fishing rod in my hand, I learned early on about the wide variety of fish that inhabit the murky waters. Some species live here year-round. Others just come to spawn, migrating hundreds of miles up the bay and throughout the watershed from the Atlantic. Some of these silvery visitors grew up here and left home in their youth to travel the Atlantic from Florida to Labrador. They are natives, returning to lay their eggs for the next generation in the place where they were born. Then it's back to the high seas.

In the 1950s and 1960s it was possible to catch your limit in a morning on the bay. But today nothing is biting. My line is slack and flutters in the slight breeze. Yes, fishing can be boring. I sit back in my seat and watch a seagull fly lazily overhead, then follow a gelatinous sea nettle drifting by, and a one-inch long, water boatman skimming across the surface of the olive-drab, brackish water. "Where are the fish?" I ask Dad for the third time this morning. He smiles. We both know they're still down there somewhere but for some reason not here where we are this morning, or at least not biting what we have to offer. In exasperation Dad and I have tried many different artificial lures and numerous spots already, some in close to shore and some way out, miles from any landmark. No luck.

It's hard for me to believe, on a slow morning like this, that the Chesapeake supports more than 3,600 species of plants, fish, and animals. Imagine the complexity of such an intricately interwoven ecosystem of birds, insects, algae, fish, crabs, and all the other life forms in the air, water, and sediments of the bay. Captain John Smith described it as "frequented by otters, beavers, martens, and sables. Neither better fish, more plenty, nor more variety for small fish had any of us ever seen in a place." Today, of the 348 species of finfish and 173 species of shellfish, only a few have had significant commercial value. During the eighteenth and nineteenth centuries, the main shellfish harvest consisted of oysters, clams, and crabs. The fish were rockfish, shad, menhaden, and sturgeon. Markets existed for eel and diamondback terrapin, the Maryland state reptile, but there is a moratorium on terrapin and other species now. Though the total catch is down dramatically from the past, the bay still produces 500 million pounds of seafood each and every year. These are big numbers, and just thinking of them stimulates some primal urge in me to take the day off and go back out to try my luck at catching a few more. That is what brought me here today. The wide variety of fish is one of the things I like most about the bay; whenever you go fishing you never know what you're going to catch.

And just like that the line snaps taut and something starts tugging. Quickly leaving my daydreams, I jerk the rod and set the hook, my first bite of the day. "I got one! It's big!" I'm shouting, even though my father is less than three feet away. Dad, who is normally a study in peace and patience, stealthily moves into action. He shifts the other lines out of the way and maneuvers the boat, so all I have to do is play the fish until he tires and bring him in to the side. I reel in the line, wondering what on earth is on the other end this time. The fish, realizing that something is wrong and indignant that I'm trying to bully him to the boat, takes off on a straight run directly away from it. Nylon line streams out from the reel. I set the drag a little tighter hoping to slow him down. My mental picture of a large bass is getting larger with each passing second. Trying to overpower the fish, I turn to Dad and say, "I knew there was one hiding in that grass bed."

"Take it easy. Let him tire himself out. Just keep some pressure on the line." Dad clearly wishes he was playing the fish, though he's pleased to see me so excited. He's the real fisherman—I'm just along for the ride. Sure, I enjoy catching fish, but there are too many days that our luck is bad, and I spend much of the time thinking of all the other things I could be doing. But at this moment, I have a fish on my line and it isn't one of those little ones that I normally catch. As I manage to reel it in closer to the side of the boat, a long nose pierces the surface of the water.

"What on earth is that?" I ask.

"Gar," Dad replies, disappointedly. I take it personally, even after all these years, as if it was my fault that a gar took the line instead of a bass. Disheartened I reel the line in slowly, until the worn out fish is alongside. Dad scoops it up with a net. It's the strangest fish I've ever seen, pencil-shaped and about three feet long. Dad calls it a longnose gar. I have seen little-ten inch gar skipping across the surface before but never one this size. Gar means spear in Old English, and the fish is appropriately named. These very skinny creatures boast long snouts with needle-like teeth.

Their skin is also tough, enough so that early settlers and Native Americans used it for abrasives and shield covers. They hunted them with bow and spear since gar tend to hang about in shallow waters waiting for smaller fish to swim by. That made gar easy to spot and to spear. The record for gar in the Chesapeake is sixteen pounds—can you imagine a sixteen-pound pencil? Gar, together with sturgeon, belong to a primitive order of armored fish. Armored sturgeons eight feet long have been caught in the bay. In contrast to caviar, the tasty egg roe of sturgeon, the roe of the longnose gar is *extremely poisonous*. After admiring the uniqueness of my catch, we agree to throw it back into the deep. Neither of us interested in cleaning such a bony and unappetizing meal.

Normally when we went fishing, Dad moved the boat around trying to find the right spot—the right depth, the right amount of grass cover, and a place where bait fish lived. In recent years though, we've learned there is another factor to consider, one that is man-made. We now know there are dead zones throughout much of the main stem of the bay. Dead zones are large areas with huge algal blooms that deplete waters of oxygen, areas where most fish cannot live. Dead zones are caused by too much nitrogen running off our lawns and farms during storms, leaching into the groundwater from our septic systems, passing through our sewage treatment plants, and airborne nitrogen deposited on land and in the bay from car exhaust. In these places only a few fish like the longnose gar can live because they can breathe air. Their specialized swim bladder allows them to gulp air at the surface in order to supplement oxygen that is normally taken in through the gills. It's ironic that the more primitive fish may be the best prepared for living in a future of increasingly contaminated waters.

A fisherman can sit in a dead zone forever without catching a fish. Last year oxygen-depleted dead zones covered forty percent of the main stem of the Chesapeake. Although they are mainly found in the deeper parts of the bay, tides and wind can shift them up onto the shoals. Now when fishing on the bay you need to know where to find a healthy habitat. Our poor storm water, fertilizer, and waste management practices are limiting the healthy habitat for fish and other species. We're literally suffocating a wide range of species and pushing them out of the bay.

FLY FISHING WAS DAD'S favorite pastime. He always tried his fly rod unless it was just too windy. He even tried fly fishing when the fish weren't jumping, that is, when the fish weren't feeding on insects hatching on the surface. A fly fisherman tries to match the hatch by using a dry fly that looks like what is hatching. I picture him in the back of the boat, a well-worn, dirty bass cap on his head, dried saltwater spray on his bifocals, biting off one of his hand-made flies from his line and tying a new one on with a specialty knot that secures fly to line. Then it was back to casting, rocking the boat back and forth with each deliberate wave of his arm, trying to get enough line out with each forward cast to lay down the nymph, streamer, dry fly, or wet fly right where he wanted. It was a beautiful sight to watch him cast, even if it didn't always attract a strike from a greedy bass.

On slow days, I learned that it was not beneath Dad to make do with whatever it took to bring home dinner. After tying and retying his favorite homemade flies onto his line without a bite, Dad would begrudgingly switch to a spinning rod. An hour or two later, with no action on his wide assortment of spoons, MEPPS spinners, and imitation minnows, he would start attaching live minnows, bloodworms, or pieces of cut up clams or baitfish, anything to induce fish to bite. If things were really dead, I recall him putting a float and lead weights onto his trusty bamboo fly rod. He would drop the line complete with minnow over the side and wait for the float to move while continuing to cast with his spinning rod. Sometimes we even resorted to trolling. Now, there is nothing wrong with trolling, many boats do it. It just wasn't his style, much too passive.

In spring, summer, and fall we fished in the lower Susquehanna River, the Susquehanna Flats, Bush River, the Choptank, the Chester, the Pocomoke, Kent Narrows, the Magothy, the Potomac, and out in the main stem of the bay. I recall several times getting stuck on the Flats at the mouth of the Susquehanna at low tide, the motor clogged with grasses. Dad would manually clear the propellers while I jumped overboard. Stranded in one to two feet of water, miles from shore, our only option was to wade through the thick aquatic vegetation and drag the boat to deeper water. Sometimes that was easy, at other times our bare feet sank into the mud and silt up to our knees, and each step was a struggle to pull free from the muck. In contrast, speeding over the Flats at high tide, watching the giant gold fish (carp) dart off as we zipped by, was magical. I would lean over the bow and drag my fingers through the water as we flew along.

The cheapest way to fish in the bay is on a head boat. These boats take out anyone willing to pay the modest fare for renting a rod, all the bait you will ever need, and a space by the gunwale. Head boats carry ten to forty people, standing shoulder to shoulder. Everyone stands near the sides of the boat with a sturdy rod in hand—we're not talking light tackle here. No casting allowed; just drop the bait over the side, lower it to the bottom, and wait for a bite. Try to imagine forty people standing around the sides of a boat, each with a line with multiple hooks in the water. When there is a breeze or when the tide is changing, half of the lines drag beneath the boat.

Picture what happened when the bait on the fishing line of our friend, Lindsay Chase, got scooped up by a cownose ray. It sped away with its powerful wings, stripping line off Lindsay's heavy reel like nothing could stop it. The ray began to circle the boat. Lindsay raised his rod and line high above everyone's head, shouting to us all to pull our lines in. But it was too late. Within seconds everyone thought he had a whopper, since every last line was caught up in the melee. As quickly as he could, the captain cut the line, letting the ray go free, hook and all. He then spent the next half hour slowly and methodically untangling the other lines, and cursing his bad luck, and that damned ray, under his breath. I thought it was all very exciting.

To increase the odds of catching something, the pragmatic and taciturn head boat captains will often chum for fish. Chumming involves cutting or grinding up small fish, clams, or any other concoction the captain thinks will serve as bait. He throws the chum overboard hoping to attract fish with the smell of blood and carnage. This will sometimes produce a feeding frenzy and lead to lots of activity for everyone.

I chummed once with my kids on a small, saltwater pond. My daughter Anna and I used a seine net to corner and capture a school of three-inch-long minnows in the shallow end of the pond. We then outfitted the whole family with rods, lines, red and white bobbers, and hooks with minnows securely attached. Wading out on a sandbar in the middle of the pond, everyone cast their lines out into deeper water, where the bigger fish were supposed to be. Everything was quiet until I threw the rest of the minnows out there, too. The placid surface suddenly churned with twelve- to fourteen-inch white perch gobbling up minnows. Within a minute each of us had a bite, and we all started pulling in fish. Anna's line and bobber disappeared, streaming out away from the sandbar. When she finally pulled it in, the biggest fish of the day came with it. The perch had been so greedy and caught up in the feeding frenzy that he had missed the minnow completely and swallowed the entire red and white bobber, which was too big for him to spit out again.

On one trip Dad and I pulled up to a cluster of small boats that had gathered around a head boat. It's an unwritten law of fishing that boats tend to gather together. If the fish are biting, boats stay in the vicinity. If they're not biting, boats move on. Therefore a cluster of boats is usually a good sign. The head boat's captain threw buckets of chum overboard, and it wasn't long before his customers were pulling in a fair number of rockfish. The tide was moving at a good clip, and the wind was up. We floated over the hot spot as the head boat moved on, and before long, fish were hitting our lines as well. The captain didn't seem to mind that we benefited from his efforts. We felt like sea gulls picking up the scraps. The Chesapeake treated us well that day.

Even on good days, it's hard to imagine a smorgasbord of 348 different possibilities of fish hiding down there, swimming through the aquatic grasses. At best, I have landed only a few dozen species over the years. Thinking back on it, I was pretty narrow-minded. When I went out I usually claimed, a little pretentiously, that I was going fishing for rock, blues, or shad. These are the première sport fishing prizes. We went after them because they can be large, they put up a good fight, and at times lots of them "run" up the bay. Rock or stripers are local names for striped bass. They grow as large as sixty pounds or more, and blues get up to twenty pounds, though the average size for both species is much smaller. On good days, if we were lucky, we brought back a few and sometimes even an ice chest full of these sports fish. The trouble of course is that you cannot count on catching them. Far too many times I didn't. Fortunately, on those days, when the rock or blues weren't "running," I often ended up with a potpourri of other fish. Such is the beauty of the bay.

The most common catches to make it to our table back home were catfish, yellow and white perch, bass, and bluegill. Crappie, croaker, carp, sea trout, spot, eel, drum, flounder, pickerel, and rays also showed up on our lines, on our stringers, and in the bottom of our boat. On one outing, with no luck casting on the surface, we changed our tackle and switched to bottom fishing. The only bottom dwellers biting that day were blowfish. Once in the boat, they indignantly puffed themselves up and watched us while we tried to catch something more dignified.

BLUES RUN UP THE BAY in schools containing dozens of fish, often all of the same size. They are voracious eaters and will chop up schools of menhaden or even cannibalize schools of smaller blues. When fishing with Dad, our main interaction with blues came on days when by chance one of us spotted a flock of gulls diving, circling, and calling, and we found ourselves "seagull chasing."

"There they are!" I'd shout.

"Get the lines in," he'd reply, starting the motor and steering us toward the action. As we approached the flock, he'd shut off the motor just in time to coast close to the gulls, trying not to get too close and scare off whatever was churning the water beneath. What we usually found were baitfish schooling and jumping near the surface, trying their best to get away from a school of greedy blues who were corralling them and tearing them up, leaving small pieces for the gulls. We fished the edges and the middle of this fury, usually landing a few snapper blues feeding on menhaden. The blues were almost always the same size, typically twelve to sixteen inches long. Since we fished with light tackle, we could rarely land or even hold on to a large blue for very long. Invariably they'd bite right through our lines. Almost as quickly as the frenzy began, it ended. The storm was over. The gulls dispersed or settled down, floating calmly on the water as if nothing had happened. Like them we waited, fishing the old patient way and keeping an eye out for another flock of diving gulls.

Striped bass (rock) and shad have both been major commercial fisheries along the East Coast and provide a lot of fun to sport fishermen in the bay. Historically the main shad and rock spawning areas were the fifty-plus freshwater rivers that feed the Chesapeake. It is estimated that seventy to ninety percent of the striped bass in the Atlantic Ocean spawned here. Rock have been so important in the Chesapeake watershed they were selected to be Maryland's state fish. During the 1970s and 1980s, we overfished the rock, and in the late 1980s the states put a moratorium on catching them. Today the populations have recovered and appear to be healthy under new and stricter regulatory limits. Over a million rock were taken last year in Maryland, divided equally between commercial and sport fishermen. Most of the charter boats that go after these fish still work out of Chesapeake Beach, Tilghman Island, Solomon's Island, Rock Hall, Deal, and Annapolis. Depending on the time of year, the limit is either one or two rockfish per day, and they must be over a minimum length, eighteen or twenty-eight inches. It appears that regulations and limitations on the number of fish taken are now a requisite for keeping the fisheries at healthy levels.

Shad are one of the bay's legendary fish, often referred to as "poor man's salmon." Like salmon, shad make major runs each year up their natal rivers to spawn, and at these times are fairly easy to catch. In contrast to salmon, they are very boney and difficult to eat. They are also a principal feedstock for rockfish, so the health of one population is related to the other. In the distant past, long before I was on the scene, shad proved to be one of the biggest harvests in the entire watershed. The Susquehanna, the largest spawning ground for shad in the country, had annual runs exceeding tens of millions of fish. That number dropped dramatically as dams were built and especially when a series of major dams were constructed across the main branch of the Susquehanna in the nineteenth and early twentieth centuries. The annual spawning run that had taken place for thousands of years was cut off overnight. Imagine the shad the following spring, heavily laden with eggs, stopped at the foot of a dam, unable to reach the thousands of miles of freshwater habitat upstream where they were born and which was needed for the young to survive.

One of these dams, built in 1928 at Conowingo, Maryland, serves as the roadbed for U.S. 1, which runs from Maine to Florida. Driving across this old dam has always been exciting to me. On the northwest side lies a tremendous reservoir, the waters of which splash over the sides of the dam and onto the road on windy days. Look out the other side of the car to the southeast and you'll find a steep drop to the boulder-strewn river bottom below. The dam is 4,648 feet long and rises 104 feet above the rocky riverbed. The dam and hydroelectric plant harness the power of the Susquehanna, controlling how much water goes downstream. This site was an attractive location for a dam because the water rushed through the "Smith Falls" area of the gorge before the river widens and enters the bay a few miles to the southeast. It captures enough hydraulic energy to run seven turbines, the output of which is second only to Niagara Falls. Hydroelectric power is considered clean energy, and power captured from the river at Conowingo generates a significant part of the regional power supply. But the cost has been high. The dam stopped the spawning runs, depleting the shad fishery and other fisheries dependent on the shad. A whole industry was destroyed. Millions of fish that had swum up the bay to gain the freshwater of the mighty Susquehanna were stopped dead in their tracks.

In the 1990s the utility that owned the dams took steps to assist the fish in their spawning runs. It spent $60 million to build elevators to lift fish over three of the major dams on the Susquehanna and a fish ladder at the fourth. The system built at Conowingo was the largest fish lift in the country. Similar efforts were undertaken on other rivers. To date about sixteen of Maryland's 1,000 dams have been modified to allow some fish to pass upriver to spawn. Unfortunately, these efforts have not proven to be very effective in getting many fish upstream to their historic spawning areas. Only a few thousand make it past all four obstructions on the Susquehanna each year. Even if they make it upstream, the fish have to be able to get back downstream through the dams and the turbines to return to the ocean. Only a few make it.

These were not the first dams built in the watershed. Before coal and oil became our main energy sources, mills were run by the water captured behind small dams. Milldams were everywhere and disrupted the fisheries on a local scale. So the problem is not new. There are even records showing conflicts with Native Americans who, before European settlers arrived, had lived in part on the fish swarming up the rivers in the spring but who lost this food supply when the dams were built.

Shad were the most important freshwater fish in America. Second only to saltwater cod in the numbers caught, shad were highly valued along the entire eastern seaboard. Fifty million pounds of shad were caught annually during the last years of the eighteenth century. Easily salted and pickled, the shad were stored and shipped inland or overseas. Time and again the fish proved their value by sustaining our ancestors through difficult seasons. Many villages and farmers, on the brink of starvation after a long, cold winter, were saved by the spring runs that came literally right to their doorsteps.

I remember as a kid seeing men, women, and children along the banks of the Susquehanna and Deer Creek with dip nets. These four-by-four-foot nets were hung from a long pole cradled in the notch of a tree. The tree served as a fulcrum so eager fishermen standing on the banks could easily lower their nets into the water. Periodically they were lifted in attempts to catch the shad as they migrated upstream. It looked so easy! The other extreme was the way they fished in earlier times. Commercial fishermen stretched gill nets, up to a mile long, across the river to catch shad as they came upstream. Gill nets hung from floats at the surface and reached down to depths of up to thirty feet. Any large fish swimming upriver were likely to be snagged. Fish attempted to swim through an opening in the net, but those too big to fit all the way through could not back out because the netting caught in their gills. The technique was effective. The single greatest catch ever recorded was 10,000 shad in a single net.

From time to time "shad wars" broke out. Building dams and other obstructions to help catch fish limited what folks upstream could take. Pennsylvania even had a law on the books that made dams illegal. Of course, enforcing it was difficult in such a large watershed, especially during the frenzied few weeks in April when millions of silvery, thirty-inch-long fish were running up the rivers.

George Washington harvested shad in the Potomac River at Mount Vernon. He sent scouts out in the spring to keep an eye on the river, and when the call came, his slaves and servants put aside their chores and set out a long seine net. They then pulled it in and separated herring from shad. Records from Mount Vernon show a harvest of one million shad and herring in a six-week period. The shad were used for personal consumption, while the herring were salted and sold to merchants or stored to supplement rations for his slaves. Most diets were heavy on pork, herring, cider, and ale. Washington sold five hundred barrels of salted herring annually to Alexandria merchants, who shipped it to the Caribbean to feed slaves there. This business was limited by the amount of salt Washington could buy to dry the fish and the quality of the nets he used. Some years so many fish were caught that some were used as fertilizer for his crops.

I find it hard to envision so many fish, especially on days when my luck is bad. As a result of dams, water quality, and fishing practices along the Atlantic seaboard, the shad population has dwindled. There has been a moratorium on shad fishing for years, and that is unlikely to change in the foreseeable future. The good news is that, though it was once close to being placed on the Endangered Species List, the shad population has rebounded a little due to an extensive effort at re-introduction in some areas and the building of structures that allow fish to bypass dams.

Since the shad fishery failed in part as a result of damming the rivers, in recent years discussions have taken place concerning the possibility of removing more of the dams in the watershed. Many are obsolete and not used for power or recreation any longer. In theory, the fishery could recover if we removed them and cleaned up the waters. It has been estimated that if the dams were removed along even one of the moderate sized tributaries, like the Patapsco, 16,000 shad and 160,000 herring could return to spawn annually in this river alone.

The challenge is that removing dams is not an easy or inexpensive thing to do. A lot of sediment is stored behind them, and some dams have the beneficial effect of capturing silt and nutrients that run off our lawns and farms. More nutrients are not what the bay needs right now. If we removed the dams we would also have to significantly improve our storm water management practices.

Removing some of the dams and stopping the nutrient runoff that causes dead zones would be two important steps for rebuilding the fisheries. That together, with improved waste water management practices and fewer emissions from our power plants and cars, would greatly help in cleaning up the bay. Just think, if the fisheries came back it would be a clear sign that as a society we were capable of taking the necessary actions to restore an important natural resource. It would also be a large step toward re-establishing some balance between man and the natural world.

What can be done to bring back the fisheries? The first thing is to learn more about the fisheries by visiting www.dnr.state.md.us/wildlife and www.asmfc.org. As discussed above, re-establishing traditional migratory routes, managing the harvest, and reducing the nutrient mix in the bay are the three main steps that will help all the fisheries. We can all do something to reduce the nutrients that we dump into the bay. Excess nutrients feed the algae that produce the dead zones. Algal blooms also kill the grasses and the filter feeders that are necessary to maintain the health of the bay.

Individuals can help by reducing the amount of nutrient-laden storm water that runs off our lawns and farms. We can do this by installing rain gardens, bioretention ponds, infiltration ditches, and adding more trees and shrubs to open areas. We can use native plants that require less fertilizer and less watering. We can reduce fertilizers we put on our lawns—apply them only in the fall, and only if necessary to recover from summer stress. We can drive less and drive hybrids which contribute fewer nitrates to the bay. Or we can do away with our lawn, plant trees, and create instead an environmentally friendly garden of native plants.

Governments can require reduced emissions from cars and our fossil fuel-powered electric generating stations. They can manage the harvest to ensure that fish populations stay at healthy levels. They can remove some of the dams and the legacy sediments on the tributaries to the bay.

Corporations can find better ways for reducing and treating runoff from farms, suburbs, construction sites, and urban centers. There will be a growing market for redesigning landscapes to capture rain water and allow it to filter into the ground.

Chasing Crabs

The Algonquin Indians got it right. Their name for the bay, which we interpret as *Chesapeake,* meant the Great Shellfish Bay, from which they took oysters, clams, and crabs as a major part of their diet. Even though the feast has diminished, shellfish still enjoy iconic status in this region. The blue crab, which is arguably the most famous of the creatures harvested from the bay, has become the symbol for everything good about what a bard in the 1950s first called "The Land of Pleasant Living." What could be better than a relaxed, summer afternoon crab feast at the shore—or anywhere?

Like the spirit of the coyote in the southwest, blue crabs have been elevated to near mythical status around these parts, not merely because they're so tasty but also because of certain qualities they exhibit. For example, crabs typically offer us only quick glimpses of their shadowy shapes before disappearing into the murky, blue-green waters. We sense that they're always down there watching us, trying to steal our bait, but when we look they just slip away. We've mythologized what we assume are their personal traits. I grew up thinking of crabs as wily and wonderful.

Crabs must be wary, because like most other bay creatures they are not just predator but prey, consumed in turn by sharks, rays, sea turtles, eels, bass, gar, catfish, and even croakers. Life in the Chesapeake can be dangerous, but somehow through their tenacity they persist. Scientists estimate that at this moment there are close to 200 million crabs in the bay, busily cleaning up anything that falls to the bottom. They are our covert housecleaners, keeping an eye on everything, and picking up anything that falls to the bottom.

Crabs are born fighters, and human-crab encounters are therefore always a challenge. Invariably when I try to remove a crab from a bushel basket, at least one claw grabs onto the edge or to another crab and hangs on with the persistence of a little sister. Many times I've tried to pick up a crab and come away with a whole chain of them, all holding onto one another with their claws. Even when the fight is lost and a crab is cornered in the bottom of the boat, he will fight on to the end, scampering side to side like Muhammad Ali, raising his front claws in defiance, challenging me to try to pick him up. I often feel like Goliath to a scrappy little David one-hundredth my size. Yet somewhere in the back of my head I have this fear of crabs, based on the story that "if a crab latches onto your finger, he will not let go until sunset." I believe it. As a result I've always had a great deal of respect for these feisty little crustaceans.

Growing up on the shores of the bay, the blue crab culture permeated my family's thoughts, activities, and dining experiences. We enjoyed crab mythology so much that my Dad proudly wore crab ties and tie tacks. My mom sported crab silhouettes on her scarves and hats. We bought untold knick-knacks, just because they had crabs printed on them. We wore crab tee shirts, unless we were lucky enough to have an authentic blue and white, Johnny Unitas jersey with the number "19" printed on it. The State of Maryland even adopted the crab as its motif for tourism marketing campaigns.

On the rare occasions when my family went out to eat, we ordered crabs or rockfish, another Maryland delicacy. Mom and I would splurge on our joint birthday ordering both delicacies together in a delicious dish of crab-stuffed rockfish. At other times it was baked crab imperial, broiled crab cakes, steamed crabs, sautéed soft-shell crabs, or stewed she-crab soup. Why even go out for dinner, we thought, if you weren't going to order crabs?

The family's favorite crab shack, at least until it burned down, was Gablers on Bush River. No menu, and no utensils, just steamed crabs and beer. They carried Pabst Blue Ribbon and National Bohemian by the returnable bottle. The place was nothing more than a camp kitchen, a large, closed-in porch with windows all around that tilted up to the ceiling. Even on the hottest summer days, a breeze off the river cooled the patrons. We'd sit at long tables with other customers, eat crabs, drink beer, and watch the sun set over the estuary. For the fancier crab dishes we had to visit the Blue Bell, Gordon's of Orleans Street, Obrycki's, or

Phillips' if we found ourselves in Ocean City, Captain Bobs in Chincoteague, or Harrison's on Tilghman Island.

The best times were when friends or family came over to our house for a picnic in the summertime. We'd invariably serve a bushel or two of steamed crabs. Yes, there might have been a few hotdogs, and lemonade for the very young, but there was little choice on what you were going to eat if you were *grown up*. Just picture a four-by-eight-foot picnic table under a spreading maple tree. The table is covered thickly with newspapers, old copies of the *Baltimore Sun* or the now defunct *News-American*. Wooden mallets for cracking the crab claws are scattered about the table and crabs are piled high in the middle. What a sight they are—bright, red-orange crabs, coated with layers of brown, spicy seasoning—surrounded by a dozen hunched over bodies, all hands busily engaged in crab-picking. What a way to spend a beautiful sunny day—friends, crabs, and the whole lazy afternoon ahead of you.

At those raucous afternoon gatherings, friends who had never immersed themselves in a pile of steamed crabs, and who probably came dressed a little too nicely, would sit next to one of the more experienced pickers. Aunt Mary from upstate New York just stared at the pile for a few minutes, chatting nervously, not knowing where to begin. She came from a farming family that rarely ate seafood. In her nicely pressed white blouse and white skirt she seemed hesitant even to sit down on the redwood picnic bench for fear the stain might wear off. But one thing you can't do at a crab feast is be left out. You get a seat and then it's off to the races. You've got to jump in to be part of the fun. There's a lot of peer pressure.

"How do you eat these things?" she finally asked that first time. I smiled, knowing there is no right way and certainly no instruction manual. It's really an acquired talent. You just have to watch someone for awhile and try it yourself. But I liked Aunt Mary and wanted her to like crabs, so I decided to coach her a bit. Give her a few pointers to get her started.

"Roll up your sleeves and get a beer," I said with only a quick grin. The truth is that I was too engrossed in picking to look up for more than a few seconds over the next several hours. This should not be considered rude. It's just a basic requirement when picking crabs. You have to pay attention to extract the tiny morsels from fragments of shell. As she was eyeing the stack of crustaceans, I said, "Get a big one." I wondered if she was really ready for this. I seemed to remember she didn't drink beer. Well that would change quickly. I watched as she picked through the pile to find the largest crab left. Daintily she pulled it from the stack by tugging on a claw.

"That looks like a good one." I showed her how to grab the top of the orange shell with her left hand and turn the crab over, exposing its white underbelly.

"Use your right thumb to peel back the apron." I explained that crabs with narrow aprons that looked like the Washington Monument are males—we call them "jimmies"—and they tend to be heavier and have more meat. Females are called "sooks" or she-crabs. They have rounded aprons that look more like the dome on the Capitol. "Now slide your thumb under the apron and then under the shell. Pull the shell off as you go."

Aunt Mary now had a twinkle in her eye. "They smell delicious. Am I doing this right?" I waited quietly for a moment, allowing her to enjoy the full experience of dissecting her first crab. She sprayed her blouse with seasoning as she tore off the shell, but she persevered. She kept saying "Oh dear!" as the spices got all over her hands and face. I knew she would be hooked as soon as she got her hands messy and sampled a chunk of crabmeat. It's a very visual, tactile, and aromatic experience, not to be rushed. It always amazes me that no matter how fastidious a person may be in the rest of his or her life, most people enjoy and really get into the mess of picking their own scraps of food. It must be a basic survival instinct hidden deep within each of us. I also watch to make sure newcomers do not cut themselves on one of the sharp edges of the crab's shell. You don't want a fresh, open wound with all the spices, which include salt and red pepper, that get on your hands. It will burn and take much of the fun out of the afternoon.

I warn Aunt Mary to be careful. "The seasonings are good but can burn your lips." Of course that's what the beer is for. Some people like the seasoning so much they lick their fingers while picking. Some are careful not to. I didn't tell her that no matter how careful she was, she would still have burning lips by the end of the afternoon. Furthermore, her skin and digestive tract would remember this meal for days to come. "Now break the two halves of the crab apart and remove the stomach sac, intestines, along with the dead man's fingers, and the yellow-green tomalley that looks like mustard." We discussed whether to eat the tomalley. Again I watched her carefully out of the corner of my eye, for this is another hurdle for most people. I've gotten used to it, but the first time through all these innards must look awfully strange and uninviting.

Next comes the tricky part that requires a bit of skill—pulling off each leg in such a way that you coax out as much meat as possible. "Start with the back fin. Pull it out at an angle. See the big lump of crabmeat that comes with it? That's the biggest and easiest bite you'll get." I glanced over to make sure my protégé was not wasting any of the precious meat. I also checked her discard pile. Anything discarded is fair game for the hungry. I did not hesitate to help myself.

She downed her first big bite of back fin. Her expression showed even more determination to master the art of picking crabs.

"The next trick is to break open the joints on each leg in a way that lets you get the most meat." This I knew was an art that only comes from much experience and a little hunger. You've got to crack the small legs with fingers or teeth at just the right point, not too close to the joint. It's a lot of work for little gain. I've heard folks complain, "you could starve to death while picking crabs." Four to six crabs will only yield about a cup of meat. I passed Mary a nutcracker and told her to use it for the big claws. She did fine cracking them and was excited at the size of the morsel in the claws relative to the small legs.

I told Aunt Mary that her final challenge was to break open the cartilaginous carapace and excavate the remaining meat. By this time her lips would be burning and she should have fallen in love with crab picking. When she asked for a beer, I knew we had won another convert. I glanced at her blouse. Yes, it was covered with flecks of crab meat and seasoning, but I didn't say anything, she just looked like the rest of us now. I also noticed she was taking a big swig of National Boh and looking around the table at everyone else's progress. I'd never seen her drink beer before, but after a sip I saw that smile spread across her face and realized that she was pleased with herself and completely hooked.

In addition to being very tasty and lots of fun, crab feasts are great for conversation. One normally is picking and looking at the crab the entire time, so it's easier to talk. No need to look at someone else. My father always claimed to drink a bottle of National Boh with each crab, and since we often ate a dozen crabs apiece this normally quiet man became quite animated and engaged in debates on subjects he would seldom visit away from the crab table. In fact he became quite the devil's advocate, especially when his three brothers were around. The four of them were always a good source for provocative family history, though Dad claimed that these stories, even when true, were served with plenty of embellishment. I learned more about his youth and the foibles of other members of the family over long, hot afternoons picking crabs than at any other time in my childhood. It was our time for passing down family stories.

During my adolescence and college years, crabs feasts proved to be one of those few times we could delve into emotionally charged subjects like Vietnam, drugs, Johnson, and Nixon. We could say our peace and share deeper thoughts without retribution. I learned about my Dad's philosophy of life, women, work, and religion—all around a table filled with steamed crabs. I don't think I would have known the man if it wasn't for those hot summer days, picking away at a long table filled with family and friends.

So eating crabs was a great deal more than just about sustenance. It was all about community and persistence. I think those of us who stayed at the table the longest must have acquired crab-like traits. I know my sister did. She was always the last to leave. It took tenacity to get your fill of crabmeat. I think that's why I find eating steamed blue crabs more fun than eating king crab or Dungeness crabs from the Pa-

cific. Sure blue crabs are known to be sweeter and the Old Bay Seasoning makes the crab tastier, but it's the patience and expertise required to
keep from starving while picking that puts steamed blue crabs atop my
culinary experiences.

MY FAMILY DIDN'T just eat crabs—we knew how to catch them as well, and
of course, the tastiest crabs were always the ones we caught ourselves.
During the summer, there were days when our sole mission was to catch
a bushel of crabs and bring them home for dinner. Catching a bushel
full was not always easy, but it was always a good ambition if you had
a free day by the shore. Over the years we tried everything to reach it.
We settled upon three basic strategies and even then, sometimes they
worked and sometimes they didn't. The one we most commonly employed was from a boat, because Dad would always rather go fishing
than crabbing. But he was wise enough to know that fishing was not
always successful, and crabbing increased the odds of bringing home
dinner. So whenever we set out to go fishing, we were also prepared for
crabbing just in case we had bad luck with fish.

"They're just not biting today. Let's see if there are any crabs down
there."

Dad, who is sitting in the back of the boat and trying to make the
most out of the day with his fly rod, looks at me for a moment and then
smiles. "This may not be such a good spot for crabs. But then again,
you're right, it can't be worse than the fishing. Go ahead and get the
cord out of the tackle box. Make up a couple of lines." Delighted that
he's agreed, I reel in my fishing line as fast as I can and set my unpro-
ductive spinning rod out of the way in the bow. Turning around without
rocking the boat too much, I open the tackle box and get the cord out.
At one end I tie heavy lead weights and a frozen chicken neck. On other
occasions, I've chopped up eel and some of the junk fish we caught, but
today we planned ahead and picked up frozen chicken necks on our
way down to the water. Any bait will do since crabs are omnivorous and
will eat almost anything dead or alive, but chicken necks are traditional
crab bait in the bay country.

I drop the weighted line over the gunwale and let it settle to the bottom. It's only eight feet down, but with the murky water it's all mystery, all unexplored sea bed, all potential. I tie the lines to every available seat and oarlock and give each line a few feet of slack to adjust for the tide. Excited about catching crabs, I get carried away and set out six lines hanging from our twelve-foot skiff—I was serious. Over the next hour I keep busy and optimistic, checking each line in turn, lifting them slightly, feeling if the weight has changed, hoping not to miss a crab, hoping we will drift over a hot spot where you can get some action on all lines on a regular basis. But unfortunately, on some days there is no action, and this was one of those days. We went home skunked.

I remember having better luck when crabbing from a pier with my cousin Bucky. We were the same age, the same height, and we both loved being outside. We hung out together when down by the water. One day when we were ten, I was lying on my belly on an old creosoted, splintery, wooden pier, with my head and upper body hanging over the edge. Sweat was dripping off my nose and making little ripples in the water below. All I had on was a pair of red Speedo racing trunks, which I largely lived in during the summer. Bucky, who had fair skin and was already sunburned, was wearing shorts, a tee shirt, and a hat, and his nose was covered with white zinc sunblock. My back was darkly tanned and peeling and my throat was dry, but I didn't care; I was focused on crabbing. The sun was hot, the cicadas and mourning doves were singing, and the dragonflies were keeping a close eye on things. Nothing else was happening. Eisenhower was president.

My line descended down three feet before it even hit the surface, and then another six feet into the murky water near one of the pilings holding up the pier. I was watching my line intently. I could swear it was moving ever so slowly away from me. From my long experience with such things I just knew that at the other end a large male blue crab was trying his best to steal my bait.

Ever tried to outfox a crab? You're on one end of a cotton cord and even though it could be your imagination, or the tide, or the small waves lapping against the pilings, you believe down deep in your salty veins that something's tugging on the other end. When you threw the line in, just a chicken neck and some lead weights were attached to it—nothing alive that could move on its own. But now the line is moving.

"Chicken necking," as locals call it in the bay country, requires knowing where to go, a little bit of skill, and a great deal of patience. Everyone has his own technique, but all agree that the line has to be brought up very slowly so the crab doesn't suspect what's happening and let go. His greed when chewing on the bait must exceed his concern about being slowly lifted toward the surface. My goal therefore is to outsmart this crustacean. After all I am Homo sapiens, modern man, the intelligent one, the master of the universe, and he is but a lowly, eight-ounce, bottom-dwelling scavenger. He does have his advantages. He has ten legs and swims sideways, propelled by his back set of flippers. The middle six legs can be used for detailed foraging or gently cradling a mate while she goes through her final molt. The front legs are called claws because they have large, sharp pincers on them to protect him from predators or to break up prey. These claws can also hold onto a chicken neck.

So I decide to make my move, ever so slowly, and start to retrieve my line. Hand-over-hand, I raise the line—lead weights, chicken neck, and phantom-like cargo—to the surface, inch by cautious inch. At first a chicken-necker feels tugging from the crab. The tugging either continues or the line goes slack. From years of crabbing, I instantly know when I have lost my crab and let the line drift back to the bottom. This time the line feels heavier than when I threw it in. Yes, I have one, so I continue to raise my quarry ever so slowly to the surface, praying to the gods of the Chesapeake to let me catch this fellow for dinner. Fortunately, the crab knows that he's got a prize and he is holding on for dear life and for his own dinner. Sweat blurs my vision and my eyes strain to peer into the murky depths. I want to be the first to see *the other*, my opponent in this aquatic tug-of-war. Visibility is poor, and much of the line retrieval is done blindly. When a shape finally comes into view I anxiously whisper to my crabbing partner, "Bucky, I've got one! Get the net, quick, scoop him up."

Waiting for the Crabbers. (Courtesy of Alice Webb, the artist.)

But Bucky knows what to do without being asked. He has noticed my intense concentration, the careful hauling of the line, my mumbling to myself with barely concealed excitement, and has dropped his line to come over and help. He scrambles and tries to reach over or around me without tripping or falling into the water. Bucky is good. He lowers the net into the water behind the crab, then deftly pulls up line, sinker, the remains of the slightly mauled chicken neck, and one, king-sized, green and blue crab with gleaming white underbelly. He shakes the net and this twisting collection of claws and bait drops into a bushel basket sitting on the pier. There is a momentary shuffling of the half-dozen crabs already in the basket and then silence as they embrace in a network of clasped claws. I put the lid on the basket and throw my line back in for another one. We keep at it till we have half a bushel, and it's time for dinner.

Back at the house our mothers get out a big steaming pot, a double boiler, and put it on the stove. They fill the bottom with water or beer. Once it comes to a boil in the lower pot, we layer the crabs in the upper one with ample amounts of salt and Old Bay Seasoning. This is the tough part, moving crabs from basket to pot is a challenge that tests the best of us. When we grab one crab, more than likely he will have taken hold of another or the side of the basket. Crabs are stubborn, often able to outlast me in a tug-of-war, it sometimes takes brute strength to separate them. One crab of course, always manages to get loose on the kitchen floor, scampering sideways to hide under the table or the chairs. As I approach, he rises up to defend himself, waving his two-inch pincers on the ends of six-inch arms back and forth. More than once a crab has *gotten me*, seizing my fingers and at least momentarily winning the battle of wits before ending up in the pot. But they all end up in the pot. The crabs steam until their green and blue coloring turns a bright orange, usually after about twenty minutes, and the victors can sit down to enjoy.

On most days, chicken-necking from a boat or pier produced a crab feast. I have even had days when we caught several bushels of large male "jimmies." But sometimes, being confined to a boat or a pier only produced small female sooks, or males that were under the limit of five inches across the shell. Fortunately, at some critical point in my child-hood, we discovered a third option for catching crabs. It involved aban-doning ship or pier completely. Dad and I, and sometimes my sister and mother, would jump overboard in shallow water, tie an inflated inner tube to our bathing suits with a piece of crab line, and squeeze a bushel basket with a secure lid into it. Each of us took along a chicken-wire crab net on the end of a five-foot wooden pole.

We had two options. The first was to walk along in the shallow water where there were lots of reeds and try to net doublers, peelers, and soft-shell crabs. Doublers are pairs of crabs: a male crab carrying a female around, holding her beneath him with his smaller legs, and wait-ing for her to slough her shell so they can mate. Peelers are hard-shell crabs about to slough their shells. They do this up to twenty times per year in order to grow. Once they bust out of their shells they are called soft-shells and are considered by many to be a delicacy. Soft-shells are often sautéed and served whole between crackers or two pieces of toast. With all ten legs hanging out the sides of this sandwich, it makes a real culinary experience and proves you can eat just about anything.

Our second option was to wade into deeper water, two to three feet deep, and keep our eyes open for clear sandy spots in the weed beds. Of-

ten granddaddy-sized crabs sit in these spots sunning themselves, waiting for lunch to float by. As we approached, the crabs typically raised
their pincers high in an attack stance. That revealed a flash of their white
bellies. As soon as we saw the flash, we'd plunge the crab net down on
top of them, scooping them up, grass and all. That often proved to be
the easy part. Getting the crab out of the net and into the basket was
harder. He often held fast to the netting with his claws, or used them to
keep me at bay. If he was enmeshed in the netting I could reach in and
secure him at the one place on his shell that was safe to grab. It must
have been a design flaw, but the crab has an Achilles' heel or at least an
Achilles' back fin. If you grasp a crab with thumb and forefinger just
where the back fin meets the shell, he cannot get at you with his claws.
Once you had him, you had to pull him free from the netting, and once
you did that you had to lift the basket lid and toss him in without letting
the ones inside escape. This was often a challenge. We kept the crabs in
the basket moist on hot days by layering them with bay grasses.

While catching crabs in this manner, our bare feet commonly felt
clams buried beneath the silt. These were easily recovered with toes,
fingers, or the crab net, and therefore we often returned with an appe-
tizer as well as the main course. Small littlenecks or cherrystone clams
are delicious steamed and dipped in butter; large quahogs are good for
chowder. Wading in shallow bay waters is also quite therapeutic—the
sun on your back, the warm waters soaking your limbs, long grasses
stroking your legs, feet sinking into the silty bottom. Just standing still
in the shallows is a treat. Minnows and small fish come up and nose
your legs, dragonflies and damsel flies land on your arms, swallows
skim the surface, and small gar will skip across the top of the water. Not
a bad way to spend the day.

So summers on the bay were pleasant, productive, and always spent
outdoors. As a boy I felt I could subsist on my own, taking pride in
knowing how to catch enough to eat. There was something fulfilling
about being free to explore the world of the bay and knowing how to
bring home dinner.

Things have changed a bit since the 1950s. Childhood today seems more about a fear of the outdoors and a focus on indoor electronic activities. Yet it's not just our lifestyles that have changed, so has the bay itself. It's as if we have forsaken the natural world. We are letting it die. The crab population has declined significantly, the waters are murkier, and there are fewer aquatic grasses. Our method of chasing crabs on foot no longer works in many areas. Crabs require clear water and shallow water grass habitats where they can hide and hunt. Former Maryland state senator Bernie Fowler has publicized the problem of water clarity with his annual "Wade-in." For the past twenty years he has been staging an event in the Patuxent River at which an increasing number of concerned citizens wade into the water until they can no longer see their feet. They measure this depth every year and use it as a kind of barometer of water quality. This June event on the Patuxent is now replicated in a dozen other rivers around the state. The resulting data is referred to as the "sneaker index" for measuring water clarity. Over the past few years this method has documented a downward trajectory in bay-wide water clarity. As a result our kids don't get the opportunity to chase crabs the way we did at their age. They have become one more step removed from living on and living with the land.

Although the catch has dropped off in recent decades, the bay is still heavily crabbed. Commercial crab pot operations produce about a third of the blue crabs eaten in the U.S. However, the resource management goal of 200 million crabs in the bay, necessary for a stable crab population, is not being achieved. As a result this fishery like most of the other Chesapeake fisheries is now in collapse. This is probably the result of over-harvesting and poor water quality, the collateral effects of unchecked human population growth. Nutrients from cars, lawns, and fields, and siltation from development and other human activities cause the waters to become murkier and foster algal blooms that restrict the sunlight needed by aquatic grasses. Algal blooms often lead to fish kills—from toxins algae release into the water and from depleted oxygen levels when the blooms decay. The bay is now much more susceptible to the oxygen-depleting effects of nutrient loading because filter feeders like oysters, clams, and aquatic grasses have been greatly reduced in numbers. Large "dead zones" with little or no oxygen no longer support the wide array of organisms that crabs feed upon. The loss of underwater grasses also means there are fewer places for crabs to hide when they slough off their shells. Given these declines in the quality of the habitat, we might be forced to restrict crabbing even more to protect what is left of this once glorious fishery.

I wonder about the future of crabbing. Crabs have been wily and tenacious enough to survive sharks, rays, eels, and bass, but are having a hard time with the growing numbers of humans in our watershed. They will need all the tenacity we ascribe to them if they are to adapt to the harsh and degraded environment we are creating for them. We simply have to reduce our impact on the bay if the crab is to have a fighting chance. I wonder if we have learned enough about tenacity and persistence in our centuries-old struggle to catch, cook, and eat crabs to now do what it will take to save them. Our children are missing out on a way of life that is vanishing before our eyes. It doesn't have to disappear. If we just learn to change our ways, children will once more be down on the edges of the bay, chicken-necking from piers, chasing crabs in the shallows, picking away happily at a crab feast, and participating in all the other wonders associated with living by a healthy and productive Chesapeake Bay.

What can be done to restore the bay's water quality and fisheries? In addition to the landscaping suggestions in the last chapter, we must stop thinking of streams, rivers, and the bay as places to flush the residue of our society.

Individuals in suburbs and rural areas can replace aging septic systems with new nitrogen-reducing systems. All of us can help reduce the strain on waste water management systems by not dumping garbage, fats, oils, and grease down our sinks. Garbage disposals in our sinks should not be used at all. (See Appendix A for details on composting.) Nor should we dump medicines or pharmaceuticals down the drains.

Governments will have to upgrade most of our public waste water treatment systems and provide grants to assist residents in upgrading their private septic systems. They should restrict all development near shorelines.

Corporations can develop and promote the use of technologies that contribute fewer nutrients to the bay. These include hybrid vehicles, better septic and sewerage systems, some forms of alternative energy, and water insoluble fertilizers. As individuals come to recognize and appreciate the significance of our actions, demand for sustainable technologies will increase.

The Atlantic Flyway

Finding myself with an hour free from meetings, I walk down to the water, close my eyes, and, blanking out the drone of cars in the distance, listen to the sounds of nature. Today is one of those special days, when all outdoors is erupting with life. I'm not sure why this happens. Maybe it occurs on days when the sun finally emerges after a cold or wet spell; birds, squirrels, and people rush forth to enjoy the sunshine. Special days also seem to happen just before bad weather: a scurrying of activity to gather food, a few last breaths of open air, and the last glimpses of sunlight before we're forced indoors, or into the thicket. Either way, it's magical when all of nature turns out to enjoy itself and celebrate on a sunny day.

The birds and squirrels out and about in the woods and along the shoreline seem oblivious to my presence. I'm the invisible man, standing still and watching. Two squirrels, chasing each other at full speed, almost run smack into me before taking a sharp, ninety-degree detour to the right. Birds chatter back and forth in the brush and in the trees. They seem to have a lot to say today. People pass me on the path. They too are chattering with one another, and scampering about in running shoes and on bikes. They are clearly enjoying themselves, and like the squirrels, they appear oblivious to all the other species out on this special day.

Then it happens—a crescendo takes shape overhead as several squadrons of geese arrive and circle the lake. One squadron, wings downward, glides in for a closer look or a landing. Another small group of seven hones in on my territory and passes directly over my head. Like the others they communicate with a fair bit of honking, but it's not the honks that attract my attention. There is something else, a certain rasping beat, like a broom sweeping the porch. I search each of their flapping, undulating bodies for the source of the sound. The birds are so close I want to reach up and stroke their soft, white, goose-down bellies. Then I look more closely at their wings. There it is! The fourth bird back on one arm of the V is different; she proves to be the musician. Her right wing is missing several feathers, and each down-stroke produces a beat that complements the vocals as she struggles to keep up. Swoosh, swoosh, swoosh, and off they fly, not to be heard from again, at least not by me during this hour by the water. Yet, the rustling of wings has lifted my spirits for the rest of the day.

I remember other crisp winter mornings, years ago when I was a teenager, driving around the top of the bay and down the Eastern Shore. I was usually with a group of men, riding in a van, heading out to hunt quail along the edges of soybean fields. Half of us were generally dozing as we passed the Bohemia and Sassafras rivers and the towns of Georgetown and Galena. It's been years, yet the names are still etched in my memory from those sleepy morning drives. On some trips, the sun would be blocked, and the sky would darken as Canada geese, snow geese, and a wide variety of ducks took to the skies of the great Atlantic Flyway. Flocks of birds stretched from one horizon to the other, creating layer upon layer of waterfowl. It was impossible to count or even estimate how many birds were in the air at one time. Perhaps there were a million, blanketing the sky like that. I have not seen that phenomenon in years. It was breathtaking and one of those times in life, like peering at the stars on a clear night in the mountains, that puts in perspective one's place on this planet.

There are fewer migratory birds now than when I was a boy because of our disruptive activities. One of the main problems facing the birds is the loss of food owing to the degraded water quality of the bay. The loss of submerged aquatic vegetation such as eel grass is a real problem for ducks and to a lesser extent to geese. Aquatic grasses are disappearing as the result of algal blooms and warming waters. Geese have had to adapt to grazing on lawns and in fields. Normally, the diet of waterfowl would consist of plankton, vegetation, and invertebrates in a healthy bay.

A second problem is the loss of habitat, especially along shorelines and wetlands under pressure for development. Too many of us want to live by the bay, and some species of ducks, like the black duck, are not tolerant of people. Over-hunting has also been a problem. In times

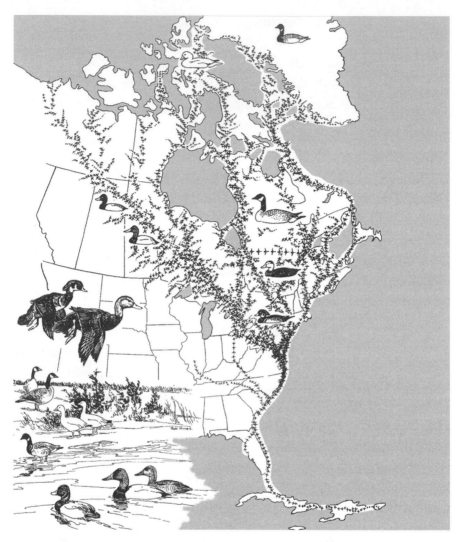

The Atlantic Flyway. (Courtesy of the U.S. Fish & Wildlife Service.)

past we have simply shot too many birds and damaged the health of the population. Today hunting is tightly regulated and monitored in an attempt to better manage the species that remain. In addition to the hardships waterfowl encounter here in their winter homes is the fact that their summer breeding grounds in the upper Midwest and central parts of Canada are also under siege. Our increasing population and growing demands for food and biofuels has increased pressure to turn much of the Prairie Pothole Region, which runs from Nebraska up into Alberta, into farmland. This area is ranked first among the twenty-five most important and threatened waterfowl habitats on the continent. A great battle is taking place. Our population growth is threatening the existence of many other species that we need to maintain a healthy and balanced biosphere for all of us.

The Chesapeake is the winter home of more than thirty species of waterfowl. Fowl and waterfowl have had a long history with humans. "Fowl" generally refers to birds we raise, such as chickens and turkeys. "Waterfowl" generally includes geese, ducks, and swans, which are fowl that have been domesticated but are also strong swimmers. With medium to large bodies, historically they have been important food sources and continue to be hunted as game or raised for meat and eggs.

Of the million waterfowl that migrate through the Chesapeake each year, the majority are Canada geese. They arrive sometime in late fall or early winter and leave each February and March on their way to nest in the Hudson Bay region of northern Canada. One day I spent an hour counting the size of the flocks flapping their way north and noticed several that contained more than a hundred geese. They migrate at speeds of thirty to sixty miles per hour and fly in a V-formation whenever possible because it conserves energy. Try watching geese flying in formation to see how often the lead changes. Traveling in a V allows them to fly seventy percent farther than when flying alone. Evidently as the lead bird tires he or she drops back, allowing a fresh leader to take the point. Wing speeds and heart rates are slower for the non-lead birds. If you look closely you will see that each bird flies slightly above the one it is following. This positioning reduces wind resistance, allowing each bird to take advantage of the lifting power from the one to its front. It also provides them with a better view and greater ability to communicate with one another. I wonder what we can learn from geese. Aside from team bicycling races, has anyone used these benefits of teamwork to inspire humans to share the lead? I would like to join a group that believed in constant sharing of the lead and constant communication,

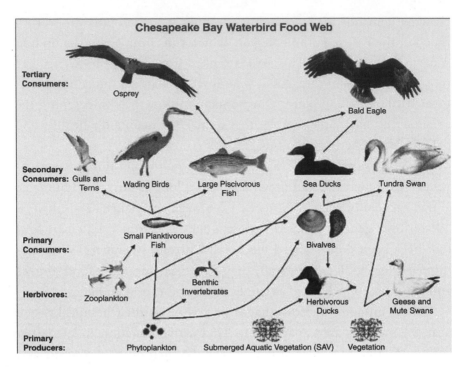

Chesapeake Bay Waterbird Food Web. (Courtesy of the U.S. Geological Survey.)

especially if it led to each of us getting seventy percent further ahead in whatever it was we wanted to do.

About 100,000 Canada geese remain in the Chesapeake watershed year-round. These resident, non-migratory birds have descended from geese that were introduced into the bay from the Midwest to attract migratory birds. Hunting reserves imported them and used them as live decoys. Wildlife refuges imported them to bolster their numbers of waterfowl. Unfortunately, these geese are genetically not wired to migrate and have become permanent residents. They have adapted to the changing landscapes of suburbanization, enjoying large expanses of short grass for food, a lack of natural predators, and the luxury of people feeding them. Problems arise though, when too many resident geese settle in one area. Farmers don't particularly like them, for during the year they eat as much as a full-grown sheep and cause quite a bit of crop damage. Surprisingly, each goose also generates a pound of droppings every day.

This results in nutrient overloading of waterways, public health concerns at beaches, and polluted drinking water. Their numbers become a safety hazard near roads and airports. Resident geese differ from migratory geese in that, with no need to fly, they live longer, breed earlier in life, and lay larger clutches of eggs. It doesn't help either, that so many people feed them. Dependence on humans for food limits the wide variety of their natural diet. It also encourages an entire flock to stay close together, which can spread disease and harm the environment.

Each spring we watch with some apprehension as the resident Canada geese raise their large broods of young near our home. There are more and more every year. Bass and snapping turtles claim a few goslings in the spring, but so many have made it that they are damaging the local ecology. A marked loss of wild rice has already been observed in our tidal wetlands as the result of overgrazing by resident geese during the summer. This was an important food for a range of other water birds, whose numbers have declined in recent years. The habitat is clearly out of balance.

Since man created the problem by importing these geese, it's appropriate for humans to manage the habitat by removing or at least reducing the number of resident geese in it. If we don't, how will nature respond to an overpopulation of geese? Will they die from disease nurtured by overcrowding, will coyote or other predators move into the area, or will the habitat just decline to the point where the geese will move on to greener pastures? I hope we will not let it go that far. It's time to step in and tinker again; to try to get the balance right this time by removing the resident geese. I wonder if there is any possibility that we could encourage the offspring to leave home and fly away with their migrating cousins. That's highly unlikely, migration being one of those things geese learn or inherit from their parents. It would be hard for them to strike out on their own, but it's too bad they'll never have the chance to visit those faraway, ancestral nesting grounds, way up north in the Arctic.

In contrast to the decreasing numbers of many other migratory birds, the snow goose population in the Atlantic Flyway has gone up four-fold. Snow geese can be identified by their white wings with black tips. There are now typically 100,000 migrants each year. The exotic mute swan population has also taken off in the past few decades, having grown from a few that were released in the 1960s to thousands today. These birds are considered to be invasive and problematic in that they also live here year-round and eat up to eight pounds of submerged grasses per day. One mute swan became the local bully in the water near our home, chasing other birds away. He disappeared last year and all of a sudden we seem to have more herons breeding here. This year we have been enjoying great blue herons, green herons, night herons, and a great egret. Nature is always trying to adjust to the changes we introduce.

Three types of ducks appear regularly around the bay: dabbling ducks, diving ducks, and sea ducks. Like geese, ducks have webbed feet, short legs, and most have wide, flattened bills. Most also migrate seasonally and depend on agricultural areas, bay bottoms, and wetlands for food. Diving ducks are fun to watch. They have large feet and short legs near the rear of their bodies that propel them underwater in their search for aquatic vegetation and invertebrates. They often pop up a long way from where they went under. Diving ducks also put on a show when they take off because, like geese, they must first gather speed by running across the water's surface before taking flight.

Once airborne, ducks are fast, having been reported to fly at speeds over seventy miles per hour. The bay's diving ducks include the canvasback, redhead, greater and lesser scaup, and ruddy duck. The canvasback is the most abundant diving duck in the Chesapeake region. They migrate from Alberta, Saskatchewan, and Manitoba, Canada. At one time canvasbacks consumed wild celery almost exclusively, but the sharp decline in wild celery caused canvasbacks to shift their diet to small clams. The redhead, a close relative, is not as adaptable. These ducks continue to feed mainly on submerged aquatic vegetation, which has been declining in recent years. Consequently, only small numbers of redheads now use the bay for habitat and breeding. Most winter farther south in order to find food. I rarely see them any more.

In contrast to the diving ducks, dabbling ducks have small feet located near the front or middle of their bodies. This allows them to dunk their heads and necks underwater to feed off submerged aquatic vegetation. Dabblers, like geese, look like bobbers floating on the water with their tail feathers sticking straight up while their heads are submerged during feeding. Dabbling ducks can take off vertically and can walk easily on land but are not good divers. Local dabbling ducks include the American black duck, green-winged and blue-winged teal, mallard, northern pintail, and American wigeon. The black duck and mallard are the most abundant dabbling ducks in the bay, but while the mallard population is increasing, black ducks are declining, apparently because they have not been as successful in adapting to human interference. Resident mallards also adversely affect black duck populations by competing for nest sites and food, or through hybridization with black ducks. I regularly see these hybridized ducks in the water near my home.

Sea ducks normally live in the ocean but frequent the deeper parts of the bay along the old and now submerged Susquehanna River gorge. They dive much deeper than other ducks in search of mollusks, invertebrates, and fish. Like diving ducks, they must run along the surface to take off, with the exception of the bufflehead and the beautiful hooded merganser, which can take off vertically, like dabbling ducks. Sea ducks include the long-tailed duck, common goldeneye, bufflehead, white-winged, black and surf scoters and hooded and red-breasted mergansers. The food quality at depths of twenty to forty feet where these birds feed has declined dramatically in recent years from the occurrence of anoxic dead zones in many of the deeper parts of the bay. The decline of mussels and oysters in these dead zones has contributed to the parallel decline in the number of sea ducks in this region.

The bay is also frequented by birds similar to ducks, like grebes and the common loon. The latter is a large bird with a dagger-like bill for capturing fish and aquatic invertebrates. It has webbed feet, located far back on its body, that act like propellers, helping it to dive to depths as great as two hundred feet. Grebes are small birds with very small tails. The pied-billed grebe is found in shallow water and marshes, while the horned grebe is found in tidal rivers and open bays. They eat fish and invertebrates and their lobed feet with flattened claws help them swim and dive.

Goose and duck hunting is still a thriving sport in the Chesapeake. Guides and outfitters can set you up with a hunting experience on private land. You sneak out before daybreak and hide in blinds set up in cornfields and on rivers along the flyways. Your hideout will be surrounded by decoys, and the guides will try to call the waterfowl into range with goose and duck calls. Unfortunately, the warming climate is wreaking havoc on this business as well, since migrating patterns are changing. The traditional hunting season is now missing the main bird migrations. Hunting regulations have also been implemented to minimize the impact of over-hunting, which was a major problem in the past. For example, in Maryland migratory game birds may no longer be taken with traps, snares, nets, crossbows, rifles, pistols, swivel guns, fish hooks, poisons, drugs, explosives, or stupefying substances, all of which methods have been used in the past. In the old days, waterfowl were harvested with king-sized punt guns and multi-barreled battery guns that could knock down scores of birds with a single firing. Today, migratory game birds may not be taken with a shotgun capable of holding more than three shells or larger than 10-gauge. Non-toxic bird shot is now required for hunting waterfowl and other game birds such as coots, rails, and snipe. *Only 6 ducks per day can be taken per hunter which may include no more than: 5 long-tailed ducks, 4 scoters, 4 mallards, 2 wood ducks, 2 redheads, 2 scaup, 2 canvasbacks, 2 hooded mergansers, 1 pintail, and 1 black duck.* I am not sure why people shoot wild ducks and geese except for the excitement of bagging a bird. Whenever Dad brought home a goose he shot for Christmas dinner we used to give him a hard time. They were the toughest birds we ever ate, and we had to be careful picking through the meat because it was often full of lead shot that could crack a tooth.

There is no hunting on the water near my home, a small, man-made lake that feeds into the Little Patuxent River. That is one reason why we see so many birds flying low overhead and swimming close to shore. But the lake is surrounded by houses, and some residents don't take very good care of the local watershed. Each year parts of the vegetation buffer zone around the lake is cut down to improve someone's view of the water. People don't realize the harm this illegal pruning does to the water quality and the life in the lake. Other residents fertilize their lawns and mow their grass so short that storm water runs right off into the lake, without filtering through the soil. Because of these practices, the lake is dying and clogged with algae, invasive grasses (probably from aquarium cleaning), and debris from back yards. Fortunately, a movement is afloat to rebuild the buffers and encourage the planting of more native plants and shrubs. Still, changing people's behavior is a slow process.

Although the fish may not be doing so well, birds still like the place. Over the past year I counted an average of two dozen resident geese and about the same number of resident mallards and hybrid ducks here in the summer. Each winter we are visited by dozens of migrating geese who often are forced to fight territorial battles with the resident geese to re-establish their winter home. It's a noisy and exciting time of year. We also become the winter home for about a dozen ring-neck ducks and occasional canvasback, redheads, pie-billed grebes, loons, and hooded mergansers. Most of my neighbors enjoy watching the geese and ducks land, swim around on the water in family groups, and feed off the underwater vegetation. I've learned to differentiate the gander with his low-pitched "ahonk" call from the goose with her higher pitched "hink" call. I've seen mated pairs greet each other, communicating back and forth so rapidly it sounded just like one goose talking. The mergansers, ring-necks, and grebes entertain us with their disappearing acts when diving for food. We try to guess where they will surface.

I hope all of these species will continue to adapt to the changing climate and habitats and don't permanently disappear in the near future. Wildlife has no choice. It must respond to our actions. Sometimes it can adjust, sometimes it cannot. When we put more and more stresses on our—and their—habitat, a healthy relationship with other species that share the bay with us becomes difficult to manage.

What can be done to help migratory waterfowl? There are many good sources for information on protecting waterfowl such as Ducks Unlimited (www.ducks.org). The loss of habitat and aquatic grasses important to waterfowl and other species could be addressed by the following actions.

Individuals can help create and preserve more wetlands by supporting land trusts and insuring that our local governments enforce existing regulations designed to prevent shoreline development. We can also help restore the health of aquatic grasses by reducing storm water and fertilizer runoff. We can help by supporting water quality, storm water retrofit, and reforestation activities and legislation throughout the watershed.

Corporations can help by finding cures for the diseases that attack the filter feeders in the bay or by finding aquatic grasses (and oysters) that can flourish there.

Governments can help by managing the numbers of exotic and invasive species (resident geese and mute swans) to limit their detrimental impact on our dwindling resources. They can also help by reducing population pressure in waterfowl breeding grounds and here in their winter homes.

Winter on the Bay

Before global warming got out of hand, our winters were colder. Snow lasted for weeks, and many of the freshwater rivers froze over. In especially cold years, even the brackish waters of the Chesapeake froze over as far south as the mouth of the Patuxent River. I distinctly remember being invited to a friend's house to go skating in 1962. My folks said fine, unaware that it was not our plan to skate on a pond. Mom would never have let me go had she known that we were going out on the bay. I doubt it even entered her mind. My friend, Greg, had told me, but even I figured he was kidding, so I didn't mention it to my parents. When I realized he was serious, I began to feel anxious. It was hard to imagine the bay being frozen enough to skate on. Would I have the nerve to skate very far from shore?

Greg, who lived near the mouth of Bush River, led the way down to his pier. We were in a cold snap and it was indeed very, very cold. The temperatures had been hovering around zero for the past week. The ground crunched as we walked, and within minutes my nose and fingers grew numb. I glanced at the bay and as far as I could see there was ice, quite rough along the shore, but it did look like we could skate farther out. Momentarily forgetting that it was saltwater, I convinced myself that it must be safe.

Greg and I slipped, stumbled, and climbed over the rough ice along the shore and worked our way out along the pilings of what used to be a dock. The wooden pier was in shambles, having been heaved up off its moorings by the ice. Just past the pier, the ice was flatter. The farther out we skated, the smoother it became. It was hard and seemed quite stable. Yes, I was scared, but I was so focused on not falling and on keeping warm that I managed to follow Greg out away from shore. He was small, spidery, and fast. I was bigger, and my ankles were already sore from trying to balance on the single blades of the skates. We saw other people down the shoreline looking like they were having a great time, so we headed off to join them. There is nothing like peer pressure to make one jump into a situation. Along the way we stopped to examine the damage to other docks and areas where the ice was piled up high. A small group playing hockey with makeshift sticks, brooms, and a can of StarKist tuna called for us to join them. With no hockey sticks, we just waved and kept moving, past families who were slipping and falling and pulling kids on sleds.

Farther out from shore, we saw makeshift huts constructed right on the ice, with smoke rising from their peaks. Getting our ice-legs, we raced each other out to the sheds. I won. As we glided to a stop, a man came out of one to relieve himself on the lee side of the hut. He invited us in, and since it was cold standing in the wind, we joined him and his two brothers inside. A kerosene heater and smiles all around welcomed us into their cozy abode. Simply being out of the wind felt good. The brothers sat around three holes bored through the ice. Dressed in Carhardt overalls, they were relaxing on lawn chairs with a half-empty case of beer beside them. It was eleven o'clock in the morning. Clearly they were proud of their castle and planned to make a day of it.

The bluish-white ice, about eight inches thick, seemed a little less permanent as I peered down the holes into the clear, cold water below. I grew uneasy staring into the chilly depths and wondered if eight inches of ice could hold the five of us so close together. Slowly I edged back, closer to the wall. Each hole was outfitted with a hand-made rig with a flag over it, and with a heavy line going down into the water. The brothers had already pulled in half a dozen nice-sized fish and smoked at least a pack of Kools based on the number of butts strewn about the icy floor. The oldest brother pulled in a perch while we stood there, and I asked him what if they caught a really big fish that couldn't fit through the six-inch hole. They all laughed and said if that happened they would get busy really fast and cut a bigger hole.

Greg and I left the warmth of the hut, too young for beer, cigarettes, and stories of the good old days; after all we were twelve. The sun was now out, and feeling adventuresome, we skated on, letting the breeze push us farther out across the bay. We felt free, brave, and full of ourselves. At noon we realized we were tired, hungry, and several miles from shore, so we came to a stop to talk about where to go next. We were a bit disoriented, being about midway between the eastern and western shores. The horizon seemed the same no matter which way we looked. While standing still, realizing how far we were from shore, a loud crack like a rifle shot ripped through the ice. My heart sank into the depths of my toes, my legs shook, and my confidence vanished. It felt like an earthquake erupting beneath my wobbly knees.

We bolted, assuming the ice was about to open up and we'd slide into the icy water. Running on the serrated tips of our skates, not caring which shore we got to as long as we made land, we didn't slow down to glide on the runners for at least a hundred yards. Then came another rifle shot, and fresh images of the ice opening up right behind me. At any moment I could be swallowed up and frozen beneath the ice. Halfway to shore, with our legs cramping up, we pointed in different directions trying to figure out which cove to aim for. Finally we found the right pier and skated in, bouncing over the rough ice and collapsing on the shore. We lay there panting for several minutes, sweat running down our faces.

Eventually we turned to face the bay and saw that the ice had not opened up at all. People were still out there, and someone was even driving a car out on it. We looked at each other, puzzled. Later we learned that the ice had been adjusting to the sun. That causes stress cracks to form, but the cracks do not open up or cause a shifting of the plates. Nevertheless, we felt safer on land and slowly removed our sore feet from the skates before going inside for hot cocoa and lunch. I never told my parents about being out on the bay, about the guys drinking beer, or about the cracking ice. I just told them how much fun I'd had skating with Greg.

Since that day I have heard ice break up on lakes and ponds a number of times. I find the sound eerie and beautiful. It reminds me of rippling a sheet of tin or the haunting sound of whales, multiple frequencies with broad wavelengths that flow right through you and the very ground you're standing upon. It's an unforgettable sound, and I wish everyone could hear it so long as he or she is standing firmly on the ground.

During that day on the bay, I learned a great deal, about the musical properties of ice, about taking risks, and that fish still bite in the winter. All important lessons. I had never really thought about where fish go when the bay freezes over. How do they adjust to the temperature? How do they breathe?

It may seem counter-intuitive at first, but water actually makes a very good shelter for many animals in the winter. When the weather gets cold, some species move to the bottom of lakes and ponds or, like crabs, into the deeper channels. Cold-blooded animals like frogs, turtles, and many fish adapt themselves to the winter cold. Some fish have the luxury of migrating to warmer climates. Others have to resort to hiding under rocks, logs, or fallen leaves. They may even bury themselves in the mud. Nearly all North American turtles spend the winter underwater. Even some terrestrial reptiles withdraw to aquatic habitats for hibernation, where they become dormant. Fortunately, cold water holds more oxygen than warm water, and frogs and turtles can breathe by absorbing oxygen through their skin. In winter there is more oxygen available because the algae blooms die off and the dead zones go away.

So there are significant advantages to wintering in ponds or in the bay, the most striking of which is the behavior of water itself. Water is capable of absorbing and storing tremendous amounts of heat with only a slight increase in temperature. It cools off just as slowly as it warms up, meaning that aquatic life undergoes relatively moderate fluctuations in temperature. Another quirk of water is that at thirty-nine degrees Fahrenheit it achieves its greatest density and sinks to the bottom of ponds. This microclimate at the bottom is quite comfortable for turtles and other creatures that hibernate.

The terrestrial wildlife around the bay deals with the colder weather in different ways. On my walks through the woods in the dead of winter, I notice a wide variety of tracks. I regularly find evidence that deer, squirrels, fox, coyote, otter, muskrat, beaver, and rabbits all stay active during the winter. I am always intrigued at the numerous, often circuitous trails through fields and woods left by these mammals. They may live in holes in trees, dense brush, or underground when it's really cold, but they come out and forage for food whenever possible. Because it's harder to find food in winter they have to change their diet in order to survive. Deer eat leaves and grasses in summer and twigs and seedlings of deciduous trees and other low growing plants in winter. As beaver have made their resurgence in this area, I have seen more and more trees, especially white oaks down by the water, that have been girdled a foot or two off the ground by their gnawing.

Squirrels are often out and about chasing one another in their mating rituals in mid- to late winter. This chasing may be necessary for stimulating ovulation in the females since squirrels don't breed when they are confined in a cage. I once watched two squirrels run full-tilt to the end of a limb. One forgot to stop and fell thirty feet to the ground, landing within a foot of where I was standing. She quickly got up and raced away. When I looked up the other squirrel was hanging by his back feet, as though he was contemplating whether she was worth a thirty-foot fall.

Skunks and raccoons typically go into a period of "light sleep," curling up with their family members in a den. Although they sleep away the winter snuggled up, they do go out and forage at times. Their systems and body functions don't change as much as those of the true hibernators, but their activity slows way down. When I was a kid I caught a raccoon in this slow state once. My dog had cornered it and held it at bay until I could go get a crab net and a burlap bag. I captured the raccoon and took it home for a pet.

Chipmunks, mice, woodchucks, and bats do hibernate during the winter. Their body temperatures, heartbeats, and breathing all lower, so they use very little energy. They live off their stored fat. Woodchucks can drop their body temperatures by thirty degrees. A mouse drops its heartbeat from five hundred beats per minute to thirty.

I've often wondered where insects find winter shelter. Do they just go into holes in the ground, under the bark of trees, deep inside rotting logs, or into any small crack they can find? Every type of insect has its own life cycle, and different insects spend the winter in different stages of their lives. Many are dormant, a time when growth and development stop and the insect's heartbeat, breathing, and temperature drop. Some spend the winter as worm-like larvae and others as pupae, changing from one form to another. Some insects die after laying eggs in the fall; the eggs hatch in the spring, and everything begins all over again. One of the most interesting wintering processes is the formation of a gall, a swelling on the stem or branch of a plant caused by certain insects, fungi, or bacteria. These produce a chemical that affects the plant's growth in a small area, forming a lump. The gall becomes its maker's home and food source.

The farmhouse in which I grew up also served as winter headquarters for the blacksnakes on the farm. We encountered them or their transparent skins when we climbed into the basement crawl spaces to fix our plumbing or to run new electrical lines. Some grew to six or seven feet and as round as my wrists. Snakes, in general, hibernate during the winter in dens deep enough to be free from frost. They can be found in narrow crevices in rocks, animal burrows, holes under trees and stumps, under wood piles, and as we learned, in basements. A number of species, e.g., black rat snakes, timber rattlesnakes, and copperheads, commonly den together. The black rat snake was called the pilot blacksnake because in the spring it was believed to "pilot" the way out of the den for the rattlesnake. Now we think that snakes leave a scent as they leave the den so they can find it again when they need it. I always enjoy seeing snakes show up again in the spring. It's usually in April when snakes such as the ribbon, garter, northern water, black rat, or the corn snake appear along the paths and streams near the bay.

All life forms have developed complex routines in order to live with the climatic patterns of this region. It is pretty clear to all long-time residents that these patterns are changing, as illustrated by the fact that the bay doesn't freeze over like it did just a few decades ago. How will this dramatic change and the other effects of global warming affect the lives of the creatures in the watershed? They will attempt to adjust. Let's hope their food sources adjust as well, or in the near future we'll see the decline of some of these species in the Chesapeake. For the moment, we just don't know what the ripple effect of a changing climate will be.

What can be done to reduce the impact of climate change? To prevent harm to other species as well as on ourselves, we have to stabilize the number of people and reduce our emissions of greenhouse gases. We can lower our individual carbon footprints by reducing the amount of energy we use.

Individuals can help by doing those things you hear about all the time: using programmable thermostats, upgrading heating and cooling systems, turning off lights and appliances, switching to compact fluorescent bulbs, insulating attics, walls, and crawl spaces, driving high-efficiency, hybrid cars, driving less, consuming less, and buying local. A good way to start is by having a home energy audit performed (see Appendix A).

Corporations can find ways to offer these goods and services at a low cost and in such a way that most people and most companies can and will implement them. If they can develop the solutions, they can provide better technologies to everyone on the planet.

Governments can provide information, incentives, and leadership to encourage all of us to reduce our energy. They can incentivize research into better solutions and lead the global community toward adopting international goals, treaties, and cooperative efforts.

Part III

The Watershed

The Chesapeake Bay watershed is large and diverse, collecting waters that fall on parts of six states. The glacial terrains of New York, the coal mines of Pennsylvania, the poultry farms on the Delmarva Peninsula, and the streets of our nation's capital all drain into the Chesapeake. Rain falling on farms, factories, and probably even on your house, lawn, and driveway flows along countless streams and rivers that crisscross the land and eventually mixes with the saltier waters of the bay. The water quality, biodiversity, and health of the bay and its fisheries are all related to every part of the habitat throughout this vast, fifty-million-acre watershed. We are all in this together. What each of us does affects the rest. Our actions do matter. So let's leave the bay and explore the streams, the woods, and the other inhabitants of this intricate, interconnected ecosystem.

Down the Patapsco

Captain John Smith was the first to write about the beauty of the bay and the richness of her tributaries. Sailing north from Jamestown in 1608, he and his crew explored and mapped its major features and encountered the Native Americans already there. Some of the more than fifty rivers that empty into it now bear English names like James, York, Avon, Miles, Chester, and Gunpowder, others Native American names like Rappahannock, Wicomico, Nanticoke, Pocomoke, Potomac, Patuxent, and Susquehanna. Much has changed since Smith first saw these rivers, and at the same time, much has remained the same. Smith described the region as one "of deep, ancient forests, strong, proud people and water teeming with life." I've been on many of the rivers and find there is still very much left to explore and write about. There are indeed forests along some of the tributaries today, and in many cases, strong, proud people, especially the watermen. I'm not sure anyone would characterize the bay today as "teeming with life," but I was curious to find out how much wildlife can still be found along the rivers. I wanted to take the time to get to know at least one in more detail, to see how it is holding up to all the changes imposed by our growing population.

Early one summer my younger daughter Leigh and I found ourselves involved in the Patapsco River Valley. She worked weekdays with city youths on the downstream, estuarine parts of the Patapsco as an intern at Living Classrooms Foundation headquartered in Baltimore's Inner Harbor. At night she returned and told of building wooden boats, sailing, and harvesting oysters aboard a skipjack. At the time, I was volunteering at Mt. Pleasant Farm, headquarters of a local land trust, the Howard County Conservancy, where the same city kids came out to have a dry land watershed experience. The farm near Woodstock, Maryland, lies between Davis Creek and East Branch, two small tributaries that feed into the Patapsco. At night I shared stories with Leigh about the area's history and how the conservancy was trying to preserve land and maintain a variety of habitats.

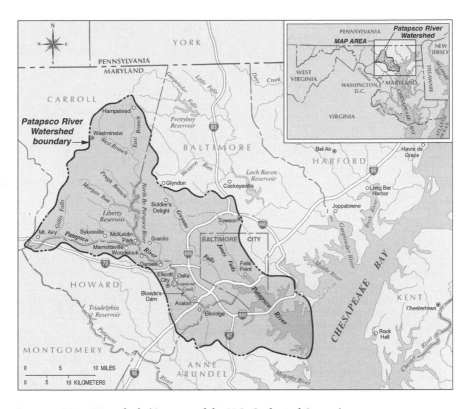

Patapsco River Watershed. (Courtesy of the U.S. Geological Survey.)

As we listened to one another's experiences, it became clear that we both had fallen in love with the nature and lore of the region. We made a pact that summer to explore the entire length of the river together on our weekends. The ensuing walks, canoe trips, and overall exploration of the valley exceeded our expectations; we saw more through each other's eyes and reactions than we ever would have learned alone. It was well worth having a common passion during the brief span of a single summer. I didn't know if we would ever have such an opportunity again.

IT'S LATE ON A FRIDAY NIGHT, early in July. Leigh and I are sitting at our kitchen table, perusing several maps and books to get a better sense of the Patapsco. Excitement is in the air as we lay out our plans to explore a river from end to end. The maps show that the river zigs and zags for thirty-five miles through the heart of Maryland. Leigh suggests that we start in the west, walking and paddling eastward with the flow of the water. I protest that this is the easy way, and not the direction the first settlers took. She wins—we only have a few weekends, not years, to complete our trip. We noticed on the maps that in the west the river meanders through the rolling Piedmont farmland, then cascades along a narrow river valley until the waters drop across the fall line onto the flat Coastal Plain at Elkridge. There it becomes tidal and "navigable" and once served as a port to the open sea, to England, and beyond. The main branch of the Patapsco River is joined by the Gwynns Falls and Jones Falls tributaries, forming the harbor that has served Baltimore so well for almost three centuries.

We learned from reading a fascinating book by Hal Sharpe (*The Patapsco River Valley: Cradle of the Industrial Revolution in Maryland*, 2001) that during the eighteenth and nineteenth centuries the river served as a vital center of industry. Ruins of numerous mills lie along its banks west of Elkridge, nineteenth-century entrepreneurs once attempted to harness the falling waters to power factories. Most of their dams and industries were eventually damaged or entirely destroyed by rampaging floods. The river's gorge has since been allowed to recover and is now protected and enjoyed as forested parkland. The more we read, the more eager we become to go out and discover the soul of the river for ourselves.

The next morning, the first Saturday in July, we set off to explore the South Branch of the Patapsco. The river is hidden in one of the fastest growing parts of central Maryland. We drive through terrain that is rapidly changing from cornfields to suburban houses, schools, and stores. This is an area bustling with families that have dropped into a landscape quite foreign to them. They are immediately caught up in the business of modern life and know very little about where they are living, about the dirt beneath their feet. They will need time before they can develop a sense of place. As we drive along, I wonder how long it will take these new arrivals to acquire a real feeling for the land where they are putting down roots.

As we descend into the valley on this hot July morning, we cross one of the bridges that pass over the Patapsco, barely noticing the river at all from the confines of our air-conditioned car. After parking in the micaceous riverbank dust along the CSX railroad tracks, we climb out into the heat and humidity of a Maryland summer. Leigh leads the way, pushing through head-high cattails, trying to get down to the river's edge. Walking is treacherous, the brush full of thistles, cobbles, ground-hog holes, broken branches, and beer bottles. I trip and lose sight of her for a few seconds. When I catch up, we look at one another, each having second thoughts about our goal for the day. On the banks our ears are full of traffic noise and locust calls. Sweat streams down our faces. Dust and pollen make our eyes itch.

"Whose idea was this?" Leigh asks. She is smiling, but at that moment it felt like another fine mess we'd gotten ourselves into.

Without answering, I take the lead, trying to drop down into the riverbed at three or four places without success. The buffer of trees and brush here is actually quite healthy, protecting the river from rampant runoff and the casual interloper. Finally we find a narrow deer path and easily make the descent.

Once we've reached the water, I swear I am not going to climb up on the dusty banks again. What a change a few short steps can make. The temperature in the shaded river bottom is much cooler, and the air is moist. Leigh and I wash the dust from our hands and faces. The water is cool and clear. We relax and smile at one another. We've discovered a sanctuary away from the heat and the bustle of suburban life. We think for just a moment about our friends, many of whom are spending their weekend on the highways or at the mall.

Leigh heads downstream, and I follow, making our way slowly toward Sykesville. Watching her, I realize we're acting more like amphibians than mammals, walking in and out of the water as we go. We both started with dry shoes. I was wearing my hiking boots and Leigh had on an old pair of sneakers. Now our shoes squish on every step, sucking water in or squeezing it out. Our feet stir up silt, leaving muddy clouds in our wake. The water level is low, and we find it difficult to walk along the artificially narrow riverbed. The water here is full of boulders and debris from the railroad embankments that border the river's edge. Over the past three centuries, it has been separated from its natural floodplain by the building of roads, railroads, and bridges—and not just a single road or railroad embankment either. In many places there are two separate railroad beds built along this river, sometimes on opposite sides. Where once, before the railroads, the river meandered lazily back and forth in its valley, naturally dissipating the energy of periodic flood-waters across a wide floodplain, now in some places it is forced to follow a straighter path, becoming a big man-made ditch if you will.

I can just imagine that in this straightened channel, storm waters run-ning off from cleared land and paved development do not have the chance to calm their fury in broad, S-shaped meanders. This unnatural constraint has been disastrous in the past and was one cause of the numerous his-toric floods. I imagine that as the climate warms and the county is further covered with houses and pavement (increasing storm water runoff) fu-ture floods will be even more devastating.

Leigh proceeds downriver, sometimes carefully stepping from rock to rock and other times giving up all pretense of staying dry and just wading in the water. Between the boulders, the bottom is gravelly in some places and in others filled with silt. Leigh runs out of stepping stones and wades through a deep pool, her pants getting wet up to her pockets. The duct tape she used to patch the rip at her knee gets wet and deserts her.

Once we settle into a comfortable pace walking along the stream valley, we realize that it's full of life.

"Look at all the fish!" I call out as a school of minnows and a few larger fish, up to nine inches in length, dart across small pools in the river bed.

"Watch out for the gnats," she replies, spitting out one she acciden-tally nearly swallowed. Leigh goes off on a side creek and as I hustle to catch up with her, small brown creatures dart across the shallow pools.

"Hey look at this!" I assume they are minnows, but on closer in-spection see that the big one is a crayfish. I have found crayfish under stones before, but rarely have I seen them in the open in broad daylight. When I flush out another school, I see that they are all crayfish—handfuls of them! A large one and half a dozen smaller ones scatter across the pool, probably a mother with her young. I move upstream and find more clusters of these freshwater crustaceans. I've never seen so many before. It's July, in the middle of a dry period, and we've got lots of action in just six inches of water.

In the river, the sounds of traffic and insects are lost. All we hear is gurgling water, birds calling, and shouts of discovery from one another. It is almost like magic, as though we have been carried far away from normal life here in the suburbs of central Maryland and plopped down in the middle of a wilderness full of living things but devoid of other people.

Leigh calls me over to the other bank. She has found near the shore a slimy, brown, rust-colored residue, an iridescent, oily sheen floating on the water's surface. "Dad, what's this?"

I walk over wondering if this iridescence indicates an oil spill. I mix it up with a stick and it does not coalesce like an oil slick would. "It's probably iron bacteria. That's a naturally occurring micro-organism that blooms when oxygen, water, and iron mix together."

Leigh looks at me suspiciously and asks "What's your confidence level?"

"About an eight," I reply with a smile. This is a new development in the family, a way to check in on how sure we are about a statement. It works very well and no one is offended. Educated guesses are OK as long as we know the level of certainty of our statements. A confidence level of eight out of ten is pretty good.

As we slip and slide our way downstream, the banks become more natural, and less affected by man. I notice holes along the bank, small ones that appear to be the size of snakes, larger ones that could accommodate muskrats. A few smooth, slippery slides down the muddy banks and into the water suggest the presence of river otters. Numerous damaged white oaks and other trees near the water prompt us to look for beaver and beaver dams. We wonder where all these reptiles and mammals are today. Is it too hot for them? Are they sleeping? Are we making so much noise that they have time to hide as they hear us coming?

During our walk we catch glimpses of a bluebird, several bright yellow goldfinches, a pair of kingfishers, and a scarlet tanager, a bird I rarely see out in the open where I usually walk. I feel as though I have entered a sanctuary that Mother Nature has created to protect a few species from man's transformation of her planet. Habitats come and habitats go; some species make it, and some don't. Clearly the habitat struggling to survive in this narrow stream valley is vastly different from the farmland and suburban settings just a few yards away. I feel an overwhelming sense of gratitude to the people who preserved this valley as a park back in 1907 and for all who maintain its 14,000 acres today.

For a mid-afternoon rest, Leigh finds a granitic rock ledge jutting into the river. We sit partly in the sun, and partly in the shade, our boots and socks drying for a few minutes in the sun as we eat apples, cheese, and bread. I smell the wet woolen socks, the wet earth, and honeysuckle along the banks and watch the water rippling over sandbars, eddying behind boulders. The water seems pure and clean, rushing through tight channels and then dallying behind rocks in pools. Bubbles form in the sluiceways where the water tumbles over itself, then quickly pop as the water slows. A cool breeze is drying my skin, alternating with the heat from the sun filtering through the leaves. There is so much to see, hear, feel, and smell in this place that we relax and try to take it all in, absorb it to help us later calm our busy lives.

As the day passes, Leigh observes, "This place is so close to home, why haven't we been out here before?"

It's a good question. We have lived within a few minutes' drive of this beautiful sanctuary, and yet I've never brought my family down here for a walk. It's close, it's free, and it makes for a wonderful afternoon of exploring and sharing. Strange how my family, like many others, has gotten so wrapped up in structured and in many cases commercial events that we haven't made the time to discover the world all around us.

There was a time when kids would naturally gravitate to the local rivers in the summer. We may not have had air-conditioning back in those days, but like many kids we did have a swimming hole. Ours was on the Gunpowder River, and going there was the high point of a hot summer day. According to William Ellicott, who wrote in 1910, the Patapsco Park was initially created "because it offers an alluring opportunity for a ramble in the woods or a walk by the river, and has become a favorite sylvan resort of large numbers of our people." No longer, I'm afraid. Air-conditioning and electronic entertainment have taken away the need. I wonder how many of us realize what we're missing.

"Time to move on," Leigh announces. We resume our walk downstream, continuing our exploration. The rough going forces me to pay attention to each step. Even so, I keep glancing ahead and into the canopy above, trying to see everything and hoping not to miss something wonderful hidden in the foliage. As we come around the next bend I freeze, teetering on a wet boulder. I point quickly downstream and make a muffled alarm to raise Leigh's attention. She looks and eventually sees what has attracted my curiosity—a full-grown, great blue heron stands perfectly still in the shallow water just ahead, blending in with the background.

As we watch, Leigh suddenly slips off her boulder and splashes into the river. The heron reacts by lifting off in a manner that is at once graceful and awkward. His movements are otherworldly, certainly not something you'd see during the normal everyday rat race. Once airborne and floating about six feet above the water, he glides downstream for a hundred yards and alights in the shallows. Again he becomes a motionless statue, allowing his features to blend into the background foliage. Standing still and tall, he is hard to identify among the reeds and branches. Our great blue repeats this pattern each time we come too close, not wanting to expend too much energy, but not wanting us to disturb his fishing. Being a fisherman, I relate to his feelings about intruders.

Leigh, recovering from the fall, stumbles out of the water, her arms flailing about as she tries to catch her balance. I see the same awkwardness and grace in her long limbs as in the heron's. Her youthful athleticism lets her quickly recover her balance in a way that can only be fully appreciated by an older, less fluid soul—one who must appear much more awkward and far less graceful to the heron if he has been watching.

The heron wins our game of catch-up as he disappears from sight with a last glide downstream. It is late in the day, and as we come to a railroad bridge we decide to climb out of the South Branch and walk back along the tracks to our car. An easy exit. Once up on the track we are surprised to see the gaping mouth of a tunnel. Above the entrance is the word SYKESVILLE. Inside we find a plaque honoring the designer and engineer who built it in 1902. What a surprise to find a tunnel here, one a hundred yards long. We had completely missed this engineering marvel while sequestered within the banks of the river, just like those who don't drop into the riverbed at all would have missed the natural wonders we've just enjoyed.

As we admire how well-built this old tunnel is, I wonder why so many who live close to this beautiful, significant, and historic river valley have rarely taken the time to get to know it, to explore the meanders, the falls, the dams, the tunnels, the pools and eddies, the riffles, fauna, and flora. And why has it taken *me* so long to find my way into this sanctuary? Why do we ignore the rivers that carved our landscape and drain the rainwater from our lawns? Are we just too busy with superficial activities to drop into the riverbed and really get to know this vital part of our community? The river's health reflects the health of our community, our ecosystem, our ecological niche. If we all took the time to get to know a river, we just might become better stewards of our environment.

As Leigh and I walk back to the car, the river disappears behind a curtain of invasive ailanthus trees. We are back on man-made tracks, focusing on our normal reality. The stream recedes from our consciousness. Our minds, no longer completely engrossed with the river valley, turn to other things: going home, mowing grass, preparing dinner, going to work. Then, as if we needed another reminder of the wilderness that lies just a few feet away, our friend the great blue rises high above the trees and emits four hoarse, primordial squawks on his way back upriver to his favorite fishing hole. We stop and watch him, now feeling in some strange way connected. We are fortunate to have discovered this sanctuary, the lair of the great blue heron and the scarlet tanager, hidden away in the middle of Maryland, and we are thankful that it still exists after so many years of abuse.

ANOTHER SATURDAY MORNING, and I wake up early. A hard rain fell during the night. It's time to canoe the Patapsco from Daniels to Ellicott City. This is the most exciting run on the river and includes shooting the dangerous breach of the old Union Dam. I wake Leigh; we eat, and then untie the red, Old Town canoe from its roost hanging from the rafters in the garage and load it onto the car. I lash it around the middle, and Leigh clove-hitches it, bow and stern. We used to over-secure the canoe, but now with experience, we have become minimalists, not wasting line, knots, or time. Throwing the paddles, life vests, and water jugs into the old blue caravan, we drive off holding mugs full of steaming chai. We don't really need the caffeine because we already have an adrenaline lift just planning to challenge this section of the river with its rock gardens, riffles, and dams. You can run a canoe down the whole river, but just west of the fall line it's best in winter and spring and sometimes even in summer if you catch it within a day or two of a good, hard rain. Today would probably be our last shot for the summer.

We want to start at Daniels, but first we drop one car at the parking lot behind the grain mill in Old Ellicott City. This is where we will "take out" later in the day, if we make it that far. Then we drive upriver to Daniels. A fisherman is wading in the shallow water and casting into the turbulent pool below the dam, and a family is starting a hike upstream. It feels good to know that others are enjoying this, too. We lift the canoe off the car and wade out onto a pebbly sandbar, a good start. The paddling is easy and we enjoy the slow pace along this first stretch. We stop once or twice to pick a few blackberries along sunny stretches of the bank, and at one point flush a doe with her twin fawns from the shrubs.

We notice along the banks a series of stone walls—foundations of houses, mills, and factories peeking out from behind kudzu and grapevines. The old buildings are gone except for these ruins, lost to multiple floods that tore off the upper stories, the walls, and the roofs. Hundreds of people used to live and work here. Some perished in the floods. Now vines and trees dominate once again, reclaiming the original look and feel of the valley.

The going is good along this stretch though we scrape and bounce along the pebbly bottom in a number of places. It would be harder to run later in the day as the water level quickly rises and then falls following a rain. One of the major changes we have imposed on this river is that of creating an erratic water level. Without man's involvement, rainwater naturally soaks into the ground and migrates down to the groundwater table. The water then flows through the ground to the banks of streams and rivers and slowly and continuously recharges the water flow. This allows water to be filtered and purified by the soil and helps maintain a constant flow of water throughout the year, resulting in a healthier riparian ecosystem. By paving over so much land we've created conditions where far more rainfall regularly flows across impervious surfaces right into storm water culverts and directly into streams immediately after a storm. This change to the natural hydrologic system has resulted in greater flooding and scouring of river banks, and more drastic variations in riverine water levels. As a result, the natural river habitats are damaged by unnaturally high water following rains and low water the rest of the time. It also results in more silt and fertilizer from farms and yards washing into rivers and the bay. A move is currently afoot to change our storm water systems. By building rain gardens, bioretention ponds, and planting trees and shrubs we can restore the health of our rivers by helping rainwater filter into the ground and not just run off into the bay. It won't be easy, but with enough individual and political will it can be done. We built rain gardens and bioretention ponds at the conservancy when we constructed our new Environmental Center, and they are working well. Good conservation methods could be standard for all buildings. We hope everyone will soon see their importance and implement these practices on their own land and especially on all future development.

The beauty of this place quickly draws my attention back to all the life around us. Jays, mockingbirds, redwing blackbirds, and catbirds fly by only to hide in the dense grapevines and sweet-smelling honeysuckle hanging from trees along the banks. We debate whether we see a Baltimore oriole or not and are serenaded by a couple of noisy crows. Our reverie is jolted by a coal train with four engines. As its forty cars rumble by, we read their names, which suggest faraway places, large mountaintop strip mines, and worldly destinations. Allegheny and Western, Chessie, Baltimore and Ohio, Santa Fe, Illinois Central, CSX, Union Pacific. The air resonates with screeching metal as the train rounds a curve. It disappears as quickly as it came, leaving us deafened long after it has gone. Leigh had covered her ears. Bird songs can't compete with a freight train.

Just below the high bridge of the Route 40 overpass are the remains of the old Union Dam, which is breached on the right and navigable by canoe, though it can be dangerous in high water. I have a lot of respect for this sluiceway. Just a few years ago, right after a major storm, a couple tried to float down the river in a rubber raft. They never made it—their bodies were found at Union Dam. Fortunately the water is not that high today. As we approach the dam, we pull off to the sandbar on the right and walk down to the breach. The current is strong, and gravity sucks the water down a three-foot drop into a vortex that has a reputation for not releasing its prey. We'll have to hit it just right to avoid the rebar and not get stuck in the standing wave. The excitement of running this channel overcomes my fear of getting caught in it, so we go back to the canoe and shoot the rapids holding our breath. It is thrilling and terrifying. We keep our paddles stroking hard, thankful that the mass and length of our eighteen-foot canoe carries us through the worst of the rapids on the river. I don't want to think what would have happened had we capsized.

The river from here down to Old Ellicott City can be fun if there is adequate water. On this day we make it in record time. The water is just high enough that we don't have to get out but low enough to require a lot of maneuvering. Lots of buffalo-sized boulders in this stretch make

The B&O Railroad Station in Ellicott City. (Courtesy of Alice Webb, the artist)

for an exciting whitewater trip past Dickey Mills at Oella. Large, spotted sycamores line the banks, and groves of beech and oak cover the sloping hillsides. Scraggly sumac and royal paulownia trees, with their large leaves and pungent lavender flowers, hug the railroad tracks. A millrace can be seen running from Union Dam along the east side of the river down to a mill that has been completely erased from the landscape.

At Ellicott City we pass by the B&O Railroad Station and the old trolley stop that brought people from Baltimore out to the country. The old track has been removed, but the path offers a beautiful walk from Old Ellicott City up to the Benjamin Banneker Museum. I recall reading in my grandmother's diary that back in 1911, while my grandparents were courting, my grandfather would bring her out here on the trolley to climb the hills above Ellicott City and watch the sunset. It must have done the trick, because they were married the following year. I've lived here a long while but have never taken the time to climb these hills with my wife to capture the same view. Where has all the romance gone?

Just below the bridge into Ellicott City we take out and load the canoe onto the pickup car. If we'd had more time we could have gone on downstream. There is another twelve-foot dam at Thistle where the better portage is on the right, and after another half-mile stretch there's the twenty-five-foot Bloede Dam. Shortly thereafter you get to Elkridge where the river is tidal. We will complete it all someday, but now it's time to go back upstream to our other car and drive home for dinner. We inch our canoe-laden car through the traffic and all the steamy sidewalk shoppers in Old Ellicott City. I'm amazed at the contrast—wall-to-wall people here on the hot pavement and only a couple of yards away we had the cool, refreshing air of the river almost to ourselves. It doesn't make much sense.

IT IS OUR LAST WEEKEND together, one of those hot, sultry days in the middle of August. There is absolutely no reason to be outside except that we have learned a secret this summer. We know that this is the very best time to appreciate the joys of a Piedmont river valley. Leigh had been wondering about the wide expanse of green she drove over each day as she took Interstate 95 into Baltimore. Like so many others, she had only seen the lower area of the Patapsco Valley Park from the concrete canopy of the interstate. It was time to explore the floor of the valley, far below the steady stream of speeding cars on the highway.

With a water jug and a bag full of nuts we're off to explore another section of what has become our favorite river. We head downstream from Ellicott City to where River Road crosses the Patapsco at the old Simpkins Mill. This was the site of a cotton mill, built around 1822. It made cotton duck sails for the Navy and merchant ships sailing out of Baltimore—a good business when cotton duck was replacing hemp as material for sails. Today this old mill sits abandoned just downstream from the Thistle dam. There is no easy, legal place to park, so we make do on Hilltop Road. Dropping down onto the left bank of the stream, we start hiking southeast by walking on top of a large sewer pipe that serves as the bank along this stretch. Although it intrudes on the beauty of the streambed, this sewer main has dramatically helped clean up the river. The Patapsco, like most rivers in the seventeenth, eighteenth, and nineteenth centuries, served as the open sewer for Ellicott City and beyond. It's just too bad that gravity-fed sewer systems have to be in streambeds.

By the time we reach the water's edge we are hot, and the cool air from the shaded valley instantly rewards us for making the trek. We cross under an active railroad bridge and, glancing up, see the mouth of a tunnel with the name ILCHESTER cut into the stone above its cavernous entrance. Farther downstream we climb up another, lower and older railroad embankment where the railroad bridge had been washed away. This bridge has now been replaced by a walking bridge. Yes, there have been two railroad tracks laid along this river. The lower, older one is marked by a smooth trail and lots of granite blocks that supported the early train tracks. Granite was also used along with marble to build the bridges in this area. One keystone documents its completion in 1869, considerably earlier than the 1902 date recorded on one of the tunnels of the upper, active railroad track.

Along this section, the river has cut a deep valley through the contact zone of the Ellicott City granite and the Baltimore gabbro complex. The older, darker rocks were intruded by fingers of magma that cooled to form gray, granite veins and pegmatite with very large, lustrous, gray quartz and pink feldspar crystals. The largest crystals, as big as a foot in length, can be found on the north bank of the Bloede Dam.

The river along this stretch, though relatively low, still has plenty of water in it, but no people. It's just too hot for most folks to be out and about. It is indeed hot, but this is the place to be. The valley is not stifling at all. It's rather pleasant. We think of taking a dip but don't feel the need as much as we did before we entered the riverbed. As we walk along the trail, we finally do encounter one couple in the water. They clearly *get it;* she is pregnant and floating peacefully, and he is clearing the bottom of large rocks.

"What are you up to?" I call out to him.

"Just building a dam. Next year I bring my son here to swim," he claims with a big smile on his face. I bet he will come back.

In this part of the river we see larger fish. In general, the dams, even with their fish ladders, keep most of the big fish from coming very far upriver. I've heard that Hickory Shad make it up to Bloede Dam along with yellow and white perch, but few make it much farther. There is talk

The Patapsco Flow. (Courtesy of Alice Webb, the artist.)

of taking out Union Dam and possibly the ones at Bloede, Daniels, and Simpkins as well. I try to imagine thousands of shad running up this river valley and wonder if that would bring people out to catch them.

I tell Leigh there is a controversy about developing this section of the park. One local group wanted to build a better path along this section, but the Sierra Club was against any more incursions into the greenway, which is also an important corridor for animals.

"What's the matter with a dirt path?" Leigh asks.

"The argument for paving is that a paved path and a footbridge would make it much easier for folks of all abilities to do the entire stretch from Avalon to Ellicott City," I reply. We both agree it would be good to enhance and increase the width of stream buffers, with fewer paved areas and less intrusion by man. At the same time, if people don't have the chance to go out into nature, they may not realize its importance and the need to do something to preserve it. It's a fine balance: preservation and access. We need both.

That summer ended all too quickly. We ran out of weekends. Many of the river's stretches will have to await our return. Fortunately, we now know that whichever section we choose to explore will be worth it. At times we felt we were deep in the wilderness, the first to walk along the river, and then we'd stumble onto the ruins of a mill built well over a hundred years ago. The train abutments kept transporting us back to the start of railroading in the 1830s. The scoured out sections of the river, on the other hand, returned us to the present and the need for better storm water management in our own back yard and in the yards of the millions of homes, streets, and businesses in the watershed. We now have a greater appreciation for the need to once more permit storm waters to filter into the ground so they don't just flush down our rivers after a storm. We realize that if these waters were allowed to pass through the soil they would be cleansed, cooled, and would slowly feed the springs and streams, restoring healthier habitats throughout the year.

Leigh and I pledge to go home and plant more trees and shrubs to hold rainwater and allow it to seep into the soil. We commit to do our part. We want to come back here someday and see a healthier stream along its entire length. The Patapsco, like the bay's other tributaries, is indeed a wonderful place to explore, to escape to, and to reawaken the senses; it's a great place to learn about our planet and see what we've done to it. We will return again and again, whenever we get the chance.

Judging by our experiences along the Patapsco, very few people drop into the river valleys and explore the tributaries of the Chesapeake. This is probably a local symptom of the nationwide addiction to electronic media, our focus on structured activities and lives, and possibly even a fear of the woods. We found the river a wonderful respite from the chaos of modern life. I hope others will find it and help put their lives in balance. Exploring the Patapsco certainly made for a memorable summer.

What can be done about our general ignorance of and lack of appreciation for nature? We were surprised at how few people we encountered along the Patapsco River, which lies within a short drive of several million people. Evidently, we do not get out into the woods much today because we have too much structured time and spend much of our free time engaged with electronic media. There is now a national movement, fueled by interest in Richard Louv's book *Last Child in the Woods: Saving Our Children from Nature Deficit Disorder*, to encourage families to get outside more (www.cnaturenet.org). Here are a few of my suggestions for creating opportunities for your family, friends, and employees to spend more time outdoors.

Individuals and families can begin by just starting a daily or weekly regimen of going outside. This can be enhanced by adopting and exploring a tributary close to your home or checking out local land trusts, environmental organizations, nature centers, and schools to see if they have open space available for exploring. Ask if there are maps for you to use, or order a topographic map online (www.mytopo.com). For advice on how to make your own back yard healthier and more interesting see the appendices.

Corporations can enhance the health, creativity, and productivity of their employees by encouraging them to spend thirty minutes outside during the day. Create paths and arbors on your property and provide maps to local trails. Hold retreats and meetings at nature centers. Include an outdoor activity at all corporate functions.

Governments can encourage more outside activity by having interconnected trails, maps of places to walk and bike, and a regular series of events that use these trails. More outdoor educational opportunities should be provided for all levels of learning.

The Value of Trees

Twelve board members sit uncomfortably around the conference table. They normally gather here in the farmhouse on Mt. Pleasant Farm for more uplifting discussions on such things as preserving land or planning new educational programs. But today everyone's a bit tense. The board of the Howard County Conservancy, a local land trust in Woodstock, Maryland, is about to take a vote on whether to cut down one of the oldest trees in the state.

The tree is special. It's a majestic tulip poplar with a trunk twenty feet in circumference and a spreading canopy that dwarfs the old farmhouse in which we're meeting. It stands out above all the other trees on the hill and is something of a landmark. People come here just to get married under this tree. It's featured on the conservancy's logo and stationery. Nobody is happy that it has come to this. After all, we are on the board to preserve the land and our history, not destroy it.

When Senator Clark, the octogenarian chairman of the board, is asked about the tree, he replies, "Just 'cause some of us are getting old, doesn't mean you have to take us out and shoot us." Of course, his remarks make us feel even guiltier. This is a big deal for each of us.

The meeting is called to order. After some routine business, the hard-working executive director is asked to give her report on the health and prognosis of the tree. Everyone turns to hear the details, hoping for some glimmer of hope, some reason, some excuse to save the tree, even if it's only for a few more years.

"We've now had eight arborists evaluate the tree. They all recommend it be taken down." The silence is palpable. Most of us stare blankly ahead. She continues, "I think we have to conclude that it can't be saved. They claim it's unsafe. There is nothing more they can do."

For the past ten years since the conservancy became stewards of the property, experts were hired who pruned, fed, and wired many of the grand old tree's main branches together. The tree continued to split right down the center and could fall at any time. You could stand on one side and see right through the center to people on the other side. It's amazing that it is still standing.

"Why can't we just wait till it falls naturally?" one member asks.

The director replies, "That would have happened a long time ago. Fortunately we've been able to maintain it up to this point with the wires. Now it's too risky. We are, after all, an outdoor education center and five thousand school children come out here throughout the year. We can't take the risk that it would fall and injure anyone."

So the tree came down, and everyone was sad to see it go. Only a very large stump remains. To me it was like an old friend, one I had been caring for over the years. I will not forget it and often think about the parties, ceremonies, weddings, and all the history that passed beneath its branches. What famous people stood in its shade, and what events took place under this old, stately tree?

This experience also makes me think about how our view of trees has changed over the years. For much of our history our economy was based on cutting trees down. They were either in our way or a resource to be harvested. In contrast, we're now starting to recognize that trees may have even more value to us while they're living. Especially if our population continues to grow, we will need even more trees to filter our air and water and provide habitat for many species beneficial to our life here on earth. That life would be quite different, possibly even impossible, without trees.

So what's the value of a tree? That is a complicated question. Certainly an old, majestic tree that comes with a bit of history has cultural value. For example, the Mt. Pleasant Farm tulip poplar overhung the oldest log cabin in the area, one built in 1695 by Ranger Browne, a Patuxent Ranger. He was sent out here into the Piedmont wilderness from Annapolis to survey the region and keep an eye on the Indians encamped on the river near Woodstock. The Brownes lived here for nine generations until they were no more. The conservancy fortunately was able to take over stewardship of the historic site and its trees. This particular tulip poplar must have been planted by one of Ranger Browne's early descendants, for it turned out to have 237 annual growth rings. That means the tree was here, alive and well, during the American Revolution and the Civil War. A tree like that helps us reach back in time and touch some of the events that made us who we are today. I often take children to climb on the stump of the tree. We count rings to give them some sense of its size when Washington, Lincoln, and King were alive.

But there is more to trees than history, and the value we place on them has indeed changed over time. The first settlers, trappers, and hunters, like the Native Americans, lived off the trees. They ate the fruit, shot game nesting in the branches, and cooked with the wood. They built canoes from tulip poplar, pine, and cypress. They built homes from chestnut and oak. I've heard stories of the early days of the first European explorers, tales of fearless trappers and hunters, before man began changing the land. They tell us that "mature chestnuts were so widespread that a squirrel could travel from Georgia to Maine, jumping from one chestnut to another, without ever having to touch the ground." Forests so tall, dense, and deep that many of the colonists who emigrated from tree-starved Europe were afraid to enter them. These are the stories that excite my imagination and make me wish that I could have been here then. They also let me grasp a little better what John Smith meant when he spoke of "the cathedral forests of the Chesapeake Bay," what Longfellow pictured when he penned, "Under the spreading chestnut tree, the village smithy stands."

But the Europeans who came here to farm viewed trees first as an obstacle to survival and later as a resource to be exploited. Their real value was in taking them down. Our ancestors burned the forests to make room for their homes and fields. They removed trees so they could conquer the land, feed and warm themselves, and raise tobacco as a cash crop for the European market.

In addition to going way overboard in clearing land to raise tobacco in what became Maryland and Virginia, our forebears turned to the cathedral forests to solve England's chronic timber shortage. Very few trees were left in England by the end of the sixteenth century, and each warship in the Royal Navy required hundreds of oak trees for its construction. Many came from the Chesapeake and were transformed into the most powerful navy on earth. The tallest and straightest trees were used for masts and always earmarked for the king.

To move tobacco to market, planters needed hogsheads—large wooden barrels with axles that teams of oxen could pull down "rolling roads" to the wharves or "landings." Sawyers, who were woodcutters, and coopers, who built barrels, were much in demand. The cooperage trade employed more craftsmen than any other in the colonies. Making barrels required not only hardwood trees for wood, but softwood trees for tar, pitch, turpentine, and charcoal. Pine and fir trees were cut down and heated in kilns to extract their sap, which was then boiled down to tar, and then to pitch and turpentine. Pitch was used to seal barrels, boats, and houses.

Other demands were made on American forests as well. Charcoal, made by burning wood, was a valuable commodity. Firewood and charcoal in large quantities were needed not just for cooking and heating but also for tanneries, tobacco drying barns, iron forges, and mills. Much of the charcoal supply was shipped overseas. Cypress and cedar trees made excellent roofing shingles that were in demand in the colonies and Europe. Sassafras chips and roots were sent to England in hogsheads for tea and medicinal use. Furthermore, as planters divided up the land, they marked off parcels with "worm fences," which required enormous quantities of wood.

Iron forges, which soon produced the second major colonial export, consumed a great deal of wood as well. Iron production utilized all local ingredients. The furnaces used charcoal to heat the bog iron and oyster shell lime as a flux to remove impurities. The problem with the iron industry, like so many others, is that it outgrew its resources. A large ironworks required thirty thousand acres of forest to sustain it. No other fuel existed. Depletion of the wood supply caused many of the earliest ironworks to close in the 1800s.

The pressure on forests would not ease until the discovery and incorporation of coal and petroleum as the main fuels for powering our economy. By then, thanks to the great demand for wood, the "cathedral forests" Captain John Smith marveled at in 1608 were all but gone. Photographs from the late nineteenth century show many parts of the Great Eastern Woodlands of North America, one of the largest forests in the world, devoid of trees. Fortunately, forests in many areas of the eastern woodlands recovered as industry switched to coal and oil and moved people off farms and into cities. Now, in the twenty-first century, the pressure is back on the trees as development increases with our growing population.

Here at Mt. Pleasant, Ranger Browne cut down trees to build his log cabin, which makes up the center of the current farmhouse. He probably used chestnut logs, since chestnut has been described as the most valuable and usable tree that ever grew in the eastern United States. The fairly light wood was easy to work with and used for furniture, buildings, shingles, barrels, railroad ties, and fence posts. It was great for outdoor uses, because its high concentration of tannic acid kept it from rotting. Unfortunately, a fungus introduced accidentally by man in 1904 and peaking in the 1930s wiped out all the chestnuts in America. It is estimated that four billion trees died, and the resistant ones were quickly harvested for lumber by men who feared these healthy trees would be lost as well. That was a great misfortune, for some of the chestnuts were probably resistant to the fungi and might well have created a path to recovery for the species. So today there are none left. The fungus remains and infects young trees before they reach maturity. Chestnut trees are just one of many species lost to future generations because we failed to understand, manage, and preserve our environment.

The Brownes obviously valued trees for the shade they provided, since the farmhouse is surrounded by tall oaks, poplars, hickories, and elms. The building is without modern air-conditioning equipment and yet remains pleasant throughout much of the summer. This is partly because it's shaded all day in the summer and because Ranger Browne built the house on a hill, so it receives a breeze most of the time. Good site selection can make a big difference in a house's comfort. The U.S. Forestry Service claims that well-placed trees can cut one's summer cooling bill by thirty percent. With the high cost of energy today, that can certainly add up, making the dollar value of shade trees significant.

I can testify to the value of trees to life on a small Piedmont farm in the 1950s. When Dad bought it, ours was a working farm providing sustenance to the sellers, who had worked it seven days a week, sunup to sundown. Dad figured he could keep his manufacturing job in the city and still run the farm if he just scaled back on what they were doing and worked evenings and weekends. His plans also included free labor from my sister and me.

Our hundred acres comprised six fields, a woodlot, two barnyards, an orchard, and the yard around the house. Trees in each of these areas were there according to purpose: hardwoods in the woodlot, apple trees in the orchard, mainly nut and shade trees in the yard, and a big elm in the barnyard for slaughtering and hanging steers. No trees of any kind were allowed in the cultivated fields or pastures because shade was not desirable and fallen debris and roots could damage the farm machinery. Trees in the other areas were important and had to be well maintained.

During the late fall and early winter, most weekends involved a wood party. "Hook the tractor up to the wood wagon," Dad would say over Saturday breakfast as he finished his second piece of homemade apple pie. "I'll sharpen the blades and meet you out by the tool shed."

He could usually get me motivated if I got the tractor end of the deal. I laced up my boots and headed out with the dogs jumping at my sides, vying for attention and excited that we were all home for a day on the farm. The rusty red tractor was a 1939 Farmall that surprised me every time it started. I pulled the throttle and away she chugged, smoke and rust particles billowing from the exhaust pipe.

The woodlot was barely a quarter-mile from the house. Each of us grabbed a chain saw and pushed our way through the brambles. Our goal was to cut down hardwoods like beech, maple, and oak, but we took most anything except pine and poplar. The best woods for heating based on their BTU contents are Osage orange, ironwood, and hickory, but they were not as plentiful as the more common hardwoods. We tried to manage the woodlot to encourage the growth of hardwoods by clearing out less attractive species that might interfere with them. A woodlot, if properly managed, will last forever.

"Dad, I'm going to thin out those poplar and paulownia over by the fence."

"Fine, and on your way over there, cut up the branches that fell in the snowstorm last spring. They'll make good kindling."

We cut the tree trunks and branches into two-foot lengths and split them with mauls and wedges if they were more than six inches in diameter. Locust trees were cut to seven-foot lengths for fence posts because "black locust never rots." Large trees were often taken to the saw mill to be cut into sixteen-foot fence boards. Any live trees we cut down were left for the following year so the green wood could cure. Wood is best for heating after it has dried out. Our goal each year was to have five cords of seasoned hardwood stacked by the back door before the first snowfall. We rarely made it, so the wood parties continued into the winter. They could be fun on some days but bitter cold when the wind came up.

The trees in the yard around the house were black walnut, English walnut, a huge ninety-foot-tall pecan, and a few peaches. We harvested them all. The apple orchard presented the biggest challenge. In late winter and early spring the entire family spent many weekends up on ladders pruning back the suckers. Our hands would get so cramped squeezing the pruning shears that we had a range of tools to switch to, just to keep going. We also had the harvest to look forward to, but that was a long way off and not on our minds when halfway up a tree on a cold day in February. By harvest time, though, we had forgotten the pain and the long hours; we just enjoyed picking, eating, and juice running down our faces. We were well rewarded with a wide range of apples for pies, crisps, juice, and cider. Varieties like Golden Delicious, Summer Rambo, Baldwin, Northern Spy, Grimes Golden, and Winesap came into harvest at different times from late summer to late fall and became a major part of our diet during the summer, fall, and winter.

Dad always complained we did not get enough pies made in our house. When he discovered that this was largely because Mom disliked rolling out pie crusts, he began making the crusts himself. This resulted in Dad eating pie for all three meals of the day and before he went to bed at night, and almost always *a la mode*.

So our trees gave us food and fuel at little cost and also provided for camaraderie during our wood parties. They let us live a little more self-sufficiently than if we had lived in the city. Working with trees also gave us a healthy respect for nature. More than once when felling a mature tree, Dad and I had to scramble out of the way when it decided to fall 180 degrees from where we had planned to drop it. One never knows for sure.

Trees proved to have other value to us as well. In 1960, when the Northeast Expressway (Interstate 95) cut through the middle of the farm, we planted thirty thousand pine and fir trees as a sound break. They eventually helped hide the insult but did not completely succeed in keeping the noisy and smelly intrusion of a million cars and trucks from the once pastoral setting. As the trees grew, we thinned about ten percent of them by selling them as Christmas trees in a cut-your-own-tree operation. Although a lot of hard work was involved in pruning and managing this business, it yielded enough revenue that my sister and I could go to college.

So trees have provided a range of value to man over the years. Most people don't have the direct connection today with trees as the source of their fuel or food; nuts and fruit just come from the store. I think we've lost an important link with nature. Now that private woodlots and orchards are no longer crucial to our lives, we have forsaken trees. These days we cut them down all too easily. They appear to be relegated to the status they had when the first settlers arrived—they are in our way and obstacles to building roads, shopping centers, and golf courses. Trees are often clear-cut and their wood wasted in the name of expediency during development. Once again they are treated as if they have more value dead than alive.

Land may appear to have more immediate monetary worth than the trees planted on it, but has anyone done a cost analysis on what a tree is really worth to our society? What about all the other services it provides? Let's consider just one: storm water management. The settlers learned how expensive uncontrolled storm water runoff could be once they cleared their land of trees. A whole series of major floods occurred following the denudation of the tidewater and Piedmont. The ports of Joppa Town and Elk Ridge were silted in and largely abandoned as a result of accelerated erosion once the trees were gone. Our ancestors paid dearly for disregarding trees as agents for holding soils in place.

Today we have a similar problem. Having paved over the countryside, once again accelerating runoff, we now realize that we are killing the bay with silt and nutrients and wrecking our streams and greenways with the scouring effect of uncontrolled storm water. Then we're surprised when dangerous flooding occurs. Fixing our storm water systems around the bay through man-made mechanical means will cost us billions of dollars and probably will not work nearly so well as nature. If we calculated the savings provided by adequate stream buffers, they surely would be enormous. Leaving trees in place so their roots can hold onto the soil and their canopies can slow down storm water runoff would be a great deal more effective and less expensive than anything else we might do.

If we don't save the trees, we'll have to raise taxes to collect the billions of dollars it will take to retrofit our storm water management system. We're running up our collective debt every time we let new development get away with cutting down trees along our streams that if left standing could prevent damage to the streams and to the bay. We are in effect subsidizing current development by forcing future taxpayers to cover the cost of restoring resources that were damaged out of expediency. It is time to set the bar higher. Some jurisdictions allow trees to be cut down as long as they are replanted elsewhere. This is a good step, but it takes a long time to replace a mature tree with an eighteen-inch seedling. It's best to keep as many mature trees on site as possible. Furthermore many newly planted trees do not live very long. They are consumed by deer or drought. If our population continues to increase, we will have to continue to implement a wide range of reforestation programs in an attempt to maintain our stream buffers, forest habitats, and our balance with nature for the sake of our own health.

A simple walk along the paths around the 232-acre Mt. Pleasant Farm imparts a real sense of the value of trees and the challenge of maintaining them and other habitat today. The oldest trees found here are restricted to the steep creek banks and around the buildings. Their value to the farm was to maintain a healthy water supply, habitat for game, food (nuts), and fuel for the owners, and to provide shade for settlers and animals alike.

Unfortunately, as beautiful as the old trees appear today at Mt. Pleasant, the current forests are probably not sustainable, primarily because of the large deer population. Deer eat a great deal of the new growth, leaving an inadequate number of understory trees to replenish the forest. Streams have also been deeply incised by extensive runoff from fields that were heavily cultivated over the past three hundred years. Storm waters rushing down these damaged streams have undercut many of the old trees. The land trust is trying to manage the deer population, widen the buffers along the streams, and reforest selected parts of the farm. The goal is to improve water quality, restore stream habitat, and reduce erosion and the runoff of storm waters into the bay.

As it turns out, in addition to their individual uses as food sources, wood, and habitat for other species, trees play a very large role in providing us with a healthy place to live. A tree shading a house or in a parking lot can be valuable from the standpoints of health, energy savings, safety, and property maintenance. Every day the trees around us serve as filters that improve our air quality, carbon sinks that remove much of the carbon dioxide our society generates, and oxygen generators that allow us to continue living on this planet in this industrial age. In fact, trees obtain their entire carbon biomass from the greenhouse gases in the air and therefore are one of our best weapons against global warming.

Based on a series of studies compiled by the U.S. Forestry Service and the State of Maryland, it has been estimated that trees can:

- reduce home and office heating costs by 25 percent
- reduce home and office cooling costs by 30 percent
- increase property values by 10 percent
- reduce noise pollution
- reduce air pollution such as ground level ozone

- reduce street level particulates by 60 percent
- reduce runoff and the expense of erosion control facilities
- increase the life of asphalt paving

How can you put a price on the benefits from a single tree? Well it has been done. For example according to the U.S. Forestry Service, a single tree over a fifty-year period:

- generates $31,250 worth of oxygen
- provides $62,000 worth of air pollution control
- recycles $37,500 worth of water
- controls $31,250 worth of soil erosion
- absorbs 2,500 lbs. of carbon dioxide from us and our cars

These numbers are significant. Multiply them by hundreds of trees per acre and you will quickly see the real value of living trees and what is lost when the land is clear-cut for development. Yet, this value is rarely calculated into decision-making when considering land for development. At best, zoning laws require that every tree cut down be replaced. That is a start. Maybe it's time we incorporated the real value of trees into the site review process. It might result in our cleaning up and rebuilding the cities we've abandoned and leaving the forests alone. At the least, it might make it clearer to all of us that preserving forest habitat has a great deal of economic value above and beyond its ecological value.

The more we understand the role trees play in our ecosystem today, the more we will want to take care of them, and, in return, the healthier our planet will become. I think we owe them some respect for their contributions. Maybe it's our turn to start taking care of our trees because they certainly have been trying to take good care of us.

What can be done to encourage the planting and preservation of trees? There are many ways to preserve the trees in your community. Local forestry boards, arboretums, or Master Gardener organizations can provide you with expert advice for free (www.ahs.org/master_gardeners).

Individuals can help by supporting forest preservation efforts and learning who owns and maintains the trees in your neighborhood. You can also help by planting trees and by encouraging tree planting in your neighborhoods, nearby cities, and along highways.

Corporations can help by designing developments that preserve as many trees as possible and implementing habitat management plans on properties they own. They can also become partners with local land trusts.

Governments can help by implementing site development regulations that ensure more trees are left onsite. They can implement better regional planning that helps to focus redevelopment efforts in our cities while preserving green spaces. They can also insure that parks maintain a range of habitats and do not just become ball fields.

Foraging

No matter where I go in the watershed, when walking through the woods I automatically look for things that are edible. The yellow and white flowers of honeysuckle are the most common treat, a sip of nectar that brightens a hot summer day. Garlic mustard happens to be a target partly because it's another invasive plant that should be pulled and partly because I've developed a taste for it. There is a garlic mustard cook-off each spring at the Patapsco State Park, and it's amazing what a good cook can do with it. I normally just pull up the plants and chew on a few leaves at a time. Not bad. I've also been known to chew on sassafras twigs or roots. I like the flavor. Sometimes you'll find me chewing on tall grasses just because I used to do it on the farm growing up. Call me a hayseed if you like, but there is something about having a long stem of orchard grass in your mouth while meandering through a meadow. It's certainly relaxing and makes me think I'm a part of it all, standing out in a field, breathing the air, and chewing on a long stalk of grass.

Of course none of these offerings compare to finding edible fruit and seeds. It wasn't all that long ago that foraging for fruit and nuts was a natural part of living in this fertile watershed. Somehow we've gotten away from it. When was the last time you or your family went out to pick something wild? I've foraged off and on throughout most of my life, but I never get my fill. I don't know what spring would be like without eating purple serviceberries. I can't imagine summer without picking raspberries and blackberries, or fall without harvesting grapes, apples, and nuts. For many of us who walk the woods on a regular basis, it's always a treat to see trees laden with fruit. Even though today the cultivation of our food supply has become highly mechanized, many an ancestor knew they could live year-round on what was freely available from native plants and trees. Here are a few of my favorite free foods in the watershed. They can make any walk through the woods more fun and more flavorful.

Shadblow (serviceberry) is one of the first trees to show off its white blooms in a Mid-Atlantic spring. In fact, this ungainly, understory tree derives its name from the timing of its flowers: they open when the shad are running up the Chesapeake's tributaries to spawn and once provided a significant reminder back when shad were an important part of our lives. I look for the dainty, white flowers of the shadblow in April to convince me that spring is actually coming and then always search for these trees again in mid-June to eat their delicious blue and purple berries. I like them so much I planted a number of these multi-stem trees on the west end of my house, partly as ornamentals but also thinking I would have their fruit close at hand and all to myself. Not surprisingly, as with many of the other free sources of food, you still have to get up early and check often to beat the birds and the raccoons to the dinner table. Yes, as flimsy as the branches of the shadblow may be, I've caught young raccoons after dark up in *my* trees trying to reach the small berries at the ends of the branches. I don't actually do anything about them except ask what they think they're doing. They usually just watch me until I give up lecturing about trespass laws and then we both go back to foraging—there are plenty of berries to go around.

Mulberry trees seem to grow everywhere and rank right up there as one of the tastiest, all-natural snacks on a hot summer day. Both the red and the white mulberry trees grow like weeds and are common along hedgerows and edges of forests. They both have edible fruit. White mulberry was introduced by the colonists to feed silk worms, a business that did not prosper in this country. Dried white mulberries can be used as a substitute for raisins or figs. Red mulberries are native and make better pies, jams, and wine; they also stain hands, clothing, and sidewalks, which makes them easy to find along streets and highways. When the berries are ripe, the pavement beneath tree branches that reach over the road is stained a dark red. Both red and white mulberries can be tasty and the fruit is easily harvested, as long as you can reach the limbs. Ripe fruit should fall off into your hands. I recommend you stop and try a few the next time you pass one of these trees. If the berries aren't sweet wait a day or two, but not too long. You don't want to miss out on mulberries in season. By the way, there's no point in feeling guilty about not taking them home to share with others. They don't keep well.

Persimmon is probably the most under-appreciated fruit in the watershed. When quail hunting it was always a treat to stumble upon a persimmon tree in the middle of a long trek on a cold November day. Well almost always—it had to be after the first frost. Consumed too early, the acids of a not-quite-ripe persimmon can make your tongue swell and you won't be able to get the pithy, dry feeling out of your mouth for hours. It's an indigenous tree but the fruit of the American persimmon has never quite caught on commercially because of its astringent chemicals and very large seeds. Our ancestors enjoyed this fruit by making home-distilled, persimmon brandy. I happen to have eight of these trees in my pasture. All are nature's volunteers, brought here via the intestinal tracts of birds, raccoons, or opossums. My kids love to collect the fruit but it's hard to harvest enough meat from around the large seeds to bake a loaf of fruit bread. We manage to collect just enough every year to make a single loaf. It's a tasty tradition, but not so good that we do it more than once a year.

Grapes are probably the most common fruit found in the fall throughout the region. Growing wild are fox grape, summer grape, and river bank grape varieties which are hard to tell apart. These are the favorite food of more than a hundred species of songbirds and many mammals. Wherever still available, the clusters are eaten by birds throughout the winter. The fruit tends to be small, an eighth of an inch to half an inch in diameter, and ripens in the fall, so it provides tasty nourishment to anyone out admiring the fall colors. The grapes grow on woody vines that climb high up trees and hang over stream banks. Tendrils on the stems tend to curl around trees and shrubs and hold on while the trees grow. The long vines are great fun to hang on and swing from, though I do recall a few breaking and dropping me into the dust, thicket, or river. It's hard to guess the bearing capacity of a grapevine. It's also never good to be the largest guy in the gang.

People have collected wild grapes for centuries to make jellies and wine, and have used the edible leaves to wrap meat and rice (dolmades).

Half of the cultivated grapes in the world today come from varieties native to North America. Dad cultivated grapes for years, always making jams, juice, and wines that lasted throughout the winter. Our cultivated grapes may have been bigger and juicier, but rarely were they as sweet as the wild grapes you can pick along stream banks on a cool fall day.

Berries are manna from heaven. No matter how bad the news may be on any given day, encountering ripe berries along the side of the path restores my faith in the universe. Just to happen upon something that tasty and free helps me to step out of the rat race and take my time enjoying the bounties of nature. Berries are easy to collect and widespread throughout the watershed. Yes, it takes patience, because they are small. Yes, you have to work your way through the weeds and thorns, but what a reward, something this good without clearing, planting, weeding, or shopping. It doesn't get any better.

At times I've encountered competition while picking berries. I have shared a berry patch with bees, deer, an occasional snake, and once even a small black bear, but no harm in any of these cases. When I came face to face with the bear, he paused for a moment and then turned and lumbered into the brush. I was surprised he gave up his berry patch without so much as a growl.

The native berries I personally enjoy most are blueberries and strawberries. Introduced varieties of berries—raspberries, blackberries, and wineberries—are now almost ubiquitous if not invasive in most areas. We shouldn't complain, we should just eat them. I suppose I am to blame in spreading their seeds as much as any other critter. It would be very hard to give up these non-native plants. On the positive side, there is absolutely no carbon footprint when feasting on wild berries in season.

Strawberries are one of the first fruits to ripen in the spring, usually in early June, and are celebrated as a rite of spring throughout the watershed. Dad always had the dream of taking time off for several months in the spring and following the strawberry season from Georgia to Maine, going from one strawberry festival to the next. He never did, but he always grew hundreds of feet of strawberry plants in his garden each year.

This often proved to be more than we could eat. When asked, he replied that he had to plant enough for the wild animals as well.

The commercially available strawberry is a descendant of the small, East Coast wild strawberry, which is widespread and very tasty. It was hybridized with a West Coast variety to eventually evolve into what is cultivated throughout the country today. The small native variety is a pioneer plant that readily grows in areas that are burned over or left fallow. Since the plant is small, I used to sit down on the ground after the spring cutting of hay and collect these small, succulent fruit. It is well worth an afternoon of foraging, since they are also usually far sweeter than their cultivated cousins.

Blueberries are the fruit of a shrub that belongs to the heath family, which also includes the cranberry, azalea, mountain laurel, and rhododendron. The berries grow in clusters on shrubs that grow from one to eight feet high. Individual blueberries can be as small as a pea or as large as a marble. In color they range from deep blue to purple-black, and the skin surrounds a semi-transparent, yellow flesh that encases tiny seeds. Blueberries are native to North America, where they grow throughout the woods, barrens, and mountainous regions. Native Americans combined blueberries or cranberries with dried meat and lard to make *pemmican*, a traditional dish. I am always on the lookout for the tiny, wild, low-bush blueberries; they just seem to be sweeter than anything you can buy from the store. I've never been in such a rush that I would not spend a half hour picking every berry I could find along a trail in the woods. One of the nicest gifts I ever received was a box, a foot square and a foot high, of freshly picked blueberries. It was a friend's way of celebrating a summer spent together hiking in the woods and living off the land.

Raspberries grow on dense overlapping vines in fields and on the edges of woods. Black and red raspberries are both members of the rose family, which also includes apples, pears, strawberries, blackberries, cherries, peaches, and plums. Black raspberries are often confused with blackberries. In contrast to the blackberry, which also consists of a cluster of tiny fruit, which grow around a core known as the receptacle, the fruit of the red and black raspberry detaches from the receptacle when picked. The receptacle of the blackberry does not detach and is eaten with the fruit. Throughout the summer my family would pick wild raspberries along the edges of woods or highways and eat them in pies, jams, jellies, or sprinkled on top of cereal or ice cream. We ate them with every meal of the day and as snacks between meals.

Blackberries are also round fruit that grow on flowering shrubs or trailing vines and often leave a stain on your hands. Blackberries found in the woods are protected by large sharp thorns that can make foraging quite treacherous. My neighbor stopped by one day with a dozen thornless blackberry plants. He was so excited to have found them that now he was sharing them with friends. We planted them along the edge of the woods and they took off. Huge vines ten feet long formed arches reaching out toward the sunlight. The fruit were large and juicy. What a gift he had brought, a patch that returned every year. All we had to do was to prune back the canes in late winter and keep honeysuckle from overtaking the patch.

Wineberries, a species of raspberry native to northern China, Japan, and Korea, were introduced to North America in 1890 and are now naturalized and even invasive. The hairy canes grow to nine feet in length, and the sticky sweet fruit is encased in a husk that peels back when ripe. The fruit is about three-quarters of an inch in diameter and has an orange or red color. I do not recall seeing these berries on the western shore of the bay when I was young, but I run into them all the time now while walking along the edges of the woods. I've grown accustomed to their sweet and tart flavor and enjoy them on a hot July walk.

Many of the habitats that are good for berries have been overtaken by invasive trees, shrubs, vines, and herbaceous plant species. Edge areas today are often full of ailanthus ("tree of heaven"), paulownia ("empress tree"), Russian and autumn olive (with very strong scented pollen), and white mulberry trees. Invasive shrubs include Japanese barberry, winged euonymus, privet, multiflora rose, bush honeysuckle, and Japanese spirea. Vines have also invaded many of these areas. The most common are porcelain berry, oriental bittersweet, English ivy, Japanese honeysuckle, mile-a-minute vine (aka devil's tear-thumb), kudzu, periwinkle, and Japanese wisteria. Garlic mustard and giant reeds are herbaceous plants that are also widespread and invasive. None of these plants should be used for landscaping and decorative purposes and should be removed where they have gotten out of control.

FRESH UNCOOKED NUTS are very good for you, but no one seems to care that such a valuable food is right out the back door. Why don't we eat native nuts anymore? It must be that they're just too hard to collect and open as opposed to going to the store. Apparently we've forgotten that the foraging is half the fun.

The most commonly eaten nut a century ago was the chestnut, then an important food for man, livestock, and wildlife even though it was protected inside a prickly husk. Throughout the Chesapeake watershed, settlers let their hogs feed under these trees and compete with the deer, squirrels, and turkeys for the fruit. Nuts were gathered by the wagon load and stored for the winter or shipped to major markets in East Coast cities where they were roasted on open fires and sold on the street. Although we refer to them as nuts, the meat inside was evidently soft and starchy, more akin to grain than crunchy, like traditional nuts. Chestnuts were widely used to stuff Thanksgiving turkeys and in other festive winter dishes. Unhappily, native chestnuts are no more, though imported varieties are available in grocery stores.

When I was young, our front yard was dominated by a very tall pecan tree with English ivy growing up the trunk. Each fall we collected bags full of these oblong, thin-shelled nuts to eat throughout the winter. It's easy to peel the thin green-brown husk off pecans when they're ripe and crack the inner shell by squeezing two shells together in one hand. (That was the true test of manhood or at least boyhood in my family. The smaller kids just couldn't get their hands around two nuts at a time.) I ate most pecans raw. My mother placed them decoratively on sweet potato and squash casseroles along with marshmallows. My favorite treat to this day is roasted and salted pecans. I have no willpower and can't stop eating them if they're around the house.

Hickory nuts have always been ubiquitous in my neighborhood, but

I've never eaten them because they're so hard to open. While out in the woods I always collected these small, hard nuts to use as ammunition; no telling when they were going to come in handy. I'd throw them at trees and signs, birds and squirrels, and almost always missed. I often kept a pocketful in case I was chased by dogs, which was far more common in the days before leash laws. The great cooks claim that hickory nuts can be prepared and used in the same way as pecans, as snacks or in cooking. Evidently, their flavor makes removing the meat from their shells well worth the effort.

Black walnut trees drop dozens of one-and-a-half-inch nuts covered with a thick green aromatic husk containing a brown liquid that readily stains fingers and clothes. My family always wore gloves when collecting these large nuts and would stored them in bushel baskets over the winter until the oils in the husks dried. I would then dump them in the driveway and run over them several times with our car to remove the husks. The remaining nuts were then opened with a hammer or a vice. It's very hard to get to the edible kernel since it is enclosed in a thick, hard, ridged shell. The prize inside is a strong-flavored nut that's wonderful for baking in bread and cookies.

Most of these free foods are still out there in the woods. It just takes time to find them. Their habitats have been diminishing as the countryside is more densely developed. Whenever I ask other parents if they forage with their children, most reply that they don't have time to go wandering in the woods.

I've also heard two concerns from parents who do not let their children go into the woods at all. The first is the fear of deer ticks. They may be right to worry, because none of us want to get Lyme disease, but let's take a closer look at it. Deer ticks appear in your back yard and on your dog as well as in the woods. Only a small number of deer ticks actually carry Lyme disease, and normally they have to be on your body for some time to cause infection. Whenever you think you might have come into contact with ticks, it's always a good idea to examine yourself closely, but for a little perspective, I've never found a deer tick on me, and I go out into the woods every day.

The second concern has to do with contacting potentially hazardous chemicals. After a career in the environmental industry, I'm cautious
about eating fruit and seeds in areas where the air, water, or soil may be
contaminated. Some plants will bio-accumulate heavy metals in their
plant material. This indeed may be a problem on old industrial sites,
but it would be far less likely to occur in mature forests today. Most
of the contaminated sites of the past have been identified and either
cleaned up or are being closely monitored. Today, the use of hazardous
chemicals is more strictly curtailed, and discharges into the environment are far less common than in the past. Nevertheless, surface and
ground water both contain some contaminants, those we apply to our
lawns, use for weed control along the sides of roads and paths, and still
use on commercial and industrial sites. Some are airborne. Usually their
concentrations are very low in the soil, especially in what appear to be
pristine conditions that are only fed from rainwater. However, lead, asbestos, and other chemicals and particulates from car exhaust and road
materials can concentrate on vegetation growing beside highways.

The Wildcrafter groups, whose members collect plants and food
from the wild, advise foragers not to eat foods collected within fifty feet
of a busy highway. I also would avoid low spots such as storm water re-
tention sites where metals could accumulate. It is wise to be concerned.
Environmental health questions apply to everything we eat, whether
we buy it in a store or pick it in the woods. Today we have strict rules
regarding chemicals and how much can be emitted into the air, water,
and soil or used throughout the industrial food chain. I advise using
caution. The risks are low when foraging if we are careful where we pick
and don't make a constant diet of foods from any one source. The benefit of course when eating wild foods is that they are less likely to have
been exposed to chemicals and dangerous bacteria because they have
not been handled in any way by the industrial food process.

What can be done to preserve the tradition and enjoyment of foraging?
Nut trees seem to be everywhere in the woods. It just takes effort to go
out and find them. In contrast, many of the berries in the watershed

tend to grow on the edges of wooded areas or in meadows, which are far less common today. These areas are fast disappearing as infill development turns them into manicured homesteads. If you leave a fence line or field edge dormant for a few years, berries come out of nowhere and start producing. So there are several ways you can help bring back the enjoyment of foraging.

Individuals can work toward the preservation of a variety of habitats, especially the edges of fields and woods that would be conducive to these plants. You can also help by removing as many invasive vines, shrubs, trees, and herbaceous plants as possible and no longer using invasive species in gardens.

Corporations can clean up contaminated sites, encourage a range of habitats on lands they own, and provide access to these areas for the community during fruiting season. Pick-your-own farms have become quite popular over the past decade, and the interest in local produce indicates a growing demand for more of these venues close to population centers.

Governments can help by banning the indiscriminate use of herbicides and by ensuring that all contaminated sites are cleaned up or clearly marked. They can also help ensure the preservation of meadowland and forest edge habitats.

A Good Day to Fly

It's always pleasant to return from a trip and realize we have more birds here in the Eastern Woodlands than in most other places on earth. I've grown especially aware of this richness following trips to Central America, West Africa, and Southeast Asia, foreign forests where I had expected to hear more voices. Upon each return, I marveled at the wide variety of birds that serenade me right here at home.

On a recent trip to Oaxaca, Mexico, I rented a room from Magdalena who along with her extended family hosted visitors in her house. Around the ancient city and up in the Sierra Madre de Oaxaca mountains, I saw only a few birds. My room though, opened onto her central courtyard, and each morning before breakfast, Magdalena's elderly mother swept the floors and uncovered the birdcages. Much to my surprise, they held old friends: a mockingbird in one and a cardinal in another. There was something painfully sad about seeing woodland friends caged. These delightful songbirds are so ubiquitous around the Chesapeake Bay that many of us just take them for granted. I would never have expected to find them here in Mexico, in a cage. Yet, these divas enchanted the entire courtyard, each sharing his varied and beautiful repertoire with all in Magdalena's home. What a way to wake up so far from home.

The voices of the cardinal and the mockingbird contribute only a small part to the Chesapeake's woodland symphony. We have dozens of songbirds, and for several very good reasons. One is that we benefit from bird migrations coming from both north and south. The bay lies at a narrow point on the Great Atlantic Flyway, a migratory route for millions of birds that reaches from the vast northern boreal forests stretching across Canada south to the Caribbean and South America. A second reason is that the Chesapeake offers a broad array of habitats: the waters of the bay and its tributaries, wetlands, meadowlands, stream valleys, forests, barrens, and mountains. Birds of many types can find a home in the watershed. They like it here.

Waterfowl come south to the Chesapeake to spend the cold months of winter with us. In contrast many of my favorite summer songbirds cannot live in our winter temperatures and therefore migrate south until spring. The Baltimore oriole, for example, the state bird of Maryland, spends its winter in the Caribbean and returns in the spring to nest. They are quite common here in the summer. Just listen for their whistle in May and look up into the treetops for their bright orange plumage. Then there are the birds just passing through that we only briefly glimpse during spring and fall but who can be pretty special too. Overlapping and sequential migratory patterns make this a fascinating place to observe the comings and goings of birds with each of the seasons.

Migration is one of those not fully understood marvels of nature that allows for the survival of many species. Ornithologists believe that birds find their way south and back again by having a generalized star map in their heads, using the sun, and following the earth's magnetic field. They are specially equipped with tiny magnetite crystals in their nasal cavities that help them detect this magnetic field. Odors, sounds, and a mental picture of their birthplaces may also help them know when to stop migrating. Unfortunately, odors, sounds, and pictures are all changing as a result of fairly widespread development along many migration routes and wintering habitats. I wonder how this is affecting traditional migration patterns.

Birds follow multiple pathways up and down the East Coast when migrating. Hawks, for example, tend to follow the ridge lines of the Appalachian and Blue Ridge mountains, and the Atlantic coastline. They are looking for updrafts by which they can gain elevation. These soaring birds have also learned that they can catch man-made thermals rising over every city on the fall line. Cities generate substantial heat throughout the year, and heat rises. By gaining elevation and soaring high on one of these thermals, hawks can glide a long way toward the next city while expending far less energy. Interestingly, this man-enhanced migratory path for hawks parallels the major north-south migratory path used by man himself, Interstate 95, which connects many of the same cities.

In addition to adapting to atmospheric changes caused by heat rising from cities, some birds are now migrating at different times than in the past. Two things causing these age-old migration patterns to evolve are global warming and habitat changes.

As global warming continues, migration patterns are likely to become even more complicated. In the not too distant future, orioles could bypass Baltimore entirely and summer farther north. How sad for Maryland! They might even become the state bird of Pennsylvania or New York someday. The greater risk of habitat change is that some species will not be able to adapt. In nature, timing is everything. For example, certain bird species fledge just in time to feed on the coinciding hatch of a specific insect species. If, in the future, changes in the migration and hatching patterns of the two species don't coincide as a result of global warming, the fledglings may not live and the insects may overproduce. Should those two related things happen, the impact could be enormous, a chain reaction felt throughout the fragile interdependent web of life. If the bird species became extinct, it could not fulfill all the other roles it plays in its ecological niche, which might include keeping worms and a range of insects in check. The insects, in turn, if not regulated by the birds, could cause severe crop and tree damage. To prevent this damage, man might spray insecticides throughout the habitat, killing off a variety of beneficial insects as well. The chain of consequences could go on and on. Birds in fact have tremendous economic value to our society as pollinators, insect eaters, and rodent predators. It has been calculated that they provide $5,000 per year per acre in services to us (Robinson, 1997).

Habitat changes have had a fairly significant impact just within my lifetime. When I was a boy, many farmers left some of their fields fallow, not plowing them every year. As a result there were numerous meadow habitats. Now, with increased suburban development and more intense use of the remaining fields for food and fuel, meadowland species such as bobwhite, bobolinks, eastern meadowlarks, and upland sandpipers are far less common. Their numbers have declined precipitously due to grassland habitat fragmentation, overgrazing, development, and a focus on reforesting those lands that are preserved. In addition to the loss of meadowland, the counties around major cities like Baltimore and Washington have had a thirty percent decline in forest cover since the 1960s. This results in far less habitat for birds, although a few such as the song sparrow, cardinal, and catbird have adapted to the artificial scrub of landscaped suburbs.

In contrast to the loss of forest cover close to cities, there are actually more woodlands in other areas away from the cities. This has been good for many woodland species. Living as I do on the edge of suburban development, I routinely see more pileated woodpeckers, hawks, and barred owls now than when I was a boy. Not having grown up with some of these birds, I love looking for them in the woods today. One day I was walking along a path through the woods with a group of friends and heard the unique *yucka, yucka, yucka* call of pileated woodpeckers. They make a real racket, not musical at all. I told everyone to look up as I pointed out two large birds in the tops of adjacent trees. With time, everyone in the group saw the birds high in the canopy, with their bright red heads and distinctive black and white plumage. It was the first time any of them had seen these striking, prehistoric-looking creatures. They are similar in appearance to the probably, or nearly, extinct ivory-billed woodpeckers, though there are claims that one was recently seen in a southeastern swamp. The group was surprised by how large they are. When full-grown, males are often nineteen inches long with a thirty-inch wingspan.

We finally tore ourselves away from this pair and continued on our walk. I was surprised to hear and see what I took to be this same pair of woodpeckers twice more over the next forty-five minutes. Either they were heading in the same direction anyway, or they simply wanted to show off, I'm not sure which. I'd had a similar experience a few years before, when a single pileated woodpecker stayed in front of me, flying from tree to tree. What a treat to see these large, wonderful birds several times on a walk through the woods.

Another great conservation success story is our national bird, the bald eagle. As a boy I never saw even one on our farm. In contrast, over the past ten years I've seen eagles on a fair number of my walks around the bay. Not just ospreys but the real thing: large, white-headed, black-bodied, bald eagles. I saw my first in the area where I live while walking down the lane one day. The eagle was flying about thirty feet above the ground and coming right at me with its large wingspan and the slow, powerful beating of its wings. I stopped and watched it fly right over my head, not bothering to change course at all because I was standing there. At close range, eagles are truly majestic and a wonderful choice for our national symbol. They grow to well over three feet in length and have wing spans from six to eight feet. They eat fish, carrion, and injured or weak small animals. A few weeks later I saw another one while leading a hike near the Patapsco River. I had just attended a celebration of Rachael Carson's birthday, honoring her work in banning DDT and saving the eagle from extinction. At the beginning of the walk a participant called our attention to the birds circling overhead. I looked up and saw five on a thermal: two black vultures, two red-tailed hawks higher up, and a bald eagle on top. A magnificent tribute to Carson on her birthday.

My biggest surprise was to see an eagle land in a tree out behind my house at the edge of a large pasture owned by my neighbor, Senator Clark. With binoculars, I admired its grandeur close-up. As it turned its head, the intensity of its eyes was mesmerizing. Later that week I shared the excitement of this sighting with Senator Clark. He looked at me and gruffly said, "They're after my lambs." I'm not sure he was right, but his comment certainly set me back a step. I was excited that they were recovering from the brink of extinction (they were on the Endangered Species List from 1972 to 2007), then he laid down the raw realities of how they survive.

What a paradox. Is nature friend or foe, or maybe just a partner in this life? Controversy still rages over reintroducing the wolf into Yellowstone Park. Wolves help to manage the elk, but farmers in that area are up in arms, concerned they will lose some of their domestic livestock to predators at the top of the food chain. The more we know about our ecosystem and our responsibility not to damage it or throw it out of balance, the more we'll appreciate all of its participants.

In general I've found that once you get to know a few birds, they'll always occupy a warm spot in your heart. This is especially true if you know when to start looking for them during the year and in which habitats to look. If you are one of those people who would like to know more about birds and how to recognize them, first go get your Peterson or Sibley guidebook. Then remember that it's the miracle of migration and the need for a diversity of habitats that bring about the wide variety of birds here in the Chesapeake watershed. You won't find all two hundred species that are identified here each year on any single walk, but to help guide you, here is a sampling of what to look for depending on when you go out for a walk.

IT'S WINTER. As I walk out the lane on my early morning jaunt, a red-shouldered hawk flies directly over my head, and the first rays of the sun light up its rust-colored breast. A second hawk calls from the woods and the first one flap-flap-flap-glides to the top of the tallest poplar to join its mate. After a moment the mate dives off the perch and flap-flap-flap-glides away to the call of *kee-ah, kee-ah, kee-ah.* This is precisely why I start and end each day fully immersed in the outdoors. Whether I walk in rain, snow, or heat, something is always going on in the wild that lifts my spirits and starts or ends my day on just the right note.

As I walk on, I notice a gathering of noisy crows loitering around the cornfield, apparently discussing their plans for the day. Two stray geese make a beeline overhead to join others already in the next field down the road. Small groups of songbirds flit around the hedgerows. It must be a good day to fly.

As I pass under the large white oak at the top of the hill, I glance up and much to my surprise see nine large turkey vultures staring down at me, like sentinels. I actually smell them before I see them in the upper branches of the massive tree. They do not stir as I pass below. A hundred yards farther down the lane stands another majestic oak with seventeen more vultures catching the warming rays of the early morning sun. Two raise their wings and glide over to a third tree. I decide that it is time to end my foray this morning. I turn to jog back home but take it slowly, wanting to enjoy it all, and not become the object of the vulture's convocation.

In the winter woods and along their edges, I see or hear downy woodpeckers, Carolina chickadees, tufted titmice, white-breasted nuthatches, and Carolina wrens. In more open, brushy areas, I see various sparrow species, northern cardinals, house finches and American goldfinches. I look for hunting hawks on the tops of poles or leafless trees. I know where they hang out and look for them whenever I go by their kingdoms. Generally the smaller birds behave as though I am insignificant, fluttering around and chattering, but if I come too close they all swoosh away to another haven where they can search for food undisturbed.

It appears to me that at this time of year everyone is just waiting for spring. Tufted titmice and Carolina chickadees start singing in mid-January after a quiet period earlier in the winter. House finches start singing in mid-February. Killdeer and American robin flocks return after mid-February. The great horned owls appear on their twiggy nests, located in crotches of mature deciduous trees, in January and February. At night I listen for the tundra swans as they fly by in late February and early March. Red-shouldered and red-tailed hawks begin their courtships by the end of January and show off a variety of aerial displays directly over their nesting territories. They must believe these stunning acrobatic maneuvers—closed-wing dives and talon-grappling—can help them secure a mate. Sounds familiar doesn't it, males showing off their stuff?

Back in my study, I hear a familiar tune outside my window. My most constant companion, a particular Carolina wren who regularly lands on my porch, is paying me a visit. He is checking into every nook and cranny the siding and deck furniture has to offer. As always his movements are frenetic, cinnamon-colored tail swishing up and down, head flicking back and forth. He appears anxious, as if searching for something, then he's off again. I hope he finds it. I love the fact that he is here with me all year, since so many of his larger, fair-weather friends come and go with the seasons.

Finally it's spring, or at least some days begin to feel like it. Everyone is out enjoying the warmer weather. Things are changing by the minute. Skunk cabbage pushes its way up through the wet, winter leaf cover, reviving the woods. These hearty, purple buds and green leaves are followed by dainty spring beauties, patches of white flowering bloodroot, legions of mayapples, and occasional Jack-in-the-pulpits. New birds are returning almost every day. There will be plenty of new life to look for, no matter when I go out over the next three months. Singing red-winged blackbirds in the cattails along the banks of the stream are a welcome sign of spring. Splendid great egrets and black-crowned night herons begin appearing around the water's edge in late March and early April. Barred owls start to call more frequently, often before dawn and after dusk. I routinely watch their nests, hoping to catch sight of their young. Northern flickers and other woodpeckers are noisily engaged in courtship rituals, drumming on the side of our house at dawn, as well as on dead trees.

American woodcock conduct their courtship flights at dusk and dawn from late February until the end of April. They put on quite a show. Al Geis used their courtship dance to help preserve their habitat along the Middle Patuxent River. He accomplished this by taking whoever would go out with him to his special spot during their mating season. During the ritual the male woodcock dances around in front of his intended mate, displaying his appeal and worthiness. Then he takes flight and spirals up thousands of feet, well out of sight. Moments later the male dives back down, stopping just shy of the ground. Seems to me a bit risky and a great deal of effort just to impress a mate. Imagine what would happen if he didn't stop in time. Such a dangerous courtship can only mean true love. One day, Jim Rouse, the developer of Columbia, made the trek with Al. The show must have been spectacular that day, because Rouse set aside a thousand acres as a wildlife area.

In early spring, flocks of cedar waxwings descend on hawthorn, crabapple, or American holly trees and strip them bare of remaining fruit that has been softened by the winter weather. Sometimes the fruit is fermented and the waxwings get tipsy in the process. April also sees the return of green herons. Yellow-rumped warblers, our most common migrant warbler, show up in great numbers during the last two weeks of April. Ruby-throated hummingbirds and most of the orioles and scarlet tanagers arrive in early to mid-May.

Baltimore orioles are nesting in the sycamore tree down in the pasture this year. The bright orange and black male is a bossy bird who makes a beeline back and forth like he means business. I call to him and he often answers, sometimes showing up as if ready for a fight. He certainly does not want any other intruders within his region of the pasture. One year, a male oriole saw his shadow reflected in our glass window and battled himself for more than twenty minutes while we all sat around having lunch.

Although every week brings something new, if I had only one day to fully appreciate spring migration, I would spend it in the field during the first half of May. In early May, the hours from dawn until mid-morning can be miraculous, a sensational show featuring dozens of bird species.

Summer, and the entire gang is back and busy rearing their young. Eastern screech-owls have fledged and are calling at dusk. Fruit-bearing trees like cherries and mulberries have become hangouts for orioles, thrushes, woodpeckers, catbirds, thrashers, blackbirds, waxwings, and tanagers. Ruby-throated hummingbirds can be found down by the streams, near the flowering jewelweed, one of their favorite wildflowers. One of my favorite birds, the northern mockingbird, sits on my roof and keeps me awake by singing through the night. But the most amazing treat in the summer woods is the flute-like melody of the wood thrush. We hear them in the morning, at dusk, and whenever clouds cover the sun. I consider them our nightingales; nothing else in the woods has so beautiful a song.

Walking back the lane, I pass beneath a convention of bright yellow, male goldfinch on the telephone lines. One by one these diminutive birds flit off, rising and falling in their syncopated flight over to the tall grass of a field not yet mowed. They land on thin stalks of orchard grass that barely bend under their minimal weight. What a splash of color and motion on a warm summer morning. They must be showing off their bright colors prior to the late summer molt and transformation back to their duller winter wardrobes. But where are the females? Sleeping in? Just the males out and about, there must be thirty of them.

The bird I associate the most with late summer is the mourning dove. They also hang out on the high wires, their long, elegant, iridescent necks twisting as they keep their eyes on us grounded creatures passing below. Then off they go with the chirping of their wings. But the strongest memory I have is of their mournful calls outside my window back on the farm. I can still hear them calling throughout the long, hot, pre-air-conditioned, summer afternoons of my childhood, their voices, as slow as my tired thoughts, keeping pace with the passing of those lonely, last days of summer.

Then it's fall. Some birds begin their southward migration as early as mid-August. I see fewer birds each week. Yet the changing colors of the trees, shrubs, and grasses make every day interesting, even though I'm starting to miss my summer friends already. The broad-winged hawk migration peaks in late September, and the merlin migration peaks during the first half of October. Also, individual monarch butterflies are beginning their long southward journey at this time of year, taking to the airways an hour or two after sunrise. I see them passing by, close to the ground and as high up as hundreds of feet. Yellow-bellied sapsuckers and winter wrens show up every autumn. In late fall and early winter I keep an eye out for flocks of bluebirds and for finches in the tulip trees feeding on the seeds. The songbirds that remain will quiet down, and the waterfowl will be the dominant vocalists over the winter with a range of species blowing in at various times throughout the season.

As I get to know more and more birds, they enrich my daily walks in the woods. Their songs, their flight patterns, and glimpses of their subtle plumage at distinct times of the year make me think of the faraway places they have been. It helps tie me into the natural order of things. In contrast, not seeing certain species that used to be more common, raises my concern for the health of the planet. As bountiful as the birds are in our area, the future of many species is uncertain. Dozens of bird species have been lost since the colonists arrived in North America. Over seven hundred species remain in the U.S., but it is entirely likely that a fair number of these will be lost by the end of the century because of our impact on the planet—changes we are creating that result in habitat loss and global warming. I hope we have learned something from the birds we've already lost. It's time to *act*, to preserve their remaining habitats and slow or halt climate change if we are to prevent the extinction of our feathered friends.

What can be done for the birds? Two unique attributes of the Chesapeake Bay watershed that make it so attractive to birds are both threatened. Global warming is changing migratory patterns, and the demands of our growing population have already caused considerable habitat loss. If these two trends continue, our future will not include the same variety of wildlife. There are many things we can do to help. First of all, learn more by contacting local ornithological societies (e.g., www. mdbirds.org).

Individuals can help by getting hooked on birds and learning how best to maintain their habitats. You can also grow native plants that feed native insects and birds and install a water element in your backyard.

Corporations can do much good by reducing the use of insecticides, encouraging Integrated Pest Management, and supporting local efforts to preserve land. They can help find ways to lead the charge to slow global warming.

Governments can ensure that a variety of habitats are maintained and work to reduce global warming. A good first step is to sign the Mayors' Climate Action Plan which is being implemented in hundred of cities across the country.

Finding Fungi

There is a spot in the woods where I return each month to observe all the seasonal changes. Tall poplars reach to the sky off to my right, stately beeches guard the forest in front of me, and a mix of hardwoods borders this special spot to the left. Dogwood and serviceberry trees make up the understory all around me. I come to watch the trees bud out, to see plants emerge from the forest floor and squirrels frolic about. Throughout the spring and summer, when so much is growing, the space fills up, I can't see far and feel closed in. Then in the fall the greens turn to browns, leaves fall from the trees, branches drop to the ground. There is a general unraveling, a shedding of all that spring and summer growth. The leafy and woody discarded biomass comes fluttering down and lands in a pile of debris that covers the ground. In some places it looks like snowdrifts, all stacked up in a ditch or against a tree. But by late winter, it is gone. Whatever was there has been absorbed, soaked back into the earth. The ground is naked again. No real sign of change from a year ago. Yes, maybe the trees are a little bigger and there might be a new sapling or two, but the forest floor is bare. Something or some process has consumed all of the growth that took place last year. Sucked it up and made it disappear. Sitting there, I wonder who does all that housecleaning and where they are right now.

As it turns out, the most pervasive and probably most active living species in the forest is hiding from us. The members of this cult lie beneath the leaf cover and extend down into the soil. Some are quite extensive, reaching out laterally for hundreds of feet in all directions. Anyone who has dug a hole or pulled up a tree in the woods will have encountered these elusive but ubiquitous organisms. They form white cobweb-like mats that become intimately intertwined with the leaf mold and all the decaying matter of the forest. I have encountered them in my compost pile and under the bark of dead trees. Some varieties send up fruiting bodies, most prefer to stay hidden. They are not plants; they have no need for the sun, no need for photosynthesis. They are not ani-

143

mals. They live by stealing their energy from plants and animals. They are different. They are everywhere. They are fungi.

When looking for fungi you can find them or evidence of them on nearly everything in sight. On my walks through the woods, I see fungi growing on anything that is dead and inanimate and also on the living. They are not just on fallen branches and tree trunks but often grow symbiotically with trees, each needing the other to survive. Fungi in the form of lichen grow on the bark of healthy trees and coat large granite boulders by the side of the path. Looking around, I see the green-gray lichen on every rock in sight and on almost all of the larger trees. My eyes are becoming trained and can spot lots of mushrooms and areas where mushrooms are pushing up through leaf mold. Fungi, in all their many forms have entered my consciousness; they have become something of interest. After having ignored fungi for so long, suddenly I am fascinated with them. They have a big role to play and are essential to life here on earth.

Today, wherever I go, I'm always on the lookout for fungi, in the woods, the supermarket, or on menus at fine restaurants.

"Waiter! Excuse me. What kind of mushrooms are you serving with this dish? Do you know where they're from?"

Sometimes these questions result in blank stares and at others the chef comes out for a talk. In the cheese department at grocery stores, I look carefully at the Stilton and Roquefort, thinking in a new way about the blue fungal molds we like because of the flavor they bring to our cheese. I pick up a yogurt, a loaf of bread, and a six-pack of beer, so I can read the labels and contemplate how important the fungal yeasts were in the fermentation process of each. At fresh produce stands I try to recognize the range of mushrooms for sale. Then before leaving, I stop by the store pharmacy and pick up antifungal creams and antibiotics made from lichens. What would we do without fungi?

With this increasing interest in fungi, I begin to wonder where they fit into the order of things. Are they plants? Are they animals? I look into the research on fungi. When I grew up, fungi were part of the plant kingdom, but scientists soon realized that fungi have a lot in common with animals. Yet they are not really animals either. So the powers that be in the science community decided that fungi should have their own kingdom. It's wonderful how our knowledge of science and the natural world keeps expanding. There is so much that we still don't know, and so much we can learn by asking the right questions. Through reading, I've learned that humans are more closely related to fungi than we are to plants. Six hundred million years ago, the branch of fungi leading to animals evolved to capture nutrients by surrounding their food with cellular sacs; these were their primitive stomachs. Our fungal ancestors then developed outer layers of cells, or skins, to prevent moisture loss and act as a barrier against infection. They became the first animals.

The other fungal strain, mycelia, evolved differently, going underground for protection and forming a network of interwoven chains of cells. They have created a vast food web upon which life flourishes. In a single handful of soil there could be miles of mycelium cells if they were placed end to end. They are powerful enough to digest rocks, producing enzymes and acids that pull out calcium, magnesium, iron, and other minerals. Fungi convert the elements they garner from rocks into food for other species. They also inhale oxygen and exhale carbon dioxide. Does that sound familiar?

If you were as pleasantly surprised as I was to discover how many types of fish there are in the bay, you might be astonished to learn that there are over 70,000 species of fungi already described. Only ten percent bear fruit, which we call mushrooms, the visible part of the fungi. Mushrooms are the reproductive structures that produce spores, the seeds of fungi. Mushrooms are fleshy, succulent, fragrant, and rich in nutrients, therefore they attract animals that eat them, spreading their spores. Humans are among those animals who love mushrooms. Some of the types we eat are harvested in the wild, others are raised commercially. Aficionados gather milk mushrooms, morels, chanterelles, truffles, black trumpets, and porcini mushrooms from the wild. The most commonly eaten species is *Agaricus bisporus,* sold as button mushrooms when small and Portobello mushrooms when large. Straw mushrooms, oyster mushrooms, and shiitakes are also widely available in markets.

One of the centers of commercial mushroom growing in the country is on the eastern edge of the watershed, right up the road in Kennett Square, Pennsylvania, "The Mushroom Capital of the World."

I had never eaten a mushroom in the wild, being fearful of getting a bad one that would make me sick or crazy. In fact, scientists don't know why some fungi are poisonous and some are hallucinatory—probably just a side effect of the production of chemicals that help break down matter. But many are toxic, and it's important not to eat mushrooms unless you really know what you're doing. Having a book for identification may not be sufficient. Often it's helpful to have an expert along. Maybe it's just me. I tend to have more faith in experience than what I read in books. Pictures and descriptions can be misleading. I think that in general we tend to rely on personal communication and building trust in others. We believe in the testimony of survivors. When it comes to being poisoned or not, I would rather listen to the experts about what I should eat or *not* eat, and even then I would probably eat a wild mushroom only after the expert had taken a bite or two.

Fungi and bacteria are the main decomposers of organic matter in nearly all terrestrial and marine ecosystems. They are the first to "arrive" when a tree dies or when a branch breaks and falls to the ground. They respond almost immediately, tiny mycelia reaching up to engulf, absorb, and decompose the broken branch. They quickly move into and then live within their newly arrived food supply. This is most readily seen where the cores of trees have been hollowed out by fungi. Their job is to break down the dead into constituents that can be used again—to digest matter to benefit the living. You might say they exist to help plants live. For example, they form a powerful digestive enzyme around the network of hyphae that protect and feed tree roots. This close relationship has evolved so far that most plants today are dependent on fungi for survival.

Many trees and rocks are covered with gray-green lichen, some tiny and angular and some large and floppy. Lichen is a composite, in which a fungus and an alga have grown together symbiotically. The fungus creates the structure they both live in and breaks down the rock substrate into minerals for the alga, which in turn will photosynthesize sunlight and make sugars to feed them both. Lichen have also become very useful to man. Antibiotics and various dyes can be made from them. Some grow very slowly, sometimes only a fraction of an inch per year, and some are sensitive to air pollution and cannot be found in areas with polluted air. Now that is a real sign of intelligence.

The more I learn about fungi, the more impressed I am with their underground strategy. During the great mass extinction event of the Permian-Triassic over 200 million years ago, that strategy proved very effective. While most other species were being wiped out, the fungal population increased. They became the dominant life form. The fossil record from that time is nearly all fungi. Imagine the planet covered with fungi—no more dinosaurs, no more trees, just mushrooms. So in addition to the observation that they are in every terrestrial ecosystem today, we know they have been around for a long, long time and can be very opportunistic. So what are they up to now? Are they just keeping a low profile, hiding in the leaf mold, waiting for their chance to dominate once again?

One of the leading mycologists in the country is Paul Stamet who wrote *Mycelium Running*. I stumbled onto this book at a permaculture conference center on Orcas Island in Washington State and couldn't put it down. He has gone much further into trying to understand fungi than just ascertaining what is safe to eat, and he's made some startling discoveries, at least to me, a neophyte in understanding this new kingdom. Paul claims mycelia transmit information across their huge cobweb-like networks using the same neurotransmitters that our brains do, the same chemicals that allow us to think. I had to stop and read that again. It floored me, but it made some sense since these living organisms have been around and evolving longer than we have. He suggests that mycelia are actually the neurons of the planet. He makes these claims, offers these insights, because he appreciates that biological systems are so complex that they far exceed our cognitive abilities and our linear logic. Man certainly doesn't know everything yet. But fungi, are they really that much more sophisticated than man? I had to keep reading.

Paul offers an example of a fungus from the Pacific Northwest. Just try to comprehend the complexity of a single mycelial mat that has been identified in eastern Oregon's Blue Mountains. It covers 2,384 acres and is estimated to be over 2,400 years old. It is the largest organism discovered to date in the entire world, dwarfing whales and much larger than Aspen groves that are connected through their root systems. Furthermore, this mat has a single cell wall and is surrounded by millions of microbes with which it is in constant biochemical communication with its ecosystem. These mats may in fact be vast neurological networks. More evidence that they are fairly advanced is the fact that they produce pharmacological compounds. Based on all these lines of evidence, Paul may be right. The extensive fungal mats inhabiting our forests may indeed be sentient beings, aware, and highly evolved beyond our current comprehension. They lie there, ready to pounce on the next tree that falls, sensing changes in weather, moisture, the movements of animals, aware of all that happens in the woods. This starts me thinking about my place in the world, and who is really in charge. The next time you go for a walk in the woods, have a little respect. You are not alone.

What can be done to save the fungi? Nothing, they can take very good care of themselves. They may be the one group of living creatures that will be able to adapt easily to all the chaos man has wreaked on this planet. In fact, much of the waste we produce is consumed by fungi and bacteria. After all, their job is to break things down so the chemicals can be used to feed new life.

Corporations have an opportunity to help clean up the soil and water on contaminated sites based on the ability of fungi to break down chemicals. It has been shown that certain fungi species are effective in remediating a range of toxic chemicals on contaminated sites. As we learn more about fungi and their properties, there will be numerous opportunities to use them to meet future challenges.

Fungi lived through other mass extinctions and even had their own population explosion while everything else was dying out. So fungi may be the planet's answer to man's excesses. They will always be there to clean things up and get life going again. Maybe that is the message we should take away from our understanding of fungi. Species have perished before, but life went on. If we destroy our environment so that we cannot go on, other life forms will succeed us. Our goal is to make sure we learn to live in balance with the environment that sustains us, so we don't go the way of many species and prior civilizations and become the next course for the fungi.

Part IV

Human Endeavors

Severn River Crabbers. (Courtesy of Chris Edwards.)

Humans have long played a significant role in the Chesapeake watershed. From our first steps on the continent to the present, we have assumed the role of top predator. No other beast has bested us in the thousands of years we have roamed this land. As our numbers grew, so has our impact. We have displaced many species and in numerous cases, such as the passenger pigeon and the Carolina parakeet, driven them to extinction. Other species have been domesticated and bred for characteristics desired by our ancestors. The numbers of favored animals have grown dramatically, far out of proportion to their natural place in the ecosystem. We raise them for our own purposes and protect them from their natural predators. After years of domination, the watershed today looks much different than it did before we arrived.

As we spread throughout the watershed, our numbers and behavior changed the natural balance of things. We began to re-engineer the land and the waterways. Dams limited the migration of fish. Canals, highways, and cities changed the patterns of terrestrial creatures. Animals adapted as best they could. Some could not and are no longer common. It has always been hard to predict the consequences of our actions, and this will probably be even more true in the future. We are reaching that point where our numbers are so great, that even little changes can have significant ripple effects throughout the biosphere. Let's take a look at some of the ways we affect the health of other species that still do their best to share the planet with us.

Predators and Prey

One day, while pacing back and forth from window to door on the west end of our house, I called out to my wife, "Kathy, come take a look down the driveway. There must be a dozen of 'em!" She joined me, and we watched for a few minutes before she went back to cooking. Entertaining as they might be, the fact is that our small place on the edge of suburbia is overrun with white-tailed deer. They graze in the backyard, beat me to the harvest in our overgrown garden, and loiter out by the barn. At times while driving in our gravel lane, we've counted as many as eighteen deer calmly grazing in the fields, just looking at us as they continued munching on the grass. Fully accustomed to our presence, the deer do not even run from approaching headlights. What a change after growing up in the 1950s, when the sight of a single deer created something of a stir. In those days much of the land was cleared for farming, and farmers hunted deer for food and to prevent crop damage. Now that suburbia has replaced the farms, as well as the farmers who did most of the hunting, deer are staging a major comeback. What amounts to a population explosion threatens many other species in the watershed. Having overgrazed and destroyed the regenerative capacity of many of our forests, they have become a threat to the ecosystem. So great are their numbers that we now find ourselves forced to manage their population. We must revert to our role as predator lest things go too far out of balance. Today, white-tailed deer in suburbia present a hazard on highways, further the spread of Lyme disease, and damage natural habitats. What a difference fifty years has made.

For most of the last decade deer did not venture into our yard. We attribute this "freedom from deer" epoch to a feisty little black Scottie named Boots who cohabitated with us. Whenever she was let out the door, she tore around the house checking for varmints, and at night she ran off barking into the woods to chase the deer away. She certainly sounded fierce, and her tenacity kept the deer at bay. She was our live-in wildlife manager, keeping the wildlife in the woods and out of our yard.

But Boots passed away last year, and the deer knew it almost instantly. This year does, fawns, and bucks have been coming right up to drink out of the small fish pond less than fifteen feet from the kitchen door. Last week I watched two bucks drinking between the lily pads. They were so close I could count the points on their antlers, six and eight respectively. When they began eating the hosta plants in the flower bed, I opened the door to chase them away. For a moment they just looked at me indignantly before prancing off into the woods.

Last year the deer ate quite a few rhododendron leaves, and the plants died. This year, figuring that if nothing were done the deer would finish off all the plants in the yard over the winter, Kathy decided to do something about it. She wanted to save the plants *and* keep Lyme disease–carrying ticks out of our back yard. Looking high and low she returned home one day claiming to have found the best organic deer repellant on the market.

Kathy called me from the kitchen, "I bought this spray. It's supposed to do a great job. Can you go out and spray the plants around the house while I make lunch?"

I took the bottle and thought to myself, "Sounds like snake oil." But it also seemed like an easy solution if it was not harmful to other things. Rather than complain, I decided that here was a chance to actually do something about our local deer problem. So I took the bottle and carefully read the label. It was organic and would not add nitrates or harmful chemicals to the ecosystem; it was not supposed to harm anything else but simply keep deer away with its bitter taste.

As I walked around the yard spraying the plants, I noticed a small trickle of fluid running down from the nozzle and across my right hand. I switched hands and kept spraying, disappointed as usual with a new container that leaked. I finished the job and reread the instructions on the can before throwing it away. No warnings about disposal. It claimed to be the strongest repellent one could buy, and evidently without being toxic. I threw the container away and went in to wash up for lunch. As I was eating a sandwich my fingers accidentally touched my mouth. A strong, bitter taste immediately got my attention.

"Yuck! What was that?"

"It must be the spray. Didn't you wear gloves?" Kathy asked.

"No I didn't wear gloves. I didn't think the bottle would leak." I even tasted the bitterness when licking my lips. The spray must have coated my face as well. I got up and walked back to the washroom to scrub my hands and face even harder this time, but to no avail. It put a real damper on my interest in lunch. This was turning into a personal disaster. How long would this awful taste persist on my lips? Bad enough that I had to put up with it, but would Kathy avoid me like the plague as well? Chagrined, I turned and asked why she had picked out this particular brand.

"The clerk guaranteed it would last all winter." Oh my, I thought. This really could be a long cold winter for me and the deer.

Still, though our new backyard strategy was not as effective as the dog, most of our trees and shrubs lived. Even I managed to survive the winter. Yet our efforts did nothing about the number of deer in the watershed. It just kept them out of our back yard. Such is the problem, too many deer and no good way to manage their growing population. Our removal of the natural predators, the mountain lion and the wolf, and the reduction in hunting has resulted in this one species running rampant and unchecked. That is never good for the other species in a habitat and in some respects parallels the problem with the uncontrolled growth of the human population. We are wiping out many other species and damaging the health of our own ecosystem at the same time.

In Maryland alone there are 250,000 deer and about 20,000 car-deer accidents per year. The bucks grow as large as three hundred pounds and can create real damage if hit even at moderate speeds. Our disruption of the natural order and our inability to manage this altered ecosystem is causing, on an annual basis, the death of over 10,000 deer and injury to another 10,000, numerous human deaths, overgrazing resulting in the destruction of habitats, and insurance costs of more than $10 million. Add to that the growing number of Lyme disease cases caused by deer ticks—more than seven hundred in Maryland last year alone—and you have a major public health issue.

These days when I walk through the woods, I see little to no understory growth in many areas of the watershed. The dense undergrowth that sheltered birds, insects, and mammals when I was young is no longer commonplace. Many of our forests are no longer regenerative or sustainable thanks to grazing deer. Their vast numbers have caused many other species that depend on forest understory to die off. It's a chain reaction affecting the entire ecosystem, not just trees and birds but all the insects and shrubs that live in the forest.

Over the years I've participated in the planting of thousands of hardwood and softwood trees and shrubs, hoping to create the forests of tomorrow. It's exciting to get a group of friends out on a reforestation project. Unfortunately, it's not always easy to create a forest. One of the main reasons that some reforestation projects fail is deer eating the seedlings. While driving to work, I pass two projects that were undertaken at the same time by a developer who was required to plant eighteen-inch saplings to replace mature trees he had taken down for a housing project. One field was planted with free-standing saplings, the other had plastic tubes surrounding each sapling. It took longer for the tubes to be erected around the trees, and many of us wondered how well a tree would survive in those tubes. Well, I recently had the chance to walk the fields, and the one without the tubes hasn't a tree left. In the other, at least half of the trees are now growing out the top of the tubes. Evidently this is not a bad rate of success. Fifty percent is probably adequate, since the trees were planted very close together to begin with, approximately every six feet. It does appear that the tubes helped them get started by preventing the small, tender saplings from being eaten during a cold winter.

Many of our efforts to preserve nature will not succeed until we learn how to manage an ecosystem that is largely out of balance. Bountiful when the first colonists arrived, the white-tailed deer were largely killed off by the time of the American Revolution, and laws were then put into effect to protect them. Very few deer resided in central Maryland well into the twentieth century while we remained an agrarian country and lived off the land. All that changed when we moved off farms and into cities and suburbs. Early deer management programs reintroduced deer during the first half of the twentieth century, and they now thrive in nearly every county in Maryland, Delaware, Pennsylvania, and Virginia. The pendulum has swung too far in the deer's favor, leaving us with the opposite problem. To keep the herds healthy and our ecosystem in balance, they need a predator species. Today man serves that role. Last year, more than 91,000 deer were taken by hunters in Maryland, and sixty-one tons of meat were donated to food banks. The bow hunting season in Maryland lasts from mid-September to the end of January and annually claims about 21,000 deer. The muzzle-loader season, which is only three weeks long, bags about 20,000 more, and the regular firearm season bags about 50,000. Yet, even this amount of hunting is not enough to reduce the numbers of deer in the state to a level that is in balance with other species in the habitat.

How will nature respond? Often when a population grows rapidly, disease sets in, which brings the numbers back into balance. As a result there is often a pendulum swing in the population statistics of species.

We are watching population swings in a number of species today. Interestingly, in addition to deer, one of the other newcomers is a predator. The coyote has moved here in sufficient numbers to affect the local ecosystem. Coyote are known to be very opportunistic. They have moved in because there are no other large predators, and they are wily enough to live side by side with humans. The question now is whether they will be the answer to deer overpopulation.

The trouble with coyotes as well as other predators is that they tend to go after the easiest prey first. That includes our pet dogs and cats and some domestic farm animals. A neighbor of ours, Janet Harvey, ran a flock of some 250 sheep in conjunction with the Clarks. During the summer of 2005, she found eighteen dead sheep and was unable to account for another eighteen lambs. A local tracker found coyote prints, which are distinguishable from dog prints in that the hind feet do not follow in the tracks of the front feet. Although coyote are rarely seen since they are nocturnal and extremely shy, local residents have been reporting sightings of these large and lean carnivores that look like skinny German Shepherds.

Part of the Food Chain. (Courtesy of Alice Webb, the artist.)

Harvey and the Clarks shut down the threat to the flock by buying a Turkish guard dog (an Akbash) and putting up electric fences around the pasture, an investment of thousands of dollars. The high cost of fencing forced them to limit the size of the fenced area and thus also the size of the flock, further reducing their income from the sheep business. The good news is that their tactics stopped the attacks. The Turkish guard dog enjoys the companionship of the sheep and constantly walks the inside perimeter of the fence, standing vigilant guard over his new found friends.

The bad news is that the coyotes did not move on. No sooner had this hurdle been put in place than our small flock became the target for the local pack. We had no dogs at the time and therefore no deterrents to pre-dawn visits by the predators. Early one morning I found a dead ewe with the front left leg completely torn off along with most of the skin and muscle of the shoulder and rib cage. We called animal control. An officer came out and asked questions to determine whether it was done by a dog or a coyote. She said she had been to several scenes where coyotes had attacked livestock and concluded the damage was probably inflicted by a pack of coyotes. She could not offer us any hope or solution. A few weeks later, I found a second sheep slaughtered in a similar fashion. Not wanting to invest in the expensive solution Harvey and

Clark had pursued, we donated the rest of the flock to the neighborhood mosque, Dar el-Taqwa, for Ramadan, and helped feed hundreds of participants at the end of their fast.

Once our sheep were off the platter, neighbors to the north began to lose theirs, one at a time. Their flock dropped from eleven to five sheep fairly quickly so they bought a guard llama and put her in their pasture. A large farm nearby took a more direct approach. They staked out where the coyotes lived and shot twenty-seven of them. That seemed to end the problem for a while, but none of us expect it to be a permanent solution. Coyotes tend to move whenever a void is created. The bottom line is that we may all have to reconsider what we're raising on our farms. The sheep business is not very profitable to begin with, even before going to these extra costs. I guess the price of lamb will have to go up. As usual we will all have to learn to adjust to nature, as nature adjusts to us.

So what will the future hold for predators and prey like the coyote and white-tailed deer in the watershed? Will the coyote, once they wipe out the easily taken sheep, help bring deer into balance with the rest of the ecosystem? Coyote food habit studies regularly show consistent use of deer as food so there is hope. They could certainly take down a fawn, and a pack might take down an ill or old deer. But there is no evidence to date that the presence of coyotes limits deer populations on a regional scale anywhere in the East. As they establish themselves at the top of the food chain, coyotes will go after the easy pickings first. They will out-compete fox for small game. Diminishing red fox populations have already been noted in portions of central and western Maryland. Lesser, yet still significant, changes are expected in gray fox, bobcat, and other associated predator and prey populations. However, until coyote or some other animal keeps the deer population in check, man will have to assume the role of dominant predator. That means we'll have to employ deer management strategies wherever possible to keep the numbers down in our ongoing attempt at keeping all species in balance.

But by far the biggest challenge to our ecosystem is the other predator species currently experiencing a population explosion—us. What will curb our growth? We are clearly out of balance with most other species and are destroying many habitats including our own. With so many of us here cramming into limited space, will disease set in to stop or reverse our growth? Or can we learn how to stabilize our population so we can live in balance with the rest of the planet? Is it possible for us to learn to modify our behavior so as to reduce our detrimental impact on the ecosystems that support us? The continuing downward spiral of the bay's health suggests that we cannot or at least are not yet committed to making it happen.

What can we do to keep our ecosystem in balance? The hardest step is to figure out how to stabilize the human population. We will have to do this for the sake of our children, but most politicians won't touch the issue with a ten-foot pole. Our best hope is education on why we need a stable population in balance with our ecosystem for the health of future generations. In that way, individuals can make informed decisions about where to live and family size. As a result of the dramatic increase in human population growth over the past fifty years, all species are struggling to find their niche in our ever-changing human landscapes. Here are a few suggestions for what you can do to help keep things in balance.

Individuals can educate themselves and their friends to the importance of a balanced ecosystem without severe population spikes within any species. It would help if we all stopped feeding the geese, ducks, deer, or other wild species. We could also encourage the planting of native habitats (instead of barren lawns) at home, in the community, and at work.

Corporations can help by supporting the maintenance of a wide variety of habitats on their lands and in the communities where they operate. They could research and create better ways for managing species that are out of balance.

Governments can implement deer and geese management efforts and preserve large tracts of land where species can develop in equilibrium with one another. Since ball fields and lawns are ecological deserts, they should re-evaluate the public's need for manicured areas and allow nature to return to more of the countryside. There may be more need for nature trails in the future than ball fields, especially as our population ages.

Upland Game Hunting

Dad and I parked our van at the overgrown entrance to Rodney's property, put on gloves and hats, and walked up the gravel driveway. An inch or two of snow lay on the frozen ground, and it was cold—not a day to be outside for long. We approached the driver's side of an idling Chrysler and tapped on the window. Rodney opened his eyes, rolled down the window part way, and grinned. "Well looky here. Aren't you two a sight for sore eyes? How are you coming along, Jim?"

I peered into the car. Rodney comfortably filled the driver's seat of the once-deluxe, previously abandoned, station wagon, his body occupying the entire space between steering wheel and the swayed back, bench seat. His familiar ragged, red-plaid, Pendleton gunning shirt covered multiple layers of other clothes. A fluorescent orange Remington cap, unlaced Redwing high-top boots, and four days' growth rounded out Rodney's wardrobe.

"Fine," my father said, sparingly as always. "Just looking for another setter."

"Well, you've come to the right place. I bet you'd like to get another dog like Sky High, wouldn't you? Now there was a fine setter. You know, Jim, he was descended from General Sky, the champion trial dog for the entire East Coast. Sky sure found you a lot of quail. I remember that beautiful flag he'd hold up when he got locked in on a scent—would hold up that white tail of his in a point for an hour until you caught up with him."

Rodney spoke just like that, a continuous, slow roll of information and insight, a photographic memory on every dog he ever sold and every bird he ever shot, and those you had shot as well.

"Remember that one year when we got snowed in up at Deep Creek Lake? We got hit with two feet of snow and had to keep those dogs warm so they wouldn't freeze to death on us in the trunk of the car. Boy that was cold. A lot like today."

As they talked, or more accurately, as Rodney talked and Dad listened, I strolled around his house and yard, trying to keep warm. If I stood in one place too long the cold would slowly creep up from the frozen ground, up through the worn Vibram soles of my boots and two sets of wool socks. So I kept moving. Rodney had about an acre, all overgrown with trees and vines, set in the middle of a frozen sea of corn right here in southern Lancaster County, Pennsylvania, near the Conowingo Reservoir. Paths meandered around the place through the overgrown underbrush to various dog cages. The old brick Victorian was right out of the set from the *Addamm's Family*, a house with turrets and porches, or at least what remained of porches. Broken glass hung in the second floor windows, and plywood covered windows on the first floor. He had moved out a few years ago when everything broke down and it was just too costly to repair. His station wagon was better suited to his budget. Looking back on it now, Rodney was the only homeless homeowner I ever knew—he lived in his car.

As I walked around the house and grounds, various breeds of setters and pointers welcomed me with yelps. One area had white, long-haired English setters with black or brown spots. Another cage held my favorite, the brown and black Morgan setters with their long, sleek coats. White, short-haired English pointers with brown spots shivered in their cages, whipping their tails back and forth in greeting and to keep warm. As I worked my way around the outside of the house you could trace my whereabouts by following the racket the dogs made. It was morning and they were hungry.

Quite a few dogs ago, Dad first read about Rodney in the back of *Field and Stream,* where an ad for hunting dogs referred to him as the "Largest Breeder on the East Coast." Dad was excited that such a man was based right here near Conowingo. They'd struck up a close relationship and begun to hunt together. Each would bring two or three dogs, put these setters or pointers in the trunk of one of Dad's sedans, and either go over to the Eastern Shore for quail or out to western Maryland for grouse. When grouse hunting, they often stayed above the gas station in Ohiopyle, sharing a room for four bucks a night. But the last couple of times Rodney had gone, he hadn't gotten out of the car, saying only, "You go ahead. I'm just going to set here for a while." We knew he was getting old when he stopped hunting.

When I got back to the car, nothing had changed. I wondered if Rodney was stuck behind the wheel. He appeared to be barricaded into the front seat. The space behind his head overflowed with flattened, empty, fifty-pound dog food bags. Beside him on the front seat were all of his notes and records, through which he now looked with some physical effort while commenting on the bloodlines of the dogs available for sale.

I leaned over and looked inside the Chrysler and for the first time realized there was a short-haired pointer and about a dozen newborn pups on the floor on the passenger side. The heater was on not just for Rodney but also for this new litter. They had stayed there all night or maybe several nights, and the pups were doing fine. Rodney would get out only when he had to get water from the old hand pump, relieve himself behind the old outhouse, or feed the dogs.

Rodney began reciting the ancestry of this and that litter and Dad eventually said he would take one. He then invited Rodney down to the Conowingo Diner for a bite to eat. We got back in our car and followed Rodney down the road a few miles to a little diner that had seen several expansions over the years, though none recently. Rodney left his car running to keep the heater on and extracted himself from the Chrysler-nursery. He flowed through the door of the diner and into his usual booth in the corner, where he shared brunch on a daily basis with anyone who might stop by to talk about dogs. Sitting had become his main occupation—sitting and telling stories about his prize hunting dogs.

We each had a bowl of she-crab soup and a piece of apple pie. Rodney collected the crackers and any scraps for his dogs. When Dad and I rose to leave, Rodney said "You all go ahead. I think I'll jest sit here for a while." We said goodbye, and as we were leaving Rodney said, to no one in particular, "Jim here just bought himself one fine dog. He was sired by . . ."

I never saw Rodney after that. He passed away at the ripe old age of seventy-seven. They found him in his car, a death attended only by his dogs. I don't think he would have had it any other way.

Rodney represented a dying breed and a dying sport that was a popular and widespread tradition throughout Chesapeake country when I was young. Quail were a lot more plentiful then. Their characteristic "bob-white" call could be heard in the woods and fields throughout the watershed. I often engaged a bobwhite in a whistling conversation while walking up the lane on my way back from school. It was a way of knowing that I was back at home, among the familiar sounds and sights of the Maryland Piedmont.

Quail are one of the easiest birds to "call in." Even when I moved into my house on the edge of suburbia I could still call the quail into my back yard. My grandfather, in his later years when he could no longer hunt or even leave the house, used to stand by the big picture window whistling to the quail. More than once a quail responded, his call getting louder on each successive response, and occasionally one would fly smack into the window and fall to the ground stunned. My grandfather would hobble out the door, pick it up, and clean it for dinner.

Missing from where I live today are the sounds of game birds. Up until the mid-1980s we regularly heard the call of the northern bobwhite quail and the ring-necked pheasant. I remember whistling back and forth to quail with the familiar three-note riff and then being pleasantly surprised one day when one visited my back yard and called to me from my very own peach tree. Their call is quite loud when they're close. What sport, to be able to call in a bird from the wild to one's own backyard! More recently I've asked the county agent what happened to these remarkable game birds. I first thought that my neighbor, who had trapped foxes for years, had just become too old to trap them anymore and that an over-abundance of fox or even coyote had doomed the quail and pheasant population. The agent thought it had more to do with habitat loss and the more efficient corn and soybean harvesting equipment that left nothing behind for the birds to glean. What a loss.

The decline in bird hunting results largely from the loss and fragmentation of upland game habitat and a corresponding drop in quail and pheasant populations. The northern bobwhite quail topped last year's National Audubon Society's List of Top Twenty Common Birds in

Decline. The Audubon Society recently announced that the population of the northern bobwhite quail has declined from an estimated 31 million in 1967 to just 5.5 million today. In Maryland alone, the Department of Natural Resources reports a ninety percent drop in the quail population. Ring-necked pheasant are even rarer than quail today in the bay area. Maryland does not raise pheasant in order to introduce them back into nature, since they are actually a non-native species brought in from China in 1857. Their population, which peaked in the 1960s, is also on the decline due to agricultural practices and loss of habitat.

Quail, pheasant, rabbits, and many other mammals and birds do best in early-successional habitats—we always found them along brushy fence rows, fallow fields, and recently harvested woods. This was common habitat when I was a boy, and there were always abandoned farms on which to hunt. Our farm had at least one covey of quail, about twelve to twenty birds, living on it. To encourage them, we planted "living fences" of multi-flora rose bushes, and a twelve-foot row of lespedeza and soybeans around the edges of all of our fields. As farming became more mechanized and suburbia spread, this type of land disappeared. Farming methods today leave little cover or food for upland game, and herbicide applications have reduced the natural food supply, such as insects and the seeds of weeds. The government has offered incentive programs to farmers to rebuild these habitats, but we have a long way to go to bring back the quail.

Historically, resident upland game in the watershed included grouse, cottontail rabbit, and to some extent snipe and woodcock in addition to ring-necked pheasant and bobwhite quail. These species were generally pursued by a special breed of hunters, who trained their own dogs and hunted the edges of soybean and corn fields up and down the eastern and western shores of the bay. Last year the official statistics revealed that 1,000 hunters claimed 1,000 quail in Maryland and 10,000 hunters in Virginia claimed 66,000 quail. I would hazard a guess that there are a few more quail in Virginia, because I cannot believe that Virginians are better shots.

The quality of the dogs used also makes a big difference in hunting quail. That's why Dad always wanted good hunting dogs and took a lot of time training the pups he owned. When the pups were young he'd teach them to *hold a point* by tying a wing from a quail to the end of a fishing line affixed to an old bamboo fly rod. He'd flick the wing out twenty feet or so and soothingly encourage the pups to stalk it, freeze when close enough to smell or see it, and hold a good point until told to flush the "bird."

Some of Dad's dogs were naturals at finding birds and holding a point. When catching a scent they instinctively and immediately froze, stretched out their bodies, and locked their heads into position with muzzles pointing toward the bird. Deftly each would then lift his right or left front paw, bend his leg up close to his chest in a ready-to-pounce position, and hold his tail out straight like a flag, waiting for the next command. A well-trained dog would hold this pose for what seemed an eternity because everyone involved, man and beast, were anxious to flush the bird. Dad would coax the dog to hold the point by quietly and firmly repeating "Steady. Steady boy. Steady." Then all of a sudden the dog would pounce, the bird would take flight, and shotguns would discharge. With any luck, feathers would explode out of the sky and the dog would retrieve the bird and drop it at Dad's feet, dead but un-molested by the dog's teeth. It was not clear to me whether Dad was a good teacher or the dogs simply possessed an innate ability, but they all seemed to know just what to do when they went hunting. They pointed and flushed far more quail than we were ever able to shoot, so the dogs clearly knew their job better than their human hunting partners.

Once Dad found a good dog, he treasured it. They became insepa-rable. All the hunting stories would center on how well the dog worked in the woods and how many quail he had pointed. In fact, toward the end of his life Dad told me that a man's life could be divided into eras based on the dogs he owned. He then went on to say that he figured he was on his last dog.

I wonder, with fewer quail around these days, what is left of all those bird dogs so carefully bred for their hunting instincts. The Eng-lish, Irish, and Morgan setters and the English pointers all seem to be dying breeds. It's a chain reaction. First the habitat goes, then the wild game. With no game, there is not much reason to buy, breed, and train specialized dogs. That leaves no place for the Rodneys of the world. His poignant passing marks the end of an era.

I do wonder what happened to the dogs. I just don't see many of them around anymore, and the ones I do see are probably getting lazy. I wonder if they will eventually lose their instinct for picking up a bird's scent as they run through the woods. Will they forget how to stop on a dime, lift a front paw and tail, with their heads locked in on a quail? Will they forget why they are supposed to hold the point till their partner catches up, readies his gun, and then instructs them to flush the quarry? There has never been a better partnership between man and dog. It's a beautiful thing to watch your dog stop dead in his tracks and hold a point, waiting for you to fulfill your part of the bargain.

What can be done about species that have vanished? Habitat preservation and restoration is needed to bring back quail, meadowlark, and many other species that no longer frequent all parts of our watershed. Meadowland, in fact, is one of the most endangered habitats left. Much of the good quail habitat is being chewed up for suburban homes. Most of the land being preserved consists of wetlands or is being reforested.

Individuals can help by working with Quail Unlimited (www.qu.org) and local land trusts (http://www.ltanet.org/landtrustdirectory/) to target and preserve a wide range of habitats.

Corporations, especially utilities, that maintain major rights-of-way, can help by keeping some of their land as meadowland, to be mown only when necessary and at non-breeding times of the year.

Governments can help by ensuring that some public open spaces are preserved as meadowland and early-successional forests.

Chickens and the Bay

As I approached the weathered, blue-green hen house, egg basket in hand, a ruckus erupted from the chicken-wire windows. This was not the normal clucking that occurred each morning when I came for a visit. Something was up, so I quickened my pace. My boots, wet from the not recently cut grass, squeaked with each step. It was a moist morning in May, the sun not quite yet melting through the mist, and it was my job to gather the eggs.

I reached up on my tiptoes to the faded wooden latch and turned it ninety degrees to the left. The door creaked open and a clutch of nervous Rhode Island Reds greeted me. Stepping up into the sea of feathers, I was immediately drawn to a commotion at the other end of the row of nesting boxes. Cautiously I worked my way down the row, collecting eggs and watching where I stepped. The last box on the right was devoid of chickens and eggs. A fat black rat snake curled up in it stared at me in defiance, and the hens were not pleased. Their carrying on abated for a moment as they waited to see what I would do.

It was clearly my job to deal with this situation. Everybody else was busy. Dad was getting ready to go to work. Mom was cooking breakfast. My older sister Marsha was taking care of the horses. The question now was just what should I do. I'd seen Dad reach in by hand and grab seven-foot-long black snakes in the cellar crawl space and take them outdoors. Mom would shoot snakes with her over-and-under .410-gauge shotgun. But this time it was up to me, and neither of those options seemed right for a four-foot-tall kid. I looked around at the chickens; they clearly expected me to do something about this predator. I looked back at the snake. He held his ground, tongue flicking in and out of his mouth. By the looks of him, he had been gorging himself on eggs and was not ready to move. I felt something down deep kick into action. This was not just a snake, this was a thief. It was my job to feed the chickens and in return I was supposed to get the eggs. He had to go.

I grabbed a pitchfork that was taller than I was and normally used for removing the chicken droppings. Carefully I pushed it into the laying box and picked up the snake. He was heavy, but I was able to move this slithery bulk of poised muscle out the door, across the yard, and into the pasture. By this time I had gotten the attention of the dogs, who barked and sniffed at the snake, trying to get close without being bitten. None of us knew whether we had encountered a vicious foe. He looked comatose. The snake finally slid off the pitchfork onto the ground and quickly disappeared into the weeds. My job was done. I had met the challenge, now back to collecting eggs.

The farm was my testing ground, where I learned about predators and prey, about animals and manure, and even a little about fear and making decisions. As a boy I learned about chickens, turkeys, ducks, and geese, the art of collecting eggs, and feeding, watering, and even butchering poultry. In fact, every farm I knew in the Maryland Piedmont and the Coastal Plain raised chickens back in the 1950s. They were just part of life, and life on a farm was always about birth and death, about raising food, about nutrient management, and about recycling everything you had. We fed the chickens our table scraps, and in turn they provided us with an easy and tasty food, and as I am sure you know, fresh eggs always taste better than store-bought. I also learned how to spread manure over our gardens and fields, mix it in with our topsoil, and grow enough food for our family and the livestock on our hundred-acre farm. We had little need for commercial fertilizer, hormones, antibiotics, and all the other chemical and technical enhancements used so extensively on today's industrial farms. Our system appeared to be in balance with the land. It worked well at feeding the four of us and left us with a few eggs to sell to the neighbors.

My generation grew up and left the farms behind, and now my family, like most of the country, relies on fewer and bigger farms for our food. As our population has grown, society has spent a great deal of time and money to optimize production. The miracle of agribusiness is that we now can feed many more people today than before, and we do it with less labor and on less land. In some ways this is a good thing, a major success story. Unfortunately this optimization has gotten so focused that it does not take into account all of the costs to our society and our environment. If the process does not soon do so, it may become unsustainable and eventually fail. To be sustainable, industrial farms, like all other institutions, will have to learn how to balance economic, social, and environmental assets and liabilities. The chicken industry is trying to become sustainable. It is making progress, but has yet to meet that goal.

Let's take a look at what has transpired over the past century in the creation of one of the biggest businesses in the Chesapeake watershed, the industrialization of poultry. If we go way back to the beginning, we know that all birds descended from a prehistoric reptile called Archaeopteryx and, more recently, that all domestic chickens can be traced back to the Asian Red Jungle Fowl. Evolution has resulted in some major changes in what we now think of as the lowly chicken. However, over the last century, even faster changes have resulted from human intervention and the continuous cross-breeding of chickens. Today, the average chicken raised is more specialized, more efficient, and more economical than ever before. *Broilers*, chickens raised for meat, are about twice the size of chickens from a century ago and will reach full size in one-third the time, using one-third the feed. That is amazing. It now takes only seven weeks from egg to butcher shop to get a nice roasting chicken of four and a half pounds. *Laying hens* have also become much more specialized, and egg productivity has increased dramatically over the past century from a few dozen eggs per year per chicken to more than three hundred eggs per year. These are remarkable feats.

You may be wondering what this has to do with the Chesapeake Bay. After all, chickens are not native to the watershed, they were brought in by the European settlers. Yet they were certainly ubiquitous on the family farms of my youth, and now there are far more chickens grown each year in the watershed than there are people in the entire country. It also turns out that much of the industrialization of the poultry industry took place on the Delmarva Peninsula, that part of Maryland, Virginia, and Delaware that lies on the Eastern Shore of the bay. As a result, poultry has become the biggest industry in this area and is Delmarva's economic engine. This is partly because, from a market perspective, the Eastern Shore is a perfect location for raising chickens and turkeys. It has a relatively cheap labor force and is close to the major markets of New York, Philadelphia, Baltimore, and Washington. However, from an *environmental* perspective, it turns out to be one of the worst places to manage a large poultry industry. Of course, no one took that into account until it was too late. Environmental concerns were not then part of the equation.

The Eastern Shore boasted a sizeable soybean and corn crop. There was enough land to supply all the grain needed for a moderate poultry industry. With the vast growth, industrialization, and concentration of the poultry business over the past twenty years though, it outgrew regional resources. Now a great deal of feed has to be imported from the Midwest at a substantial cost in terms of shipping, energy, and generation of greenhouse gases.

So large quantities of nutrients are brought into the area in the form of feed everyday. Unfortunately, this is only half the problem. The chickens take in the grain and generate a great deal of manure, about twice the weight of the meat produced from these operations. Here is where the system gets out of balance. The excess manure is not all shipped back to the Midwest to fertilize the fields where the corn and soybeans are grown. Midwestern farms rely on relatively cheap fertilizers derived from natural gas. With no other place to go, the chicken manure is distributed on the soils of the Eastern Shore, and there is way too much to go around.

One problem with this situation is that some of the ground on the Eastern Shore does not hold manure well. The sandy soils are not very retentive and in many areas are already saturated with phosphorus. A second problem is that the groundwater table is very shallow and thus, every time it rains, nutrients leach from the soil and migrate into the groundwater. In large parts of the Eastern Shore, groundwater is now contaminated. So where does the contaminated groundwater go? It flows to the rivers, which flow to the Chesapeake. One outcome of contaminating rivers has been the periodic outbreak of algae, bacteria, and fungus that can harm fish and possibly even the fishermen. Large algal blooms, the toxic microbe Pfiesteria, and fungal lesions on fish are indications that things are out of balance and reverberate throughout the food chain.

Today Maryland and Delaware together raise 540,000,000 chickens every year. That's a lot of chickens. They require a lot of feed and they produce a lot of waste. To its credit, the industry knows this is not sustainable and is trying to deal with the problem. A pelletizing system has been developed that allows chicken farmers to ship some fertilizer out of the area. A biomass power plant could be fueled with chicken waste. A major education effort is also directed toward improving waste management practices. This involves spreading less manure, planting wider buffer zones to protect streams from fertilizer laden runoff, and planting cover crops to hold the soil and water in place. These are all good, responsible steps, but more needs to be done. State regulations have finally been put in place to make up for decades of poor practices.

The poultry industry faces other challenges in addition to the imbalance in the nutrient management cycle. Today, everywhere you drive in Delmarva, you see very large chicken houses where tens of thousands of birds are raised. In close quarters, disease can run rampant. To prevent that from happening, antibiotics are added to the feed. More antibiotics are fed to animals in this country so they can live in concentrated feeding operations than are consumed by humans to cure bacterial infections. Unfortunately, some of the antibiotics are passed through the chickens to the waste streams and end up throughout our groundwater and rivers. Nature's response to antibiotics is to create and favor brand new, antibiotic-resistant, strains of bacteria. This could result in diseases that affect humans and chickens for which we have no cure. Antibiotics also kill off *good bacteria* which provide a whole range of benefits. For example, some bacteria can keep fungal populations in check.

These are just two of the social and environmental issues that have become liabilities to our society for which the poultry industry is not fully accounting at present. The large poultry companies and the farmers who actually raise the birds are indeed trying to deal with these questions. To be sustainable enterprises, they will have to figure out solutions. If the industry does not resolve these issues, their action or inaction may not only cause further damage to our environment, it may have a more severe impact on the people who live on the Shore and around the world.

How do we, as individuals, encourage the industrial food industry to solve their nutrient management, chemical use, and disposal problems? Imposing more regulations is one option, but are more market-driven approaches to correcting this imbalance at hand? Should we stop eating chicken? Should we turn to other, even more local, sources for our eggs and drumsticks? Do we all switch to *free range* and organic chickens, which are offered more and more often in the supermarkets? Do we even know if these options are less problematic? Of one thing I am certain—we are not, in the near future, going back to the way things used to be. I doubt we will all go back to raising our own chickens, even though some people lament the loss in quality of food that has resulted from industrialization.

Kathy and I were not sure this was true, but we were concerned about the effects of industrialization on our food. Since we had a few acres, we thought it would be good to see what we could grow on our own land. Could we live more in balance with the land than corporate farmers? Raising chickens would be a first good step. After all, when I was growing up on a small farm, feeding the chickens seemed like an easy chore, at least one of the easier chores on my list, even with the occasional black rat snake. Besides, I had two daughters who could take over the chores now.

Our first move was to adopt a half-dozen laying hens from a neighbor. We locked them up at night and let them run free range during the day. Scampering around the yard and eating anything that moved, they kept the bug population down. They didn't require much supplemental feed, and the eggs were tasty if not produced on a regular schedule. It wasn't long, though, before the chickens attracted the attention of the local native carnivores. I just happened to look out the window one fine afternoon as a red fox ran by with two chickens in its mouth, and his mate was chasing down a third. Feathers floated in the air, and the tall orchard grass waved back and forth as the foxes flew through the fields, efficiently snatching up the awkward hens frantically trying to escape. Our experiment with raising free range chickens ended in total failure in less than a minute.

Disappointed but not yet deterred, we decided to profit from this mistake and try again. We had learned why people raise chickens in fenced-in areas, and why free range eggs and birds are more expensive. We accepted the reality that we had to keep the chickens safe and locked up in a yard of some sort.

For our next attempt we ordered a *Murray McMurray* catalogue, which has been the gold standard since 1917 for mail-ordering common and rare breeds of poultry. The trouble with this catalogue is that you can spend a long time looking at options and deals, and we did. We found out that you can buy quail, pheasant, guinea hens, ducklings, goslings, turkeys, and rabbits in addition to chickens. You can get standard breed baby chicks, or the smaller bantam baby chicks. You can order any equipment you need, or books, videos, plans, posters, and tee shirts—all the educational and moral support that one might require.

Kathy and I spent an evening trying to make just the right choice for our starter flock. After surveying the list of Plymouth Rocks, Rhode Island Reds, Silver-laced Wyandottes, White Brahmas, Sultans, Feather Footed Fancies, Blue Andalusians, Sumatras and the green-egg laying Araucanas, we opted for the pedestrian "Frying Pan Special." It felt like the safest thing to do, and we ordered fifty birds at fifty cents each. Murray McMurray even agreed to throw in one Rare Bird, a Polish variety, as part of the package. That cinched the deal.

We sent a check and within a few days the postman knocked on our door and asked "Are these yours?" There was no question that the box, complete with small air holes, was full of hungry, peeping chicks, and they were ours. We were proud parents to our new brood. In our semi-suburban neighborhood, chickens were not a common delivery. We took the chirping, cardboard container to the basement where we had a heat lamp and a small circular enclosure. We lifted the lid and were boisterously greeted by fifty-one motherless, yellow, chirping, huddling, and quite thirsty chicks. The moment we set a dish of water in the box they all flocked to it, jumping in, getting wet, showing no sense of decorum, just pure self-preservation. By the next day they were all out of the box and eating voraciously. The uproar of peeps doubled in volume any time one of us went downstairs to check on them. I felt like I was back in the primeval jungle, surrounded by the Asian Red Jungle Fowl ancestors to our fifty-one chicks.

Raising the hungry chicks was fairly easy, and we soon moved them out to the shed. I built a ten-by-twenty-foot, screened-in run for them so they could peck at the ground and eat grubs or insects that came their way. Each night they came in to roost, and each morning when I opened their door the rapidly growing, adolescent leghorns literally flew over, under, and through me to get outside. They clearly wanted as much freedom as they could find.

I wondered about the nutrient management challenge of these two approaches. Our free range chickens distributed their waste around the yard, and it migrated directly into the soil or during heavy rains migrated across the lawn and into the streams, diluted but untreated. The penned chickens' waste was concentrated and I ended up composting it over time, eventually applying it as needed to the garden. With such a small operation, I did not spend time and money on testing what happened to the nutrients. I wondered if fifty million small farms would be the better stewards of the environment than a thousand big ones. Does each large operation systematically test and monitor its effect on the soil and streams? Perhaps it is easier to train a thousand big farmers than fifty million small poultry operations. It is all about knowledge and commitment.

About the time our leghorns reached full weight we were called away for a week. The morning after we returned we were rudely awakened before dawn to the maturing roosters practicing their wake-up calls. Imagine fifty roosters and one rare bird trying to find their voices. The worst of it was that their pen was facing and very close to our elderly neighbor's house. We later learned she had been serenaded for the past four mornings. It was time; they were full-grown and ready for the next step of the journey. They were raised to be fryers, so first thing that morning I constructed a makeshift butcher shop and began killing, scalding, picking, and cleaning chickens. Chicken feathers were everywhere. I was coated from head to toe, the small pinfeathers sticking to my damp clothing and sweaty forehead and arms. The big wing and tail feathers were easy, but have you ever tried to remove the last of the tiny breast feathers from a naked, slippery bird? After a dozen leghorns, I gave up, and we took the rest out to a country butcher. Our chickens were tasty but much tougher than store-bought birds. It must have been the flying they did each morning to get out of their cage. We ate them over the next twelve months and decided, without much debate, not to do that again. Agribusiness won this round as well.

Our next attempt was to try *laying hens* again, this time inside a shed with a protected yard. A neighbor gave us four large Barred Rock hens. They were beautiful, stately birds with black and white checkered markings. I fed them table scraps, and they rewarded us with farm-fresh eggs, or at least suburb-fresh eggs, when they felt like it, which was most of the time. The hens had the time of their lives during the cicada infestation. Whenever a cicada got into their compound, all four hens made a beeline, lickety-split, and the lucky hen would gulp it down. They were fast! They must have eaten hundreds. Though I am not a snob when it comes to most foods, fresh eggs from chickens raised on table scraps and bugs can't be beat. The hens were fun to have around. They greeted us each morning with an avalanche of anxious clucks, coming right up to us when we watered or fed them. They were quieter than dogs and easier than most other pets. They actually earned their keep. Just imagine a pet that helps you reduce your garbage waste by eating table scraps, provides you with free eggs, and generates fertilizer for your garden. What a deal.

At the end of the year I sat down to calculate my costs for feed, equipment, and the effort required to raise chickens. Chicken wire, watering trough, grit and grain trays, it all adds up. The eggs did taste better, no doubt about that. The chicken meat seemed tastier, but it certainly was tougher than the chicken we buy in the store. Our cost for eggs was twice the store cost, even if you don't take my labor into account. Of course we did not have to take the time or pay the gas to go shopping, just a short walk to collect the fresh eggs. Our price for meat, once you count the cost of the butcher, was considerably higher, too. Still, the entertainment value and ambience made having chickens well worth it. Then there's the psychological value of knowing what the birds are eating, and the potential health benefits with the lack of chemicals and antibiotics in their feed. That's indeed hard to figure and will be highly subjective. The bottom line was that there is a certain satisfaction to raising your own food and knowing what the birds are eating. There is also a sense of balance when recycling wastes. We fed them table scraps and yard waste. That's a lot better than sending our garbage to the dump or flushing it down the drain. We then disposed of the chicken waste by composting and mixing the aged waste with soil in the garden to reduce the amount of nutrients that might wash off and end up over-fertilizing the bay.

I assume we will continue raising chickens for eggs, or buying eggs from neighbors. That much is relatively easy. But raising your own chickens for meat is not for everyone. Many of us will still be buying most of our food from the store. So what is the right thing to do? Kathy and I are starting to ask our grocers where the food we buy is coming from. We are learning a lot and are starting to make decisions about what we buy based on our growing knowledge of the suppliers. We know that the large industrial chicken establishments on the Eastern Shore are taking steps to be better stewards—they just have more work to do to learn how to better manage all the nutrients and chemical by-products they generate. As for meat, we've decided to cut back on eating chicken and now buy it from local, more sustainable operations. We'll do this until the large industrial food operations accept their responsibility for contaminating the groundwater and become more environmentally sustainable. They must find a way to live in balance with the fragile Eastern Shore of the Chesapeake Bay.

What can be done about the environmental and social impact of industrial food operations? The magnitude of Concentrated Animal Feeding Operations (CAFO) is clearly a major challenge facing all who live in the watershed. The free market does not always plan well or respond quickly enough to prevent significant environmental and social damage. To help encourage all industrial food operations to step up to the plate, each of us should be asking more questions about our food and our environment whenever we shop, and articulating our concerns to those companies and our elected representatives. We should support products, corporations, and governmental initiatives that improve our health, our environment, and our economy—not organizations that damage our environment and our long-term health. To keep up-to-date with the impact of the poultry industry, follow the work of the Chesapeake Bay Foundation (www.cbf.org).

Individuals can take the time to fully understand the problem and encourage more public debate in our search for solutions. Why do we not require better waste management? Who is going to restore the damaged aquifers? How can we reduce the likelihood of developing an antibiotic-resistant strain of bacteria that could cause widespread harm to our health? We should also ask questions about all the food we consume. Where does it originate? What chemicals does it contain?

Corporations can make a commitment to become more environmentally sustainable. They can adopt the "triple bottom line" form of accounting and reporting not just their quarterly financial bottom line but their environmental and social liabilities as well. They can differentiate themselves in a positive sense by taking a leadership position and showing us how they are good stewards of the land, water, air, and the food supply. The problem of chicken manure could probably be solved if it was used as a biofuel. Combustion and gasification of poultry litter and manure should be fully evaluated as on-site bioenergy sources to provide heat and power for farming operations.

Government can help by ensuring that food suppliers are operating plants in balance with our natural systems. They can require better waste management practices and create incentives for using manure as a biofuel. They can create a private-public partnership that monitors the impacts and reduces the likelihood of new bacterial strains that might be resistant to antibiotics and which could cause widespread health dangers.

A Fine Balance

The Chesapeake's deteriorating health is not a new problem. Our society has been struggling with how to live with the bay for a long time. We keep having to learn, over and again, that we cannot abuse natural systems for long. Yet we do, and consequences follow. Nature is forced to respond. We then adjust to its response, and the pattern soon repeats itself. In the process some species are lost. Others, like us, try to adjust to the changes. All of nature is forced to change as our human population continues to expand, muscling its way into every niche of the planet. Each year we use more and more natural resources that appear to be there for the taking. As we learn more about natural systems, we should start to realize there are limits. There has to be a balance, *a fine balance,* between ourselves and the rest of Creation.

The bay is at risk today because it plays multiple, important roles in our lives. It is bounteous, and we harvest that bounty. It is also a major transportation link and for the past four hundred years our waste disposal system. It is when these three quite different roles come together that problems arise. So man is constantly trying to juggle competing demands, trying to keep them all viable. Sometimes we get it right and sometimes we don't. Finding the balance grows more difficult every year as our population grows.

Let's take a closer look at transportation. From the days of exploration, settlement, and the tobacco trade up to the present, we have plied the Chesapeake with nearly every type of ship known to man. Today those ships range from sailing vessels of every description to huge container ships and oil tankers. The bay has become one of the largest and busiest deep-water ports in the U.S.

A few summers ago, I took a short and pleasant trip aboard the *Minnie V.,* a restored wooden skipjack operated by the Living Classrooms Foundation in Baltimore. We set sail from the Inner Harbor and headed down past Fells Point to Fort McHenry, passing the Bond Street Wharf and the Domino Sugar Plant on the way. The captain pointed out the sites of old canneries, docks, and factories. It became quite clear that Baltimore was constructed around the waterfront, and most of the city's early commercial activity had been focused on the shipping and receiving of goods. Author Donald Shomette, along as the guest of the Maryland Historical Society, told fascinating stories of how the Chesapeake Bay saw more naval battles and shipwrecks than any other part of the New World. His research has revealed that there are more than 10,000 recorded shipwrecks in the bay. Some vessels were scuttled intentionally at the harbor mouth to keep the British from sacking Baltimore during the War of 1812. Don's book (Shomette, 2007) offers an unparalleled view of the area's maritime history. As we did that evening on the *Minnie V.*, seeing Baltimore from a ship's deck leads to a greater appreciation of the importance of shipping, shipbuilding, and the waterfront to the city's development.

The long tradition of boating on the Chesapeake continues today. On any given weekend from spring well into fall, thousands of boats are out sailing, fishing, and moving people and goods from one place to another. Those of us born after the development of the interstate highway system and the widespread use of air travel cannot fully appreciate the significance of passenger vessels. I recall Dad telling a story about going to a conference on Star Island, New Hampshire, in the 1930s. He took a passenger steamer from the Baltimore docks all the way up the coast to Boston. The Merchants and Miners Line was based out of Baltimore and became known as the Queen of Sea Routes, serving the entire East Coast, all the way to Jacksonville, Florida. Their century-long heyday ended with World War II, the building of a road system, and the ascent of the automobile and airplane. Dad's trip to Boston took several days. When I go today, I zip up Interstate 95 in about eight hours or take a one-hour flight. Shipboard passenger travel may have dropped off because of faster options, but the port of Baltimore is still busy with commercial shipping.

Over the years, one side effect of this rich shipping history has been a great deal of ballast, waste, and oil dumped into the bay, damaging the health of the fisheries and clogging the shipping lanes. Runoff from agriculture and construction has also silted in the shipping lanes. To maintain balance between a healthy seafood industry, a viable shipping industry, and agriculture, the government stepped in and established minimum standards to ensure the success of all three. Shipping practices were regulated to reduce pollution, farming altered to reduce runoff, and fishing limits were set to keep up the stocks. These things helped, but today we still have to dredge shipping lanes on a regular basis.

After transportation, the second use of the bay is as a means to get rid of our waste, primarily human and animal. Historically we just dumped it into the closest tributary and relied on nature to do the flushing. After the industrial revolution we also flushed waste from our canning, manufacturing, smelting, and refining operations. Humans seeking to dispose of waste have looked to the bay and its tributaries and followed the old maxim: *the solution to pollution is dilution*. Even now, although most of our sewage is treated to some extent, residual fluids and particulates are still discharged continuously, adding significant amounts of nutrients and chemicals to the waters.

To its credit, the bay historically has been relatively successful at diluting our pollution. But the trouble with using the bay for waste disposal is that it has and continues to damage marine life, thereby threatening the fisheries. Interested parties have banded together to pass laws and regulations over the past two hundred years in an attempt to maintain the health of the bay, and many of the regulations have done much to reduce the most egregious pollution. For example, sewage treatment began in the early twentieth century because the powerful oyster lobby responded to illness (typhoid) spread by eating oysters contaminated with human waste. The bay had managed to deal with our waste for three hundred years, but by 1900 there were just too many of us. Our population and its waste production had increased beyond the ability of natural systems to take care of it. It was an historic moment.

By the 1960s most towns on the bay had at least primary sewage treatment systems. They have had to be continually upgraded to meet the growing demands of what appears to be an ever-increasing population and one that wastes more and more each year. The average person now uses a hundred gallons of water every day, flushing it down sinks, toilets, and drains, resulting in a tremendous load on water treatment plants. If each of us could cut back on the amount of water we use, much of which is entirely unnecessary anyway, fewer plants would have to be built. What many people do not realize is that even after treatment a great deal of chemical-rich effluent is still discharged into the bay. We are not playing this game at the level of a pristine bay, either. We are only trying to get by, keeping it just clean enough for the survival of our favorite seafood. This is a risky level at which to play. Several of our fisheries, most notably oysters, have basically collapsed.

If our population continues to grow, our relationship with the bay and its three competing roles in our lives will require even more balancing. Our penchant for uncontrolled growth is severely damaging the environment. That, it turn, limits our freedoms and our options, and forces us to change our behavior. Tom Horton has recently summarized the challenges we will face if we don't stabilize the human population around the bay (Horton, 2008). Even maintaining the status quo will require significant adjustments in how we live our lives. We will have to learn to change many of our waste-producing habits for the benefit of future generations who will follow us here in the watershed. Let's take a look at how we have tried to manage our activities in the past.

European colonists brought with them farming techniques from England but they cared little for creating a sustainable agriculture. In Maryland and Virginia particularly, early interest was in raising tobacco, a profitable cash crop that could bring a planter great wealth. One could say they sold their souls and became a tobacco empire, founded on the rising addiction to tobacco in the old country. But years of growing tobacco ruined the soil. Our ancestors had little appreciation for the value of crop rotation, erosion control, and nutrient management, so their land quickly lost its fertility. To maintain their incomes, planters constantly had to use fresh land. They brought in cheap labor in the form of indentured servants and slaves. Many smaller farmers were forced to abandon nutrient-depleted plots and move inland to convert virgin forest into tobacco fields. That worked for the first few years until the new fields became depleted as well. We have never been very good at nutrient management.

Tobacco also loosened the soil and lowered binding capacity. Worse, most farmers cut down all their trees. Without shade, the sun baked the soil, and without cover storm water did not soak in but flowed off into the rivers, carrying the topsoil with it. Major floods in 1724, 1738, 1771, 1790, 1860, 1868, 1917, 1923, 1952, 1956, and 1972, destroyed farms, villages, ships, and harbors.

Intensive farming resulted in significant silting of waterways. Two of Maryland's established commercial centers in colonial times, Joppa Town and Elk Ridge, lost their access to markets when their rivers filled in with silt. By 1768 ships could no longer sail up the Gunpowder River to Joppa Town, so the port, the county seat, and the people were forced to abandon their homes and move to Baltimore, a newer and deeper port. Joppa Town just disappeared. Those settlers were unable to find the balance between farming practices, shipping, and life on the Gunpowder.

In the late 1950s and early 1960s, when I first visited the area that was once the thriving port of Joppa Town, it was an overgrown wetland adjacent to the rolling hills of the Coastal Plain. The hills were covered with mature forests, the wetlands full of cattails, a far cry from the busy port of Baltimore. I hunted quail and rabbit in these woods. It was hard to believe this was once an important seaport in the colony. I stumbled onto little evidence that the area had ever been inhabited except for a single old, hard-to-find foundation. The Joppa Town story is a good example of what happens when man is a poor environmental steward. Did those farmers realize they were destroying their town? Probably not. They were far too busy trying to survive and get rich. Usually it is only in reflection that we recognize the damage we do. If they did realize the harm they were causing, did they even have the ability or the will to change their ways, or were they focused only on the short term, and afraid to depart from the familiar.

Erosion and the silting of rivers all around the bay continued for hundreds of years. It was well into the twentieth century before we began to change our agricultural practices, slow the loss of topsoil, and reduce the amount of silt. The first vacation my Dad took, after acquiring his farm in 1952, was spent creating a single contour ditch halfway down his fields to reduce runoff and erosion. He undertook the work at the behest of the county agricultural agent, who was promoting contour ditches and crop rotation at the time to reduce runoff and help rebuild soil fertility.

Over the past fifty years, deep plowing of farmland has been replaced on many farms with no-till methods. This involves cutting and mulching the previous year's crops and then injecting the seed directly into the mulch-covered soil without disturbing the surface. Less soil is washed away, and more carbon is sequestered in the ground. The practice has successfully reduced the amount of silt-laden runoff that had previously choked the tributaries. It is good for the soil, the rivers, the bay, and the farmers. No-till requires less labor, less fuel, and produces less greenhouse gas.

Unfortunately this change coincided with the change from animal-based manures to fertilizers based on natural gas. Cheaper, more easily available fertilizer resulted in more grain and a drop in commodity prices. Farmers, doing everything they could to extract as much from their land as possible, began to over-fertilize, following the old maxim that if a little fertilizer is good, then more is better. Spring rains arrived at exactly the time the fertilizer was applied and deposited much of it directly into the streams. That water which did soak into the ground carried the excess nutrients down to the groundwater table. Where traditional manure was used on no-till fields, it was no longer incorporated into the soil, so it too was more likely to run off with storm waters. This combination of good intentions and economic reality resulted in over-fertilizing the bay, a growth in algal blooms, and the creation of extensive dead zones early in the season. What a disappointing and unforeseen series of events. Training is now geared toward encouraging farmers to use only the amount of fertilizer they need and to inject it into the ground if possible.

Today, with increasing development and a growing population, silting continues to be a problem. To maintain the deep water port of Baltimore and not let it go the way of Joppa Town, five million cubic yards of fill are dredged from the harbor each and every year. The dredge spoil is deposited on several islands with the goal of rebuilding them to their pre-colonial size. Hart-Miller was once two islands that are now connected with spoil. Poplar Island is being restored to its 1847 size. Other spoil is put behind coffer dams that help create wetlands and uplands around the sides of the harbor. Of course silting and dredging can wreak havoc on local marine populations, so the dredging is done in a manner and at a time of year that has the least effect on spawning fish. It's a complicated and expensive job to fix these problems, and it is always better to prevent silting in the first place. But that can be expensive and difficult as well for builders and farmers. They have to be encouraged to undertake the effort.

BEFORE THE COUNTRYSIDE was denuded and the waterways clogged with silt, the Chesapeake, the largest estuary in North America, was the continent's greatest fishery. Although fishing was not initially a significant pursuit for colonists focused on the next tobacco crop, with time they recognized the riches of the bay. From there it was not long before they fished it with a vengeance, and eventually over-fished it. Production peaked toward the end of the nineteenth century. Following the Civil War, the growth of the canning business enabled the shipment of produce to markets that were farther and farther away. Widespread marketing resulted in a continent-wide demand for oysters and other seafood, a demand beyond anything the bay could sustainably provide. The annual catch of sturgeon, shad, oysters, blue crabs, and rockfish all declined over the last century due in great part to over-fishing. Rules establishing limits and seasons have helped to bring back a few of these once plentiful fisheries, but only a few.

For 150 years, Chesapeake Bay oysters have been much in demand along the East Coast and, for a time, across the nation. In the early part of the nineteenth century, New York "oystermen," who had already decimated oyster beds off Long Island using dredges, moved their large ships into the bay, where oysters traditionally had been gathered with hand tongs. In addition to harvesting oysters more efficiently, dredging tends to remove all of the hard substrate needed for oysters to attach, thus eventually reducing the yield.

Responding to the depredations of New York commercial fishing ships, Maryland restricted oystering to local watermen using only tongs or sail power. The watermen's answer was the skipjack, specifically designed to harvest oysters while under sail. By late in the century, more than a thousand of them plied the Chesapeake, scouring the oyster reefs with dredges hauled in with hand-turned winches. Records show that 125 million pounds of oyster meat was harvested in 1880. Hard as it might be for us to imagine today, at the end of the nineteenth century residents of East Coast cities consumed more oyster meat than beef. But a century later, in the 1990s, the harvest dropped to 25 million pounds, which is about a quarter of the total U.S. oyster catch. Today this once famous fishery has collapsed from over-harvesting, poor water quality, and disease. The diminished oyster population suffers from disease and invasive parasitic infections (Dermo and MSX) as well as an abundance of silt.

The invasion of the New York dredgers triggered the deployment of a series of protective measures throughout the nineteenth century. In 1868 the Maryland Oyster Police Force was formed, and in 1891 the 130 members of the oyster police were reorganized as the Maryland Naval Militia. Maryland and Virginia watermen waged a series of "Oyster Wars" over the ownership of the beds, the size of oysters that could be kept, and the collection methods used (tongs versus dredging). The conflict between Maryland and Virginia continues today over who is doing their fair share to manage and restore the oyster beds, which have never recovered from over-harvesting and which, if robust and healthy, would help filter the bay's water and keep it cleaner.

The current bright spot in the fisheries is the story of rockfish, Maryland's state fish. Rock were so abundant when I was a boy that everyone sought them and often after a day on the water brought back coolers full of fish. Soon they too had been over-fished. Their numbers dropped precipitously throughout the 1970s and into the 1980s. The state placed a moratorium on Chesapeake rock fishing from 1985 to 1990. Many watermen who relied on this fishery for a living were irate and never thought it would work. But it did. The moratorium was lifted, and strict regulations were put in place limiting the number of fish that both commercial and sports fishermen could take. As a result, the fishery has rebounded, and rockfish are as plentiful today as they were when I was a boy. The disappointing side is that fish in some parts of the bay are suffering from fungal and bacterial lesions, fish kills, reproductive abnormalities, and immune-suppression. These maladies are probably caused by the high levels of pharmaceuticals and hormones our society uses and discards down our drains and which find their way to the bay. So the balancing act continues. The number of rock may have temporarily recovered, but a great deal more work must be done to improve their health and to stabilize the rest of the fisheries.

To check out the state of the fisheries today and to make sure I knew what I was talking about, I needed the perspective of an active waterman. So I drove down the western shore, south past Annapolis, past abandoned tobacco barns and large horse farms with miles of whitewashed fences, past soybean fields and oak forests down to an area called Churchton. I left the parts of the state cluttered with elaborate malls that go on forever, bland industrial parks, and suburban sprawl. Here the stores were in older, wooden structures, conveniently placed all by themselves at the intersections of two-lane roads. They carried the essentials for everyday living in southern Maryland—milk and meat, tobacco, gasoline, sodas, and bait. This is where I found Bob Evans Seafood, a local business operated out of a one-story shed behind a modest, gray-sided house.

Turning off the main road onto the yellow gravel driveway, I passed by two weathered fiberglass skiffs on trailers sitting in the front yard with "For Sale" signs on them. My old sedan nosed its way among fish and eel pots. Around the back of the house, a man about my age sat beneath a couple of old white oaks, each about eight feet in circumference and close to eighty feet tall. They formed a canopy above the yard, a squirrel haven that shaded the house and the shop. The ground was flat and composed of sand, gravel, and acorns with a few blades of grass. Bob was working on a wire crab pot, one of many that populated the back yard. They were made of black wire that formed a cube, two feet on a side, with one-way portals for the crabs to get in but not to get out.

Bob waved me over, shook my hand, and directed me to have a seat on a weathered picnic table. While we spoke, he enjoyed his Pall Malls and had a lot to say about the efforts to save the bay. He was all for it but thought much of the money went into bureaucracy. Bob wore a dark green tee shirt, blue pants, gold chains around his neck, and a "lucky" hat. His mustache and close-cropped, thinning hair were a red roan, his face and movements animated by hard-earned opinions on what had happened to the bay. We spoke about our experiences for several hours until the rain of acorns grew so intense he invited me indoors to save our heads.

Bob serves on the board of the Maryland Waterman's Association. He grew up on a farm but spent most of his youth in a skiff on the bay. To earn a living, he learned to catch whatever was available and marketable at a price that made it worthwhile. Back in the 1960s, when there were oysters around, he could harvest a hundred bushels a day with a three-man crew. That was when the Maryland Oyster Spat seeding program was effective. Many watermen would oyster in the winter and clam in the summer. But now both of these fisheries have collapsed. Bob blames it on the demise of that program as well as the negative impact of lobbying by the Coastal Conservation Association (CCA).

Bob doesn't fish for rock anymore, either. The regulations have made it unattractive. Three of his friends have gone to jail for catching more than the current limit—two fish per man per day. It's hard to go out and start landing fish and then have to stop because of a regulatory limit. Bob's livelihood now is catching catfish from December to July, and crabbing in the summer and fall. For catfish he uses three-by-ten-foot fish pots made of a series of hoops with a mesh netting strung between them. He loads them up with bait and the catfish find their way in but cannot easily get out. Each year before he sets his catfish pots, he lays out eel traps to clear the area of eels, so they don't steal the bait out of the fish pots. He sets out sixty catfish pots and harvests about a quarter-million pounds of catfish each spring. The big catfish go to the local market, the small ones to North Carolina for the "All-You-Can-Eat" places. He doesn't much like catfish himself, the flavor is just too mild. Give him a bluefish any day, he says. "At least blues taste like a fish."

In the summer and fall, Bob crabs. He and his two-man crew set out seven hundred wire crab pots and check 350 of them each day. In spring they typically harvest about ten bushels a day and in the fall they might average twenty. A great day is a hundred bushels. Bob operates out of an old wooden boat that he has covered with fiberglass. It is forty-three feet long and thirteen feet wide. He has overhauled a surplus diesel engine from the Second World War that just keeps going. Most of his time is spent in the Patuxent.

To make enough money to raise two daughters, Bob has operated a fish shop in his back yard since 1976. His older daughter manages it now, selling fish to many of their neighbors, some representing the third generation of families that have been buying from him for years. Many of their customers have standing orders on a weekly basis. Bob claims his revenues track the national economy pretty well, seafood sales serving as a true barometer on what the cross-section of people in his neighborhood can afford.

In the center of Bob's back yard is a pile of goose decoys. During the hunting season he can often be found on a friend's property bagging his limit of geese and ducks early in the day and then going out on the bay to fish. He loves to hunt and raises Labrador retrievers for fetching ducks and geese, but he claims the geese have lost their flavor. Years ago, when there was more corn left in the fields, they were tasty. Now the geese live mostly on grass. They are tough and have kind of a livery flavor. Bob just makes sausage out of them. He invited me back in November to get a taste of his favorite waterfowl. He always has duck for Thanksgiving. His favorites are the buffleheads that migrate through at that time of year. He also used to trap muskrats, but the market for furs has been dead for the past two decades. He still traps them to eat and occasionally can sell them in New York. Muskrat is one of his favorite foods, along with bluefish. Bob also feeds his family on venison, not that he hunts deer, just that his friends and neighbors bag so many that he ends up with plenty for his table.

Like many watermen, Bob does a lot of different things to make ends meet. He even has helped the Department of Natural Resources conduct fish surveys of perch, catfish, and bass. He asked me if I knew that scientists tell the age of the fish by cutting out the ear. I didn't. I asked Bob about sea level rise. No doubt in his mind, he confirms that there is much more water in the marshes today. Places where he used to trap muskrat are now fishable. All of Shady Side, the next town over from Churchton, was underwater during Hurricane Isabel. Most telling of all is that in the past, he would usually count on losing a month each winter when he could not fish due to bad weather. Over the past few years, he has not lost a week.

So even with more and more regulations, and many of the traditional fisheries in collapse, some watermen are still hard at it, doing whatever it will take to get a boat in the water and find the fish. Judging by the crab-like tenacity of watermen like Bob, as long as the market price justifies their efforts, they will be out there chasing the catch.

MANUFACTURING HAS ALSO taken its toll on the bay's health. As long ago as early in the eighteenth century, colonists were mining and processing iron, which became the second largest export from the colonies. Most of the manufacturing of metals, though, occurred during the second half of the nineteenth century and throughout the twentieth. Today, even though much heavy industry has moved overseas during the last forty years, there is still a network of industry around the watershed, playing an important role in our economy. Fortunately, we now have regulations in place that have greatly reduced the worst effects of manufacturing on our environment.

In high school, I was selected to be an "Engineer for a Day" for my interest in science and math. That meant that I had the honor of visiting the Engineer's Club in Baltimore's Mount Vernon neighborhood and shadowing engineers around town at various industrial sites. The magnitude of the manufacturing complexes around the Inner Harbor during the 1960s was mind-boggling. I recall large warehouse-style buildings with lots of machinery making things for our economy. The engineers were all dressed in white shirts and dark ties and worked under banks of fluorescent lights. The rooms were industrial beiges and grays. I don't recall any color in the rooms or in the faces of the human cogs that ran the machines. I decided then and there not to go into engineering.

Later that same year my father took me to see the real underbelly of the manufacturing industry. We visited the "plant" where he had spent all of his working life, the American Smelting and Refining Company on Clinton Street in East Baltimore. It was the largest copper refinery in the world. Raw copper came in by ship and rail from South America, Australia, and the southwestern U.S. and was smelted and refined here in Baltimore. The workers were proud of their history, their innovations, and their products.

Everything grew dark as Dad and I were waved past the faceless guard at the front gate. We drove along muddy, bumpy roads, slowly passing a series of dingy, corrugated steel warehouses that emerged out of the gloom. Smoke breathed out of the doors and windows of these ominous gray carcasses. Dark men in dark clothes came and went, disappearing into the shadows of buildings. They were covered with soot, as were the roads, trucks, and any other object on site. We drove up to the main offices, went in, and Dad passed me a grimy hard hat and scratched goggles. Safety had to be a concern at a plant like this. People died here.

Dad punched into a timer on the wall and we went from building to building checking on production, deliveries, and schedules. Inside, the buildings were dark as well. The few windows near the tops of the cavernous warehouses were covered with years of grime. Open windows and vents were full of tainted steam escaping the heat of the building. In the casting operations building, molten, orange lava poured from hardened steel crucibles into molds, forming red-hot ingots. In the rolling operations building, sheets of copper extruded out from between two large rollers like pie crusts from my mother's wooden rolling pins. In the chemical tank building, large vats, twelve feet in diameter and four feet deep, bubbled with sulfuric acid. The fumes burned my nose and eyes. Men casually walked on wooden planks above the tanks, sweating from the heat and breathing in the noxious mixture of whatever was poisoning the air. Dad told me how one man had recently fallen into one of the vats. I kept my distance, amazed at how Dad and all the other workers spent their days in this underworld. No wonder Dad had bought a farm to come home to at night, to breathe in fresher air and rid himself of the day's toxins.

From this and the other steel, copper, and chromium plants scattered around the harbor came the emissions, the waste, and the by-products of manufacturing. Plants were built right on the harbor to more easily receive raw materials brought in by ship and rail. Their products were shipped out from these same docks. Some of the more valuable by-products, such as gold, silver, and platinum, were shipped away as well. Others were considered waste and had to be dispensed with as cheaply as possible. Gaseous by-products were emitted into the air—no smokestack scrubbers in those days. Acids, storm water runoff, and gray water were discharged into settling ponds or holding tanks or just down storm drains or sewers. Solid waste was used to fill in low spots that were once vibrant wetlands, or shipped off site to landfills. Much of the residue ended up in the bay.

For years manufacturing in Baltimore was robust, making and shipping wonderful goods around the globe. But from the mid-nineteenth century well into the second half of the twentieth, these plants contaminated the bay. In addition, a great fire in 1904 burned much of downtown. Debris was pushed into the water, creating sixty-two acres of new land now occupied by the shops and promenades of Baltimore's glitzy Inner Harbor.

Over the past forty years, we have sought increasingly tighter regulations in our attempt to find the right balance between our economy, industrial waste, and a thriving bay. Many of the antiquated manufacturing operations have been shut down and either substantially updated or replaced by new, more efficient, and less polluting plants. Much of this work is now done overseas, where, unfortunately, it is easier to get away with polluting air, land, and water. Much of the contamination that was left behind has been identified and cleaned up or is being contained and monitored. Most practices that once dumped chemical waste directly into our soil, air, and water have ended. Furthermore, every time a new construction project is undertaken, environmental assessments are conducted to ameliorate any future impacts from these old sites. I have conducted some of those assessments myself, drilling holes, collecting samples, reviewing old records, all in an attempt to discover what remains down there in the ground or in the bay today. Like a detective my job was to find out what was spilled, how far the contamination had migrated, and whether it was affecting people's health or the environment. Yes, there are contaminants left down there beneath our feet. They cannot all be economically cleaned up. Some are left in place and monitored to make sure they do not affect human health.

Air pollution continues to be a health concern in the Baltimore-Washington corridor, but we have made dramatic improvements over the past forty years. I recall walking the streets of Baltimore and smelling the foul harbor water, fumes from power plants, smoke from the stacks of manufacturing plants, and exhaust from trucks and cars prior to the age of accountability. Much of this past pollution came from plants that have been shut down, moved away, or are now equipped with scrubbers or other control equipment on their smokestacks. Nevertheless, the Baltimore region still has one of the highest levels of ozone in the nation. Fortunately, those levels have been going down over the last decade. Last year the ozone level almost fell within EPA guidelines. Most of this problem, according to the Maryland Department of the Environment, results from transportation-related emissions and from pollution being blown into the state. A large part of the improvement has resulted from new regulations requiring upwind sources to reduce emissions of pollutants that cause ozone. Now we must do our part and reduce car-related emissions.

Newer cars on the road today pollute less, which helps reduce what we spew into our air. In fact, some hybrids reduce nitrogen emissions by as much as ninety percent. Unfortunately many of these gains are offset by the fact that there are more cars on the road every year and the average person drives more. Even so, ozone levels are going down and will hopefully continue to decline as we raise our fleet-wide goals for gas mileage. In addition to affecting air quality, one-fourth of all the nitrates that find their way into the bay and which are causing the dead zones, come from nitrogen in the air (pollution and natural sources). So it does matter how much you drive and how efficient your car is. The local utilities are trying to reduce emissions from their coal-fired generating plants by spending billions of dollars on air emission controls, but as yet there are no controls to reduce greenhouse gases from power plants. Our only option to reduce those emissions is to cut down on the amount of power we use or build alternative power sources, which Marylanders seem to support—but not in their back yards (e.g., we don't have a single wind generator in the state, though that may soon change). In general, the good news is that as we recognize our contributions to damaging our environment, we take steps to limit the impact. But if our population continues to grow, we will be forced to change our behavior even more, and forced to create more laws and regulations in order to maintain environmental health.

HISTORICALLY, OUR TENDENCY has always been to exploit the Chesapeake's natural resources until we reach a point where we are clearly out of balance. In the past, when we arrived at that point, our ancestors just moved on to greener pastures, changing locations and jobs in the process. But over the past century, as our population grew, we have been forced to pay attention and try to manage our affairs in a manner more in keeping with a healthy bay. We now know it is a watershed-wide problem, and the states and the federal government are banding together to help solve it. A sampling of these efforts can be seen in Appendix E, a chronology of environmental milestones in the watershed. One section shows a list of actions taken on a national level, many of which have had and continue to have a positive effect on the water quality in the watershed.

The other is a list of actions more specific to the Chesapeake Bay. Each of these steps was necessary to achieve balance, but we still have quite a way to go before the bay could be restored even to 1950s levels.

A quick look reveals that in the four decades since the environmental awakening of the 1960s, we have undertaken a more systematic effort at reducing our impact on our surroundings. We have learned about some of the damage we've inflicted on the environment and have created incentives and regulations to change the things that caused it. Significant strides have been made during my lifetime to reduce the most overt, toxic types of industrial contamination. We are better stewards now than we were in the past. Our regulations no longer allow human or manu-facturing waste to be discharged directly into the bay. These efforts have restored some of the tributaries and stabilized parts of the ecosystem. But our unbridled population growth over the past fifty years and the fact that we consume so much more per capita has kept the bay, and many of our local species, off-balance. The watershed's human population has doubled in that time. We are clearly the biggest challenge to the health of the bay. Water clarity and algal blooms have gotten worse with the increasing amounts of nutrients that wash into the bay. We must take another step to at least stabilize and hopefully restore and regenerate the natural systems so they are vibrant once again.

Today we know how to correct many of our mistakes. Through laws and regulations we have reduced "point source" types of contamination from factories, sewage treatment plants, and military bases. Now we must turn our attention to contamination emanating from non-point or small sources—automobiles, trucks, lawns, homes, streets, shop-ping centers, parking lots, and farms. Pollution from these sources reaches the bay in the air or from storm water runoff into streams. That is where we as individuals come into play. The habits and attitudes of fifteen million people, no matter where they live in the watershed, will have to change if we are to repair the damage we have already caused and minimize it in the future. Are we talented enough to sharply re-duce our personal contributions to pollution? Yes, we are. Do we have the individual and collective will to change? That is another question.

How many of us make the connection between our daily habits and our desire for safe seafood, fresh air, a healthier bay, and a healthier planet? Do we have the will to do what's necessary to allow the Chesapeake's murky waters to thrive once again? It won't be easy given the rat race of our busy lives, but I, for one, know that I am part of the problem. So I try to watch my carbon footprint, and every day I find that the more I'm aware of my individual culpability, the more I realize what I can do to help.

Many of these steps will contribute to reducing greenhouse gas emissions in addition to helping the bay. It is the same fight. If we can save the bay, we can save the rest of the biosphere that envelops our planet. The less energy we use, the fewer greenhouse gases we produce, and the less waste we generate, the more we can live in balance with our natural resources. It's entirely up to us. We can't sit back, point the finger, and blame it all on government and big corporations. Each of us, as an individual, has an important role to play.

The bay's poor water quality is due in part to excess nutrients and runoff from agricultural lands, so we should encourage wider adoption of no-till and other environmentally sound management practices on farms. But a significant and growing part of the problem is storm water runoff from our homes, schools, and businesses. Each of us can easily reduce the amount of fertilizers and chemicals on our lawns, or eliminate them entirely. (We might even rethink the nature and necessity of "lawns" altogether.) We can also capture storm water and allow it to filter into the ground where it is needed.

Air pollution from coal-fired power plants that generate our electricity affects the bay's water quality, so, acting politically, we should encourage utilities to reduce their emissions. We can help immediately by using less electricity ourselves, and by reducing our use of inefficient, fossil fuel–powered cars.

Waste generated by corporations and governments damages the bay's water quality, and both should to do more to reduce or reprocess that waste. But each of us can re-examine our own over-consumption and reduce the waste we generate.

Many sewage disposal plants still need to be upgraded, but we can each reduce our own chemical and pharmaceutical wastes, and the amount of garbage we generate. *None* of it should be flushed down sinks, toilets, or garbage disposals, because too much finds its way to the bay. We must reduce, recycle, and dispose responsibly.

I am optimistic for the future because over the years we have learned so much about the world we live in, our impact on it, our need to take care of it. There also seems to be a growing desire around the country to maintain our quality of life by becoming better stewards of the planet. This is not a new thing. Recently, while looking through old family files, I stumbled across my grandfather's obituary. I was surprised and excited to learn that he was named the Conservationist of the Year for New England in the 1940s. I knew he was a sportsman and avid fly fisherman but never knew that he worked to preserve rivers and lakes. That made me recall all those hours my father put in on his first vacation on the farm, contouring the land so less water and topsoil would run off, his planting lespedeza and soybeans around all his fields to feed the quail, and planting *thirty thousand* trees. Individuals have been working to preserve nature for years, and many have succeeded.

We can point to any number of things that are better today here and in some other developed countries because of our ancestors, acting individually and collectively. Many rivers and lakes are cleaner, as is our air. Some suburban areas have more trees today, and some bird species once on the brink of extinction have rebounded. Even global issues such as the ozone layer have been improved, and it took corporate leadership and international agreements to make that happen. Scientists identified the causes of problems, and individuals, corporations, and elected officials responded. So I believe the bay can again be healthy. It's a complex problem, but the solution is for all of us to care, be vigilant, and make decisions every day with the health of the planet and of future generations in mind.

What can we do to save the bay? Its health and the future of its significant fisheries (crabs, oysters, shad, and rock) should be a major concern to all of us who live near (or enjoy seafood from) the bay. We now know that all fifteen million of us (and counting) in the watershed are the biggest part of the problem. We should therefore fix it. Uncontrolled population growth will continue to tax the health of our environment, but whether or not our population continues to grow, our behavior will have to evolve so that we greatly soften our impact. That demands leadership.

Individuals. Start by balancing your life right now, and then begin to encourage others.

Government. Encourage better adherence to Smart Growth principals, accelerate funding for storm water system retrofits, enhance requirements for larger stream buffers, and preserve more forest, wetland, and meadowland habitats.

Corporate leadership is necessary to finding solutions to our problems. The first step is to become a leader in your community by implementing a corporate sustainability plan and encouraging others to do the same.

A Call to Action

During my formative years, something must have happened as I waded barefoot through the silt and submerged grasses of the Chesapeake. I must have spent too much time marinating in those brackish waters. Like a crab absorbing Old Bay Seasoning while steaming in a pot, I must have soaked up the essence of the bay during those steamy summer days, because something runs through my veins that makes me different from my friends.

Ever since my childhood, no matter how many times life diverted my attention to other places, I kept coming back to the Chesapeake. Time and time again, I chose schools, jobs, homes, and even vacations near the bay. I chose a major in college that would ensure that I spent my time outdoors in nature. Then I landed a job that kept me outside, year-round, exploring various aspects and regions of the watershed. When one career path took me overseas, I switched careers in order to come back, settle down, and raise my own family here in this place that has meant so much to me.

At some point in this long love affair with the Chesapeake, something in me changed. The plants, trees, and wildlife became more than resources to be exploited. This was a new way of thinking for someone who had spent his life as a hunter-gatherer. Over time, my relationship with nature evolved, matured. I began to realize that most of the natural world around me was threatened. This meant that my way of life was at risk as well. I made a conscious decision to find ways to preserve the dwindling resources and habitats that had nourished me throughout my life. It was like a calling, *a call to action*. I wanted to see what I could do to help restore the bay for all of us who live here now, and to help preserve it for future generations.

You may well ask: What can a single individual do when faced with such an enormous challenge? It is daunting, so great that it will require significant actions on state, regional, national, and international levels. But that doesn't mean that each of us must stand idly on the sidelines. In fact, each of us will have to make a strong effort to ensure that things *do* change, for if we don't, they won't. We can be effective in the spheres of influence where we live and work. With the damage we are causing the planet today, it is mandatory that all of us—governments, corporations, grass roots organizations, and individuals—do what we can.

We have already accomplished a great deal. By collectively changing some of our wasteful ways, we have made the air cleaner, the water healthier, and there are fewer toxic waste spills. But the increasing number of people in the Chesapeake watershed requires that we be ever vigilant. Although many of us are trying to be responsible by reducing our footprints, in some areas we may be missing the larger picture. For example, most of us recycle more today than we did in the past. That's a good thing. Unfortunately we also consume a lot more, so the net result is that we're wasting more than we did forty years ago. Some of us drive more efficient cars today, but we also drive farther. I was recently disheartened to learn that our fleet-wide average fuel efficiency has not changed much in the past twenty years. In fact I was shocked. We have known that fuel efficiency is important ever since the oil embargoes of the 1970s. The marketplace is clearly ignoring the environmental and societal cost of inefficient cars to the detriment of our health and national security. This is one area where we might have to set aggressive goals for the entire fleet as a way to encourage each of us to rethink our dependency on the car and our addiction to foreign oil. It is a real tragedy that all the conservation efforts and plans created in the 1970s to get us off petroleum were thrown out during the 1980s. It was so short-sighted as to be almost criminal. We could have been energy independent by now if we had just followed the renewable energy plans created in the 1970s.

Of course it's always easier to see things that others should have done, to point a finger, or to expect government to do it all. I therefore decided to start with myself before casting judgment on others. If I couldn't change, it certainly wouldn't be fair to expect others to do so.

I began by taking a closer look at my own life. Well, that was eye-opening. I saw myself driving to places where I could have walked, or bicycled, or carpooled, or avoided altogether. I was buying more than I needed, leaving unnecessary lights on, wasting water, fertilizing my lawn. It all adds up. Clearly I was not listening to Thoreau's suggestion to live life deliberately. I had to confess that I was caught up in the rat race too, focused on my own short-term financial bottom line. Many of my everyday activities were wasteful and detrimental to society as a whole. I wasn't thinking about the consequences of what I was doing.

I just didn't get it. Even after growing up and working closely with the environment throughout my career, it was still very hard for me to take the time to assess and change my behavior. I thought that, more than most, I understood the fine balance between man and nature. But I guess not. I am now starting to realize that I cannot in good conscience continue to be so self-centered on such an interdependent planet. We are out of step with the environment, and changing that will require much more from each of us—more than appreciating nature and the role it plays in our health and well-being. There is another, larger step. It is time we grew up and took responsibility for the well-being of others and future generations.

The question now is how do we go about living more respectfully with the rest of nature? The answer of course is, one step at a time. I began by attending meetings, conferences, and discussion groups. The first thing I realized was that I was not alone; many people and organizations are trying to make a difference. By taking small steps each day, they are setting examples for the rest of us and learning how they can be even more effective tomorrow. To help define these steps, there are many online and library resources for good ideas. The EPA's web site (www.epa.gov) is always a good place to start. If you need more support, join a community discussion group. Discussion group guides are available from the Northwest Earth Institute (http://www.nwei.org/). I found the wide variety of grass root, corporate, and government activities very encouraging.

Kathy and I decided to start with our home. We quickly realized that since the kids had left we no longer needed to heat and maintain a big house. We downsized from 3,400 square feet to a condo half that size. Deciding to move is never easy, but in our case it worked out well on all accounts. For starters, it was liberating to pass on much of the stuff we had accumulated over thirty years. We simply gave many possessions to others who could make better use of them and who were delighted to receive them. As a result of downsizing, we cut our energy costs for operating our home in half. We also sharply reduced our carbon footprint, because we now live closer to everything. The mileage we drive has been cut in half, as have our auto emissions. We feel that our quality of life has not changed and in fact has improved with less daily maintenance and more free time; we both agree it has been good for us as well as the environment.

After moving into the twenty-year-old condo, I noticed that it had not been built very efficiently. We replaced many of the lights with compact fluorescent bulbs, tightened up the house with insulation, and adjusted the windows, doors, vents, skylights, and outlets. We also changed our heating and air-conditioning system to a more efficient one. Our energy use promptly dropped an additional thirty percent. Just imagine if everyone did that. Overnight power plants could cut back on burning thirty percent of the coal they use, which would dramatically lower the greenhouse gases they generate! Less coal would have to be mined and shipped, further reducing our impact on the planet. It's amazing how wasteful we are. Energy was so cheap in the middle of the last century that we got used to wasting it. We've probably been too busy to pay attention ever since. As we wake up to the fact that energy is no longer cheap, is highly polluting, and is causing global warming, I'm hopeful that we will find many other ways to reduce our costs, wastes, energy usage, and greenhouse gas emissions.

Step #1: You can probably lower your energy use and costs by 30 percent.

The next step was to reduce the amount of storm water that runs off our property. Rain barrels are usually the easiest way to slow runoff and allow the water to seep into the ground. Another would be planting more native shrubs and trees, and leaving less grass to be mowed. Where we do have grass, we should leave it at least four inches high. Leaving it a little longer will improve its health *and* its ability to hold water. As a condominium resident I assumed I would not have much say about the groundskeeping, but I found the condo board and groundskeepers to be very receptive once I brought up the matter. It turns out that the landscaping firm we use has a whole line of native plants that require less fertilizer, less watering, and fewer insecticide treatments. We also agreed to cut back on the size of the area we had been mowing. These are all good things.

An even better way to reduce runoff is to install rain gardens, bio-retention ponds, and swales that hold the water and let it filter into the ground. Now we are talking about more significant costs. These may therefore be more long-term solutions, but getting them on the table means they will be considered when the subject of renovations comes up. The biggest problem for our condo association is our parking lot of impervious asphalt. It needs repair. Storm water from this surface has caused erosion and subsidence on our property and significant down-stream scouring. We are exploring ways to change the surface to some-thing more permeable or to design ways to slow the water and possibly divert it to a nearby infiltration pond. Is this something our condo asso-ciation could fund by itself? I don't know, but it could be a likely project for collaboration with local governing bodies, since they recognize the need to retrofit the storm water infrastructure.

The most important step the condo association took was one of education and communication. We decided to gather information from individual owners on how they tightened up their units and lowered energy costs. That broadened the discussion to what else we might do to become a greener community. As awareness grows, green communities will appreciate in value relative to those that are not energy efficient and environmentally friendly. Our condo association has developed a long-term *sustainability plan* for moving in that direction.

Step #2: Most people want to know what they can do to help lower energy costs and/or reduce their impact on the environment.

As I learned with the condo association, one can often be more effective working with organizations than by working alone. Three types of entities that can create change are grass roots organizations, corporations, and governments. I first realized this at about the same time that I got a call from Senator Clark, then the chairman of the Howard County Conservancy, a local land trust (www.hcconservancy.org). He invited me to join the board of the conservancy, whose mission was to preserve land and provide environmental educational opportunities to the community. This sounded like the perfect place to focus my energy. Joining a grass roots organization would help me take another step toward accomplishing something on a larger scale.

Land preservation is at the nexus of the debate on population growth, development, and the environment. If we're going to continue to have a population explosion in this watershed, where are the additional people going to live? Historically, it has been easier and cheaper to build on open space than to rebuild our cities, so we keep eating up prime agricultural land and natural spaces and letting our cities decay. Ironically our natural resources will have to be even healthier to withstand the strain if our population continues to grow. So a major challenge for our society is to decide whether to develop or preserve our remaining land. A land trust is one place where these issues are front and center. The Howard County Conservancy's board included land developers, farmers, environmentalists, and a state senator or two. The issues raised were important to each of these constituencies, and the debates introduced us all to a wide variety of perspectives.

Since its inception, the conservancy has been instrumental in the preservation of thousands of acres. A key component of land preservation is environmental education. If you do not appreciate the value of nature to your own well-being, you might not understand the importance of land preservation and restoration. In our rapidly developing part of the watershed we found that many people had lost their connection with the natural world. Our lives have become so structured there is little time left for getting out into nature. The farm the conservancy managed and had turned into an environmental center was the only nature center in our area and yet was visited by only a small percentage of county residents. Something was amiss.

To better understand the complexity of life today and our societal relationship with nature, the conservancy invited Richard Louv, author of *Last Child in the Woods: Saving Our Children from Nature Deficit Disorder,* to speak at a local high school. We thought having him speak might be a good way to engage the community on how to help our kids reconnect with the outdoors.

The day of the lecture was cold and started out with a bit of snow. When I heard schools were closed and all events cancelled, my heart sank. We had spent a great deal of money, raised largely by a consortium of local organizations, to fly Louv here from his home in San Diego, and it was the only date he had open. It was now or never. I was on the phone at six that morning talking to the school system. They had been very supportive and I knew many in our audience would be teachers very much interested in this topic. By nine we had our answer. The snow cancellation policy was overridden, just this once; our program could go on as scheduled. Now the challenge was how to get the word out. We started making calls.

That night more than five hundred people showed up! None of us had ever seen such a great turnout for a lecture by an author in our town before. The topic had evidently struck a chord, and Louv's book had already been read by many who came. We were not disappointed. His remarks were clear and sincere, and he touched a nerve in everyone in the audience. The research is clear. Children who spend time outdoors directly experiencing life with all their senses tend to learn better, concentrate better, and deal with stress better. A whole host of modern maladies, including asthma, obesity, and boredom are exacerbated by our sedentary, indoor living.

Louv asked us, "What happened to the days when we all just ran out the door for hours of unstructured time to explore the backyard, the stream, and the woods? Why are our lives so structured today? Why is it that most of our free time is spent on electronic media and not spent outdoors? How many of the health and social challenges we face today are the result of a kind of *nature deficit disorder*?" He challenged us to take a look at our lives. Every one of us left the hall that night wondering how to change and how to help our children reconnect with the natural world. A local movement to help get kids out in nature began there that night and still energizes our community. Through Louv's efforts, an exciting movement has caught on around the country at local, state, and federal levels to ensure that *no child is left inside*.

As it turns out, nature deficit disorder is not just a problem for our children. A great deal of research on this topic has been conducted by the husband-and-wife team of Rachel and Stephen Kaplan at the University of Michigan. Their work shows that people who work all day confined to an office setting are less healthy, less productive, and less creative than their fellow employees who are able to include a brief thirty minutes of nature into their work days. Employees who can go outside each day have *less absenteeism, faster recovery from illness, greater patience and ability to cope, less distraction, more focus, and enhanced confidence, creativity, and productivity*. These results are so compelling that many corporations actually encourage their workers to develop the habit of getting outside every day. Some progressive builders are starting to think of their office buildings as portals to the outdoors and are designing walks, pathways, and gardens that are interconnected with offices and invite the employees to hold meetings or take breaks outdoors. Green Buildings, e.g., those certified by LEED (the Leadership in Energy and Environmental Design Green Building Rating System) may be a first step. The next is to incorporate environmental, physical, and mental health planning into homes, schools, and office designs of the future.

It appears that humans have lost an important connection with nature in just a few short decades, and the way we currently live our lives affects not only our mental and physical health but the health of our biosphere. We have lost touch with the natural rhythms that keep us healthy, creative, and productive, as if we have moved into an electronic sphere where we can no longer relate to the natural world. No wonder we are not sensitive to the damage we cause to ourselves and the life around us. As we learn to take better care of ourselves by getting out into nature, we will surely appreciate the need to take care of the planet that nourishes us in so many ways.

The board and the staff of the conservancy responded to Louv's challenge by presenting a range of opportunities for the community. A series of walks for individuals, families, and organizations called "Wonder Walks" were organized with the goal of simply getting people out to explore. The hope is that these walks will be a start for many to reconnect with nature. So far they've been very well attended. More and more people are learning about the work that land trusts do, and the conservancy gains more volunteers to offer even more environmental programs and to help preserve more land.

The conservancy also hosts an annual two-day environmental film festival and a series of presentations throughout the year focused on environmental education for all ages. It serves as the Green Resource Center for local schools who want to participate in the Green School Program and provides field trips to five thousand students each year. But there is so much more that can be done at the conservancy's 232-acre Mt. Pleasant Farm and the Gudelsky Environmental Education Center. The next goal is a series of "Quests" around the county so that individuals or groups can go on walks every weekend to new and exciting destinations. They are designed to gain a greater sense of place and to learn even more about wonders all around us.

Step #3: Grass roots organizations are great ways to leverage individual efforts into greater environmental awareness within our communities.

While focusing on expanding the effectiveness of a single grass roots organization, I received a call from the county to serve on the Environmental Sustainability Board, one of the first in the country. Our county executive, Ken Ulman, has pledged to make our county a national leader on sustainability initiatives. The board's job is to help identify, prioritize, and advocate for initiatives that would benefit all parts of our community. Serving on the board offered the opportunity to work with all the arms of government to help implement more sustainable programs. It also would be a mechanism for increasing collaboration between governmental, grass root, and corporate initiatives. I said yes.

From the start the board realized that the word *sustainability* is not clear to everyone. What does it mean? The most general definition we found was *meeting today's needs without compromising the future.* A more business-like definition is *understanding the true cost of every decision.* It is similar in many ways to the Great Law of the Iroquois Confederacy: *in our every deliberation we must consider the impact of our decisions on the next seven generations.* As ambiguous as the term "sustainability" may at first appear, it is the best word I know to express the movement that is now transforming the country.

No matter how you define it, sustainability is basically a systematic way to ensure the balance between economic, social, and environmental issues to the benefit of all three. To achieve this balance, a strategic planning process called the "triple bottom line" is now being followed by many of the nation's leading businesses. Corporations are beginning to realize that they must assess themselves not just on their short-term financial bottom line but on their social and environmental assets and liabilities as well. Many now realize the economic benefits of this approach and are systematically trying to embed best sustainability practices into everything they do.

As part of my preparation for serving on the Environmental Sustainability Board, I studied and visited grass root organizations, corporations, and local governments across the country. I traveled to Charlottesville, Portland, Seattle, Asheville, Washington, D.C., Baltimore, and Burlington, Vermont. I have been struck by how much is being done by grass roots organizations in some areas and corporations or governments in others. Rarely, however, have I found all three groups working closely with one another. Although there are many success stories, most places could do even more with better coordination and collaboration between the myriad government, corporate, grass root, and individual efforts taking place today. This is something our board hopes to achieve.

A list of government priorities based on the experience we gained in our county are included in the Appendix on Governmental Actions. We tried to establish specific goals in the areas of recycling, energy, greenhouse gas reduction, land preservation, better land and storm water management practices, and education. We quickly realized that there is a sustainability aspect to almost every major decision an individual, community, corporation, or government makes. Yet historically, costs and impacts have not been systematically included in past decision-making, much to the detriment of our communities.

One high-priority initiative in which sustainability is important is the redevelopment of the large mall complex into a new downtown in Columbia, Maryland. So many environmental and social issues are involved that the developer has wisely turned to a nationally known consultant to build a sustainability framework for guiding Columbia's redevelopment over the next thirty years. The consultant has evaluated energy, water, transportation, ecology, livability, and material issues. The vision is good. Now the challenge is to make it all a reality.

Will a sustainability framework adopted by the county's general plan mitigate all the ill effects on the air, water, human health, corporate health, and the health of the bay? No, but if done well and responsibly, it offers all the stakeholders the best chance to build an economically vibrant downtown without creating more economic, social, and environmental problems. If not done well, this town will end up like so many twentieth-century concrete jungles with too much traffic, air, soil, and noise pollution, and all the physical and mental health issues that result from poor planning and too much separation from the natural world. The framework should set the bar high for future development and provide the community with a way to minimize and monitor its impact. It is an opportunity to implement a collaborative process between a major corporation, local government, grass roots organizations, and citizens to create a better tomorrow.

Step #4: Our real goal is to bring all segments of our community together to create a sustainable future.

Although grass-root and governmental organizations can have a major effect on changing behavior, corporations can prove to be the most effective leaders of change. It is an area with which I am familiar, having been a corporate officer for over twenty-five years. I am well-versed in the value of strategic planning, implementation, and monitoring for creating change within an organization. Following up on the work I did with my own companies, several years ago I began working with firms to systematically incorporate better sustainability practices into their day-to-day operations. In working with a variety of companies, I have found that recasting their mission along the lines of making a difference has given a powerful boost to corporate morale and growth. Whenever I facilitated discussions with the company's key managers, there were always a few skeptics who started out by saying they had no time to worry about societal and environmental issues and were only interested in their short-term bottom lines. Most quickly came to realize the power of re-engineering their firms around the basic tenets of sustainability.

It always amazes me how many first-rate ideas are generated in these discussions. The goal, of course, was not just to come up with ideas but to place the better ideas into the context of what was possible within their firm. Companies often need a benchmark of where they stand within their industry and a plan for what they can do to become leaders. A benchmarking process helps them identify the low-hanging fruit and set realistic goals for improving their company. Once these goals have been identified, it is possible for the key managers to go back and integrate new initiatives into their strategic plans. Overall, I have found these strategic assessments to be powerful tools for helping employees and managers become more focused on achieving sustainable corporate goals.

The potential for enhancing a company's success by incorporating triple bottom line thinking is significant. *Doing well by doing good* has proven time and again to be a great motivating force. Going back to the Kaplans' research, they found that a key to an individual's health and success is having some meaningful purpose in life. Many people do not get a great deal of satisfaction from their everyday jobs. The Kaplans discovered that when employees became involved in something they felt was meaningful at work or in the community, it enhanced their performance at work and enriched their personal lives. The Kaplans described the result as "greater empowerment (a desire to make a difference), an ability to make plans and carry them out, a desire for self-discovery and self-improvement, more executive-level functioning, and superior performance." Those sound like good things for all of us. If a company can instill more meaning into its employees' lives by encouraging them to help make the company more sustainable, it's a win for the individual, the company, and our environment.

Since many of us spend more time at our offices than anywhere else, the corporate setting represents one of the greatest opportunities for changing behavior relative to our natural world. In fact, most companies are doing something in this regard already, but many do not have a systematic process in place and have not yet developed the internal champions or the business rationale for taking significant action. This seems to be a key stumbling block. I suggest that *you* might consider becoming the sustainability leader in your place of work. Make this the purpose that re-energizes your life. To gain the skills to do this, start by reading the *Triple Bottom Line, Green to Gold,* the *Business Guide to Sustainability,* and other books. The owners of your firm should be delighted, and you will accomplish a great deal for your quality of life and for the environment.

Step #5: Corporations who lead us into a more sustainable future will prove to be the most successful in the long run.

I share these experiences to illustrate that there is a lot one person can do by making the commitment and by working with others. There are many opportunities for each of us to make a difference. I hope this book has provided you with a clear call to action. The challenge is to get everyone involved. Reach out to your neighbors, your siblings, your co-workers, your boss, and your uncle Henry. Help them understand the issues, help them articulate a vision, and help them implement a solution. Send this book to them if you think it will help. Each of us must decide if we are going to pay attention to the greatest challenge of our time and act now, or leave it to others to determine our future. I believe we all are needed to make a difference, at home, in our communities, and at our places of work. If we are to change the quality of life here on earth for the better, now and for future generations, we must incorporate sustainability practices into everything we do.

Epilogue

As I hope is evident by now, my greatest fear is that we have lost our relationship with nature, that we are so caught up with man-made inventions that we are no longer grounded in the natural world. I am hopeful that during this current environmental awakening we will all reconnect with the planet and learn to appreciate the interdependence of all earth's species.

If each of us takes the time to get back in touch with nature, we will develop a better sense of place. A sense of place usually matures to a sense of responsibility and a desire to restore and maintain the land where we live. If enough of us do that, we can preserve fragile ecosystems for future generations. We can also reduce the likelihood of droughts, floods, starvation, and wars over natural resources.

I am encouraged by all the efforts I see today. Many people are deciding to make the changes necessary to preserve what is left of our natural world. It is up to us to evolve, to change our thinking and our behavior at home and on the job. By doing so, and by starting today, we can rebalance our lives and our planet. But we have to start now. There is no more time to waste. We don't want to wait until it is too late, and all we can do is lament that we could have done more.

The year is 2020. My grandchildren are running ahead of me, hopping from rock to rock, as we work our way down a fully restored Patapsco River. The water is clear and full of shad. I hear more birds than ever before. The sun shines through clear skies, and a cool breeze chills the sweat on my arms. My granddaughter stops and waits till I catch up and then asks, "Granddad, what did you do when you were a boy?"

I ponder the question for a moment and then say, "The same things that you do . . . the same things that you do."

Appendices

Appendix A
Backyard Advice

There are a number of significant steps each of us can take to help with the problems in and around the bay. You don't even have to leave home, so save gas and get involved. Start by going outside and taking a good look at your own back yard.

Water — What happens to the water that falls on your land? If you live on a quarter acre and you receive 36 inches of rain per year, which is typical for this area, then you receive more than 220,000 gallons every year, *for free!* That's quite an asset if you think about it, a natural resource that's all yours, if you can hold on to it. Like most resources though, the water tends to slip away without providing you with as much benefit as it might have if it had been properly managed.

For reference, the average American uses about 100 gallons a day, or 36,500 gallons a year. So if you could capture that rainfall, for example by using a cistern, you could meet the needs of about six people. Instead, most of that water usually runs off your roof, driveway, porches, and lawn, washes down the street into storm water drains, and then goes directly into streams and eventually winds up in the bay. Some rainwater does filter into the ground to feed the water table and some is held by the soil to nourish the plants until the next rainfall. But by typical residential design, most of it washes away. You've lost an asset, and since the water picks up nutrients on the way, the bay picks up a liability.

This is where you come in. To help more of the water filter into the ground, you can redesign your back yard or learn to manage your resources. You can use gravel or permeable pavers on your driveways, porches, and walkways. You can also use *rain barrels* on your downspouts to collect water for use on dry days. Rain barrels can be ordered via the internet or commonly from your local county extension agent. You can also plant more trees and shrubs to slow the runoff and encourage more water to soak into the ground. All of these steps will reduce runoff, nutrients, and siltation in our waterways and improve the health of your back yard.

Rain gardens can help a great deal in reducing nutrient-laden, storm water runoff. They are easy to install and easier to maintain than conventional gardens. The goal is to site them so they collect the water that runs off your roof or your driveway and allow it to soak into the ground. Rain gardens recharge the groundwater table so that streams are fed with cool, clean groundwater throughout the year.

Pick a site downhill from where water is running off an impervious surface, such as your roof or driveway. Downspouts and sump pump pipes can also be directed to the rain garden through a buried 4-inch diameter plastic drain tile. Keep the site several yards away from your house and ideally in a place that gets a good amount of sun. Create a small depression in this area, typically 6 to 8 inches deep, so that when it rains it will capture and retain a large amount of the water that is falling on your property. Use the soil that you dig out of the rain garden as a berm on the downhill side of the garden so it can temporarily hold more water. If you have clay-rich soil it is beneficial to line the bottom of the swale with gravel or sandy soil so that water can more readily soak into the ground. If designed well, the water will soak into the ground in a matter of a few hours or days. Typically, a rain garden should be about a third of the area of the impervious surface from which you are capturing the water.

Plant the garden with native grasses and wildflowers that are specially selected for their ability to gradually absorb and filter storm water. Most local nurseries can advise you which plants are best to use in your area. Mix native ornamental grasses and sedges with your perennial wildflowers to ensure the garden has a strong root mass that will resist erosion and inhibit weed growth. Water the plants well for the first three weeks. Do not fertilize. Add about 3 inches of untreated, shredded hardwood mulch to the bare soil areas around the plants to prevent erosion. You will find these gardens to be easier to maintain and require far less fertilizer and water throughout the growing season than your other gardens.

Fertilizer — Many people tend to over-fertilize their yards, and much of this wasted fertilizer ends up in the bay. Before using fertilizer, test the soil in your back yard to see if it even needs additional nutrients. Your county extension agent can help you with this. In Maryland, contact www.hgic.umd.edu. Understand what you need and how to apply it. Consider using natural fertilizers such as blood meal, bone meal, fish emulsion, cottonseed meal, and aged manures. These also add valuable organic matter to the soil. Use composted yard waste to enhance soils and the effectiveness of fertilizer application. Leave grass clippings and leaf mulch on lawns to enrich the soil. Look for products that contain water-insoluble nitrogen (WIN). Do not use fertilizer spikes, they can burn roots. Aerate your lawn to reduce soil compaction if needed, and use lime to manage acidity.

Native plants can be a big help in reducing the need for fertilizers, insecticides, watering, and expensive storm water management efforts, especially if we all use them. Plant warm season grasses (bluestem, Indian grass, switch grass) in your yard to help hold the soil and to provide healthy habitat for small animals. Allow cool season grasses (fescues, bluegrasses, ryegrasses) to go semi-dormant during the summer's heat and drought. No need to water them during the summer. Use species that attract beneficial insects such as: anise, aster, basil, carrot, coriander, dill, fennel, mints, parsley, sage and thyme. Plant layers of native plants to include grasses, shrubs, understory trees and hardwoods. For further information contact your local Master Gardeners or your county extension agent.

Composting — To reduce the strain on sewerage treatment plants and slow the filling of landfills, try composting. Breaking down garbage to something quite valuable is relatively easy and can generate wonderful supplements to the soil in your yard and gardens. Mix green and brown material along with soil from your garden and air to help the aerobic digestion of the material. Green material is high in nitrogen and generates heat to help breakdown the materials in the compost pile. Green items include grass clippings, young weeds, fruit, vegetable scraps, coffee grounds, and tea leaves. Brown material is high in carbon and serves as the fiber in the compost pile. Brown items include fall leaves, dead plants, sawdust, dried hay, and straw. Manure of herbivorous creatures such as rabbits and horses, egg shells, paper bags, paper towels, and cotton clothing can all be composted in moderation.

Mix the pile regularly to get air into it and be sure to keep the pile damp. Weekly mixing encourages aerobic bacteria to grow and break down the material. With time you will have a layer of great compost at the bottom of the pile. Do not compost bread, pasta, nuts, cooked food, newspaper, meat and meat scraps, bones, fish and fish bones, plastic or synthetic fibers, oil or fat, weeds that have gone to seed, diseased plants, or glossy magazines.

Nature Deficit Disorder — Make your yard interesting and start spending time out there. Get rid of parts of the manicured lawn and create gardens, orchards, vineyards, ponds, and places for domestic or wild animals and birds to live. There is so much you can do in your yard besides mowing it. If you spend time outdoors, you might just encourage other members of your family to do so as well, if for no other reason than to be with you. They might even come up with their own activities. You will find that your family is healthier, happier, more creative, and more productive as a result.

Planting Trees and Shrubs — Be judicious in what trees you plant and maintain in your own back yards. Some trees are better for attracting an array of fauna and flora than others. Some are better for holding rainwater and providing shade than others. Be careful how you landscape to insure that the trees remain healthy. Some trees disperse chemicals through their roots and leaves that discourage other plants from growing too close to them. Be careful when installing rain gardens or pathways that they do not injure existing trees. Many garden stores provide a landscape design service. Master Gardener organizations can provide you with a great deal of advice for free (www.ahs.org/master_gardeners). Consider planting fruit and nut trees and shrubs on the edges of your yard. In addition to providing many hours of satisfaction for your family, they often produce more than you need and make great gifts for your neighbors.

Bird Habitats — There are certainly many things you can do in your own back yard to attract and support a range of birds. This includes having a water element and a variety of native plants and shelter that attract birds. Be sure to check with your local extension agent and master gardener group for further information specific to your area. However, this backyard suburban habitat is only conducive to the nesting or feeding of a few species. Many others need dense woods or open meadowland as part of their habitat. To ensure we have a variety of species, you will have to work with others and with local organizations to make sure a wide variety of habitats is preserved in your area.

The Trouble with Lawns — Lawns and ball fields cover large areas of our suburbs, and they are close to being ecological deserts. As our population ages, we'll need fewer ball fields, so we can help get the ecosystem back into balance by converting them back into natural areas. Creating trails through natural areas close to population centers will encourage more of us to get outside and gain the benefits of a daily walk in nature. Natural areas would be better for those who are older and who like to walk as well as for the health of our ecosystem.

Chickens — If your neighborhood covenants allow chickens, you may want to try raising laying hens. It can be very satisfying, especially if you're also raising a family. Before you start, think through the process, because you have to be aware of a few important things. First of all you have to be around to feed, water, and collect eggs nearly every day. Raising any animal is not a good choice if you travel a lot. Secondly, you need a safe enclosure so the foxes, raccoons, skunks, weasels, coyotes, and hawks don't feast on your flock. Thirdly you need a system for composting and distributing the waste. Now, on the plus side, chickens provide fresh and tasty eggs, will consume much of your garbage, and can be a great source of nutrients for your garden. But don't get carried away, this is probably not a money-maker and is not for everyone.

Lowering Your Carbon Footprint and Your Energy Bills — When planting, consider planting evergreen trees as a windbreak during the winter and deciduous trees for shade during the summer. You might also consider having a home energy audit done to help you quickly pin down the areas of your home where most of your heat is lost. This is important because you may be losing much of your heat in one area that you might not have thought of fixing first. You may wonder if the effects of these individual efforts will be significant. They will be if we all do them. So once you get started, make sure your neighbors hear about how much you reduced your energy bills and how little you have to mow. Even steps like changing your lights to compact fluorescent light bulbs, turning off your laptop and cell phone chargers, getting rid of that second refrigerator, and sealing your duct work can be significant if everyone did it. The heating, cooling, and lighting of buildings is the largest single energy demand in our country, so it presents the greatest potential for savings.

Appendix B
Office Advice (Corporate Opportunities)

Firms are working on a range of technologies that will help us become more energy independent, more carbon neutral, more sustainable, and better stewards of the bay. For example, this list includes:

- construction of more dynamic buildings that generate energy,
- creating fuel from algae,
- building wave and tidal power generators,
- novel approaches to hydrogen production and portable storage,
- CO_2 capture and storage,
- more efficient electricity transmission, distribution, and storage, and
- improved chemistry and materials for advanced fuel cells.

Breakthroughs in any one of these areas will help. However, we cannot count on if and when they will happen. Therefore even if the firms where we work are not focused on these major initiatives, it surely does not mean that we have no role to play. There are many things each of our firms, no matter how small, can do to help. In fact we must all undertake these efforts now if we are to make an immediate impact on restoring the balance between our population and the rest of our ecosystem. Let's take a look at what everyone can do in his or her workplace, no matter how large or small it may be.

A great deal can be accomplished at the office, and many such efforts are already underway. Firms of all sizes are becoming "greener" or more sustainable every day. They are identifying the opportunities and the threats they face as the country retools to use more renewable resources, reduce waste, and reduce our impact on our surroundings. These efforts are often done on an ad hoc basis. An employee asks why the firm does not recycle, and then makes it happen. An executive gets a bright idea and implements it. Step by step things are happening. It is more effective, though, to take a systematic look at your firm. If you want to get started on improving your company, I have listed several references in the back of the book. To be most effective, I suggest you find a template and try to follow a systematic approach. Here are a few areas that you might want to include in your assessment to ensure that you are covering all the bases. Just remember any success at reducing energy, transportation, or waste generation helps the bay.

Market Positioning — The marketplace is constantly changing. Have you noticed the rising interest from your clients in being more sustainable, greener, more responsible? It's there. Nearly everyone has shifted at least a little bit in this direction, and many have shifted quite a lot. Recycling was not commonplace when I was a kid except for returnable milk and beer bottles. Today most of the country has some level of curbside or community recycling program. In response to this interest by the individual, many companies are requesting and preferentially buying more sustainable services. If your client is a large company, they may have green quotas to achieve. They may select a greener product over yours and even pay up to ten percent more for it. Some people make it the basis for many of their choices. I happen to go to a green auto mechanic, barber, grocer, café, church, medical practice, and service station and only invest in organizations that have a visible sustainability program in place. If you have not yet done so, maybe it's time to take a top-to-bottom look at your products and services.

Facilities — The first place to start lowering your energy costs and your carbon footprint is the energy and resources wasted right in your offices. Most companies can reduce their energy bills by ten to thirty percent. That can be real money. Energy and waste audits can reveal significant cost-saving opportunities. Just think about all the paper that is still wasted in America today as well as all the other supplies you purchase that are then thrown away. One of my auto mechanic clients told me that the amount of engine oil left in the cans after oil changes in cars all across the country each year is three times greater than the amount spilled by the oil tanker *Exxon Valdez*. So they now drain the cans overnight and collect the extra four percent that was once wasted oil. Proper landscaping can lower your watering, fertilizing, and maintenance costs, beautify your facilities, and reduce storm water runoff. Some firms have lowered their costs by collecting the rainwater that falls on their roofs and using it in their facilities.

Transportation — Firms can lower their fuel consumption by enhancing their fleets with more energy-efficient vehicles, reducing idling times, and like UPS drivers who only make right-hand turns, changing their delivery practices. Firms also can incentivize their employees to car pool, take mass transit, or telecommute, lowering everyone's costs and the requirements for office and parking spaces.

Human Resources — There is a trend today to want to work for companies who are green, have healthy workplaces, and who encourage their employees to take care of themselves and the environment. Are you one of those companies? Prospective employees look for signs of this in the corporate mission statement and vision. This "culture of sustainability" must pervade the organization and starts with employee agreements, performance reviews and compensation, and training. Your goal is to energize the entire staff to find opportunities for building a more sustainable company.

Purchasing — If you are going to be green, then you want your suppliers to be green as well. This can be encouraged by embedding preferential terms for all products that you purchase. You will be pleasantly surprised in most cases, because most vendors are providing green options. They can often offer you valuable insights on how to make your products and services more sustainable as well. Think of this as free consulting.

Raw Materials — What is the most critical part of your supply chain? Have you considered using more recycled materials at work? They may be cheaper and more reliable than conventional raw materials. Furthermore, buying goods made of recycled material supports recycling. Is it time to rethink all of the possible sources for purchasing the materials you need and depend on?

Finance — Do your records reflect your true assets and liabilities? Most firms find out that the social and environmental assets and/or liabilities are significant and that a full triple bottom line accounting and reporting process more accurately states the value of the company. Such a process may provide you with better access to financing as well as providing a mechanism for communicating to your stockholders, stakeholders, and community that you are an outstanding corporate citizen.

Environmental Affairs — When was the last time you checked the air quality in your office? Are you storing chemicals and hazardous wastes on site? Could you improve the health, creativity, and productivity of your staff by having more fresh air circulated through your office? How about plants both within and outside your offices? Do you encourage your staff to go for a walk once or twice a day? This could make a big difference in esprit de corps and staff effectiveness. We are all looking to work with and invest in firms that we think are sustainable, have highly motivated work forces, and are looking out for the health of their employees and their communities.

Appendix C

Government Opportunities

Local and state governments have an important as well as a symbolic role to play in moving our communities in a direction that will protect our local and global environments. Here are a few suggestions for making a difference and demonstrating sound environmental stewardship to the public and corporate sectors.

Energy Manager — Governments and school systems own many buildings. Many are old and not energy-efficient. Energy managers should be able to pay for themselves and create significant savings by adjusting the way most government buildings are managed. Our local school system saved close to a million dollars last year in part by offering to share some of the savings with the individual schools. That was enough to motivate students and faculty to turn off lights, computers, power strips, and in general start paying attention to how much energy they use/waste.

Fleet Management — In addition to assessing the operating practices of a government fleet, as new vehicles are purchased there is an opportunity to bring on more efficient vehicles and possibly even new fuels and fueling stations. Any fleet that is brought back to the same location each night has the potential to use alternative fuels.

Land Preservation — As our population continues to expand, there will be less and less land available. It is essential to preserve as much land as possible now, since it will not be available later. Land preservation can take many forms. The county can acquire it or help set up systems (land trusts or agricultural-nature preservation programs) to place permanent easements on a parcel in return for tax relief. If we want to have open spaces and parks in the future, we must acquire them now.

Land Management — Governments can use their own land management practices to demonstrate to others the value of native plants, integrated pest control, and managing rain water. This also presents the opportunity for different organizations on adjacent properties to work together on more efficient and better practices for managing a watershed.

Recycling Programs — Most governments have some level of recycling. The next step is to make it pervasive throughout the community so that all schools and corporations have access to recycling as well as all homes. Our community found out that by just increasing the size of the containers and adding wheels, people started recycling more.

Building Codes — Governments can establish basic requirements for forestation, stream buffers, low impact development, LEED certifications, etc. These rules and associated design manuals should be reviewed periodically and enhanced where appropriate. Any applications for waivers to these policies should be made public and only granted if greater environmental offsets are achieved.

Storm Water Management — One of the greatest liabilities we have been left with by past development is the system of flushing all rain water off sites and directly into streams and the bay. This system will have to be updated to allow more water to filter into the ground. That can be mandated for new developments. At the same time significant restoration will be required. In most cases this will take the form of a storm water utility that can provide the funds to systematically fix our current storm water management systems.

Information Clearinghouse — Since the opportunities, regulations, and incentives vary from region to region, it would be good for local governments to manage a clearinghouse for information that can address citizen and corporate needs. This one-stop resource could provide information on the local, state, and federal incentive programs for alternative energy supplies and for weatherproofing homes. It could also provide a list of local vendors, cooperatives, agencies, and utilities. It should serve as a clearinghouse for contacts, lectures, workshops, demonstrations, and other resources.

Greenhouse Gas Emissions Inventory and Climate Action Plan — Local governments should assess the carbon footprint of the county and the community as a whole. With that data they can then develop a plan for reducing carbon emissions.

Waste Water Treatment — One of the biggest uses of energy by local government is the pumping and treatment of sewage. It is also one of the major sources of nitrogen and toxic chemicals in the bay. If not recently upgraded, these systems may have to be enhanced and expanded. The government should encourage the upgrading of private septic systems as well.

Governance — How is this all done? Does it require a large bureaucracy? I think not. Most government employees recognize the need and get engaged when they have the opportunity. The technical talent probably already exists within departments. What is required is for the leadership to state unequivocally that sustainability is a top priority. Every department in government can then revise their vision and mission and start incorporating sustainability practices into their operations. They will quickly find champions to identify and implement the changes. A key advisor(s) at the executive level is probably critical to insuring that solid sustainability principals are considered in all major decisions.

Appendix D

What Can Be Done?

This book is about man's relationship with the bay, but let's step back for a moment and take a look at the bigger picture—the health of our planet. Today we are at peril because of some pretty big, man-made issues:

- global warming from increased greenhouse gas emissions
- population increase beyond the carrying capacity of the planet
- over-consumption and massive waste of resources
- loss of topsoil and farmland
- destruction of the world's fisheries, rainforests, and other habitats, all resulting in an ongoing mass extinction of species

These are daunting challenges whose solutions will require individual, corporate, and governmental actions all over the world. Many governments and corporations are trying to deal with some of these issues as a result of worldwide human outcry and concern. But it is going to take a much more coordinated effort. We have to get the message out that the health of our environment underlies:

- national security
- the price of oil
- immigration
- the sustainability of our corporations and our economy
- public health (physical and mental)
- the effectiveness of education
- the future of our civilization

So it is time we all focused on the cause of these problems—environmental degradation. In his book *Collapse*, Jared Diamond provides evidence that the destruction of most if not all past civilizations was the direct outcome of destruction of the environment. In most cases, the damage was localized and resulted in forcing the responsible group to give up their homes and move on to less damaged areas. This same phenomenon is occurring today, as documented by our move out of damaged cities, and by the continuous leap-frogging of suburban sprawl over the last fifty years. We have a tradition of just moving on once we destroy our homes. We don't stay around and put in the hard work to fix things up. The problem of course is, as our population approaches the carrying capacity of the planet, where will we go from here?

I wonder about carrying capacity. Is our population approaching the point where the planet's resources can no longer support it? The world's population has more than doubled in my lifetime, from 2.5 billion to 6.6 billion, and is on track to exceed 9 billion people before the year 2050. Of course, that prediction assumes our stressed ecosystem can last that long. The earth's carrying capacity will probably be exceeded way before we reach 9 billion people. In fact, I would argue that the carrying capacity has already been reached, since our way of life is causing a major change in the global climate (Ehrlich, 2008). This argument is also supported by our direct culpability in the alarming number of species that are going extinct as a direct result of habitat loss resulting from global warming and other human activities. We are in the midst of one of the greatest mass extinctions of species of all time. The previous five mass extinctions of a wide variety of life forms came about after catastrophic events like meteorite impacts. This one is on us.

To extend the period of human life on the planet we will have to balance our population, behavior, and technology, with the health of the environment. It may be within our means to do so, but we have a long way to go to get the whole world working together on becoming sustainable. What sort of catastrophe will be required to focus everyone's attention on such a first order issue and off smaller problems that currently dominate the news and political debate?

When I was a boy our culpability in global warming was not as widely accepted, even though the data were compelling. I remember pondering charts showing the correlation between rising temperatures and increasing emissions of greenhouse gases throughout the industrial period. It made sense even to this school kid back then. The evidence now is overwhelming. It has taken forty-plus years to convince ourselves the data are correct, the projections are realistic, and that we as a global civilization need to do something about it. Ice ages, solar flares, and tectonic movements are no longer the sole controls on our environment; it is also us and our wasteful use of fossil fuels.

The changes in the atmosphere show that too many of us are generating too much waste for the planet to accept. We have reached a tipping point. We will have to stabilize our population and reduce our wasteful consumption. This is the defining challenge of our generation, i.e., accepting the responsibility and acting now. We will have to change; after all, it is *our* environment and *our* future that we want to protect. It is time to take action.

What will happen next if we don't deal with these issues? The data suggests that twenty percent of all species will become extinct in the next thirty years, and fifty percent will become extinct in the next one hundred years. We are rapidly losing our natural support systems, our interdependent web of life. So, unless we change our destructive habits today, in addition to lowering the quality of life for our children, we will also leave them the legacy of a dying and polluted biosphere with fewer and fewer species able to live on it.

Let's start taking action today. Get your own house in order by lowering your carbon footprint. Encourage your family, friends, and neighbors to take action too. Becoming a leader at your workplace by implementing a sustainability plan. Finding out what your city, county, and state are doing and support their efforts. Join others in raising sustainability to the top of the political debate in this country and across the world—while we still can.

Appendix E

Milestones of National and Regional Progress

National Environmental Milestones

1849   U.S. Dept. of the Interior formed to conserve and develop natural resources

1872   First National Park established in Yellowstone, Wyoming

1892   Naturalist John Muir founds the Sierra Club, a nature conservation organization

1903   The National Wildlife Refuge System (now includes over 90 million acres)

1924   The Federal Oil Pollution Act prohibits dumping of oil in waterways

1949   *A Sand County Almanac,* published by Also Leopold, provides a land ethic

1962   Rachel Carson publishes *Silent Spring,* illuminating the destructive use of pesticides

1963   First Clean Air Act

1964   The Wilderness Act finally passes Congress (now has authority over 100 million acres)

1964   The Water Pollution Control Act

1968   The National Trails Act

1968   The Wild and Scenic Rivers Act

1969   The National Environmental Policy Act

1970   The U.S. Environmental Protection Agency is formed to research, monitor, and enforce environmental laws

1970   The Clean Air Act toughens antipollution laws, but fails to address acid rain

1970   The first Earth Day

1972   Clean Water Act passes to restore waterways and prevent further pollution

1972   Oregon becomes the first state to pass a bottle-recycling law.

1973   The Endangered Species Act

1973   Arab oil embargo leads to an energy crisis in U.S.

1974   The Safe Drinking Water Act

1977   Clean Water Act Amendments establish most of the 1972 CWA programs

1980   Superfund law (CERCLA) requires the EPA to oversee toxic waste cleanups

1986   Superfund Amendments and Reauthorization Act (SARA)

1989   *Exxon Valdez* spills massive amounts of oil into Alaska's Prince William Sound

1990   Clean Air Act Amendments dramatically revise and expand the original 1963 Act

1992   U.S. joins more than 100 other nations in agreeing to end production of ozone-depleting CFCs

1996   Safe Drinking Water Act Amendments greatly enhance the 1974 Act

2002   European Union ratified the Kyoto Protocol

2008   The Intergovernmental Panel on Climate Change (IPCC) concludes global warming is largely due to man's activities

Regional Efforts to Save the Bay

1868   State of Maryland creates the Maryland Oyster Police Force

1916   Maryland Conservation Commission formed

1930s   The Chesapeake Biological Laboratory on Solomons Island opens

1940   Interstate Commission on the Potomac River Basin formed

1967   Chesapeake Bay Foundation founded

1969   Sediment Control Act enacted

1970   Maryland Wetlands Act (1972 Virginia) enacted

1970   Susquehanna River Basin Commission formed

1980   The Chesapeake Bay Commission formed

1983   Chesapeake Bay Program created to reduce nutrients. Headwater states join later.

1984   The Chesapeake Bay Critical Area Protection Act passed

1985   Maryland initiates ban on phosphate laundry detergent. VA, PA, DC join later

1985–90 Moratorium on catching rockfish

1987   Chesapeake Bay Agreement signed by EPA, DC, MD, PA, VA agreeing on a forty percent reduction in controllable nitrogen and phosphorus

1990s   Maryland Critical Area Program started

1996   Maryland places bay on Impaired Waters List. VA follows in 2000.

1998   Maryland initiates a Smart Growth Policy to control runaway urban sprawl

1999   Pennsylvania enacts Growing Greener Program to clean up state waters

2000   Chesapeake 2000 Agreement signed by EPA, MD, VA, DC, PA to correct water quality problems by 2010.

2007   Virginia implements one of the country's first nutrient trading programs

References and Recommendations for Further Reading

Birding Howard County, Maryland. Material from the electronic version of this reference (www.howardbirds.org) is used with the permission of the author and of the Howard County Bird Club, a chapter of the Maryland Ornithological Society.

Davison, S. G., and J. G. Merwin, J. Capper, G. Power, F. R. Shivers. *Chesapeake Waters: Four Centuries of Controversy, Concern and Legislation.* Centreville, Md.: Tidewater Publishers, 1997.

Diamond, Jared. *Collapse: How Societies Choose to Fail or Succeed.* New York: Viking Press, 2005.

Ehrlich, Paul and Anne Ehrlich. *The Dominant Animal: Human Evolution and the Environment.* Island Press, 2008.

Esty, Daniel C. and Andrew S. Winston. *Green to Gold.* New Haven: Yale University Press, 2006.

Fuller, Errol. *Extinct Birds.* Ithaca: Cornel University Press, 2001.

Hershey, John. *Blues.* New York: Alfred A. Knopf, Inc., 1987.

Hitchcock, Darcy and Marsha Willard. *The Business Guide to Sustainability.* Earthscan, 2006.

Horton, Tom. *Bay Country.* Baltimore: The Johns Hopkins University Press, 1994.

Horton, Tom. *GROWING! GROWING! GONE! The Chesapeake Bay and the Myth of Endless Growth.* Baltimore: The Abell Foundation, 2008. www. abell.org/pubsitems/env_Growing_808.pdf.

Louv, Richard. *Last Child in the Woods; Saving Our Children from Nature Deficit Disorder.* Chapel Hill: Algonquin Books, 2005.

Mackay, Bryan. *Baltimore Trails: A guide for Hikers and Mountain Bikers.* Baltimore: The Johns Hopkins University Press, 2008.

Montgomery. *Dirt.* The University of California Press, 2007.

Peterson, Roger T. *Birds of Eastern and Central North America*, Fifth Edition. Houghton Mifflin, 2002.

Savitz, Andrew W. and Karl Weber. *The Triple Bottom Line.* Jossey-Bass, A Wiley Imprint, 2006.

Sharp, Henry K. *The Patapsco River Valley: Cradle of the Industrial Revolution in Maryland.* Maryland Historical Society, 2001.

Shomette, Donald. *Shipwrecks on the Chesapeake: Maritime Disasters on Chesapeake Bay and Its Tributaries, 1608–1978*. Centreville, Md: Tidewater Publishing, 2007.

Stamets, Paul. *Mycelium Running: How Mushrooms Can Help Save the World*. Ten Speed Press, 2004.

Stranahan, Susan Q. *Susquehanna: River of Dreams*. Baltimore: The Johns Hopkins University Press, 1995.

Tillman, J. E. and H. L. Barnes. "Deciphering Fracturing and Fluid Migration Histories in the Northern Appalachian Basin." *American Association of Petroleum Geologist Bullentin*, Vol. 67, No., 4, 1983.

U.S. Fish & Wildlife Service. *Native Plants for Wildlife Habitat and Conservation Landscaping, Chesapeake Bay Watershed*, 2003.

U.S. Geological Survey, 2008, *Open-File Report 2008-1259*, 2008.

Walter, R. C. and D. J . Merritts. *Natural Streams and the Legacy of Water-Powered Mills* in *Science* 18 January 2008: Vol. 319. no. 5861, pp. 299–304.

Warner, William W. *Beautiful Swimmers*. Penguin Books, 1976.

Wennersten, John R. *The Chesapeake: An Environmental Biography*. Baltimore: Maryland Historical Society, 2001.

Williams, John P. *Exploring the Chesapeake in Small Boats*. Centreville, Md.: Tidewater Publishers, 1992.

ABOUT THE AUTHOR

Ned Tillman has enjoyed a long career in the environmental industry and now advises organizations on how to become more sustainable. He currently serves as chair of the Howard County Environmental Sustainability Board and has chaired the Howard County Conservancy. A lifelong resident of the Chesapeake Bay area, he now lives with his wife in Columbia, Maryland.